T0340004

Women's Leadership Development

Readers come to the topic of leadership development with multiple interests—intellectual, professional, and personal—and with curiosity about how to apply concepts and tools to themselves and to support others. *Women's Leadership Development: Caring Environments and Paths to Transformation* addresses these concerns. The book offers an interdisciplinary framework of leadership effectiveness and brings this framework to life with detailed and illuminating descriptions of four leadership transformations facilitated by care-practices used in a specific leader development program. The book will be of interest to academics who teach leadership or conduct leadership research, HR professionals who are seeking fresh ideas for how to maximize the impact of leadership training for women, and anyone with a passion for personal growth and development.

Gelaye Debebe is an Associate Professor of Organizational Sciences at the George Washington University. She is also a Faculty Affiliate at the Center for Gender in Organizations at Simmons Graduate School of Management and the George Washington University Women's Studies Program. Among others, her work has appeared in *Research in Organizational Behavior*, *Journal of Management Education*, and *Human Resources Development International*. She is author of *Navigating Power: Cross-cultural Competence in Navajoland*. She also guest co-edited a special issue of the *Journal of Management Education* on women's leadership programs.

Routledge Studies in Leadership Research

For more information about this series, please visit: www.routledge.com/ Routledge-Studies-in-Leadership-Research/book-series/RSLR

Women's Leadership Development

Caring Environments and Paths to Transformation

Gelaye Debebe

Routledge
Taylor & Francis Group

LONDON AND NEW YORK

First published 2019 by Routledge

2 Park Square, Milton Park, Abingdon, Oxon, OX14 4RN
605 Third Avenue, New York, NY 10017

Routledge is an imprint of the Taylor & Francis Group, an informa business

First issued in paperback 2020

British Library Cataloguing-in-Publication Data
A catalogue record for this book is available from the British Library

Library of Congress Cataloging-in-Publication Data
A catalog record for this book has been requested

ISBN: 978-1-138-92001-9 (hbk)
ISBN: 978-0-367-78607-6 (pbk)

Typeset in Sabon
by Apex CoVantage, LLC

To Kenneth A. Reinert, Oda T. Reinert and Ayantu H. Reinert

Contents

Figure

Preface

This book is intended for readers with an interest in leader development, particularly women's leadership development. This includes organizations who invest resources in developing leadership talent, as well as individuals who are interested in the cultivation of their own leadership talents. Academics who conduct research on leadership, those who teach leadership, and leadership development trainers will also find information of value in this book.

The book provides a multidisciplinary framework of leader development. At the heart of this framework is the notion of transformational learning. Meaningful change in leadership capacity involves deep change in the structures of meaning—schemas, assumptions, and beliefs—that shape learners' habitual patterns of thinking, feeling, and acting. The book argues that these habitual patterns, which are at the core of all behavior, contribute to ineffective leadership experiences. The path to effective leadership therefore requires developing new habits. The book provides a theoretical framework for thinking about how this happens and grounds this framework in empirical data.

Although the book is specifically focused on the development of women leaders and therefore delves into how the gendered norms of organizations limit women leaders, the framework is equally applicable to men. My hope is that readers will take away insights and ideas that inspire them to experiment with their own personal leadership practice. I also hope that this book will encourage experimentation among academics and trainers that are responsible for designing leadership development programs for women. Ideally, readers will come away with a conception of leadership that is subtle, nuanced, and both intellectually enriching and accessible for practice.

Acknowledgments

This study was originally commissioned by the Gender & Diversity (G&D) Program of the Consultative Group for International Agricultural Research (CGIAR). It was carried out under the auspices of the Center for Gender in Organizations (CGO) at the Simmons Graduate School of Management. It was made possible by the CGIAR women who agreed to be interviewed. Without their stories, we would not have learned as much as we have about the impact of the CGIAR Women's Leadership Series. I thank these women for giving generously of their time and for openly sharing their challenges and strategies with me. I hope they will feel satisfied with the representation of their experiences in this book.

I also would like to express my gratitude to the former G&D Leader Vicki Wilde for initiating this study, as well as for her openness and genuine curiosity in discovering what this research would reveal. Her willingness to provide information that I needed, while giving me complete autonomy in the implementation and interpretation of the research, enabled me to represent the stories and experiences of WLS alumnae without constraints. Thanks to Pauline Bomett, also formerly from G&D, for providing all necessary logistical support.

Several colleagues at CGO provided critical support and assistance during the data collection and writing phase of the original CGIAR report. Thank you to Patricia Deyton, who served as Director of CGO at the time of this project, for asking me to undertake this research and for providing me with support and autonomy to do the work. Many thanks to Susan Sampson from Simmons Graduate School of Management for managing the web-survey and for providing descriptive results from the survey. Ashley Barrington at CGO was instrumental in diligently transcribing all the interviews. Finally, Tara Hudson at CGO provided support whenever her assistance was needed.

In addition, I would like to thank several individuals who read through drafts of the original report submitted to the G&D. These individuals are: Fabiola Amariles, Patricia Deyton, Joyce Fletcher, Gayathri Jayasinghe, Deborah Kolb, Robert Moore, Kenneth Reinert, Amelia Goh, and Vicki Wilde. Also, thanks to Nancy Hart for her patience, good humor and excellent editorial work on the report of findings submitted to the CGIAR.

Others also provided additional feedback on a couple of articles written on the CGIAR's WLS program. Thank you to Stella Nkomo who read and gave extensive feedback on a subsequent paper that pertained to a portion of the findings reported in this book, as well as Kenneth Reinert who provided feedback on multiple articles. A special thank you to Kenneth Reinert who went above and beyond, reading and providing comments on the entire book manuscript. Thank you also to Oda Reinert who assisted with formatting of the references for this book and challenged me with astute questions to embrace the full meaning of the concept of gender—encompassing the socialization experiences of both men and women—as I contemplated the implications of my findings. This insight was congruent with a sentiment voiced by many of the women interviewed in this book.

The writing part of this project was supported by a sabbatical leave granted by the Columbian College of Arts and Sciences of the George Washington University. I am grateful for this and for the efforts of the Department of Organizational Sciences and Communications for covering my classes during my absence.

Many thanks to David Varley at Routledge who showed trust and confidence in this project. By gently nudging me to push towards completion and simultaneously honoring my creative process, Mary Del Plato played the perfect editor role and was instrumental to providing a very positive experience of completing this book.

My mother Alemitu Ibsa provided unswerving and consistent strength and support. She has always been and will always be my model of integrity and womanhood. Her comments and interest in my work have sparked ideas and insights that are woven throughout this book. My sister Zewud Debebe provided sustained encouragement and a key suggestion of incorporating stories to enliven the theoretical chapters.

I cannot describe the debt owed to my husband Kenneth Reinert. He consistently believed in this and all my projects and provided concrete and unwavering daily support. He has been willing to shoulder far more than his fair share of household chores and other responsibilities so that I could complete this project. My children Oda Reinert and Ayantu Reinert inspire and motivate me to stretch myself and live up to my espoused value in the inherent merit of continual learning. I am indebted to them for challenging me to grow as a human being and giving me love and support at every leg of this journey. This book is dedicated to them!

1 Introduction

> If women don't have models of how to lead differently, they won't have a
> chance of doing leadership differently.
> —*Women's Leadership Series Instructor*

The quest to develop talent across entire workforces, coupled with the
persistent under-representation of women in leadership positions, has
led to increased demand for women's leadership development programs (Debebe et al., 2017). But a key question in this process remains
under-researched, namely, whether and how leadership training helps
to improve women's leadership effectiveness. This book does just this.
It explores the impact of leadership training from the point of view of
women scientists and managers that participated in the Women's Leadership Series (WLS), an initiative within a global agricultural research organization known as the Consultative Group for International Agricultural
Research (CGIAR). This exploration suggests that women's leadership
development programs can indeed be successful and that the paths to
success are varied and require new ways of thinking about leadership
itself.

In the chapters that follow, I describe four types of leadership transformations that resulted from WLS participants' learning experiences, as
well as the teaching and learning processes of the WLS that produced
these transformations. Through the qualitative analysis of these processes, I will demonstrate the potential for leadership training to catalyze
deep and lasting impacts on women's leadership growth and will provide
insight into the characteristics of the training that had positive, transformative effect.

When most people think of a leader, they imagine a man, and when
they think of leadership, they think of masculine behaviors (Schein &
Davidson, 1993; Schein et al., 1996; Acker, 1990; Bailyn, 1993). In light
of this, the quotation at the beginning of this chapter can be interpreted
as not only a challenge to this masculine conception of leadership, but to
one informed by the gender binary. The designers of the WLS did not want

to embrace the standard, stereotypically masculine model of leadership, but they did not want to promote an alternative, stereotypically feminine, leadership model either. Instead, they sought to create a leadership training experience for women that took gender into account and fostered the development of the unique leadership capabilities of women. Doing leadership differently involves expressing oneself authentically in the context of gendered pressures and other expectations that obscure one's capacities and potentialities. The purpose of the WLS was to help each participant understand her leadership challenges and unique capabilities, and to discover how she could express her strengths more skillfully.

The WLS was intended to apply management and leadership theory to the gendered context of organizations and women's gendered leadership experience. This is a significant departure from most leadership programs that assume leadership practice uninfluenced by social identity processes. The WLS was also a women-only leadership training program. This was to create an environment in which women could freely explore their gendered experiences and learn from one another without fear of being judged negatively and suffering negative career penalties.

While interviewing the peers, supervisors, and subordinates of WLS participants would have been one way of learning about the impact of the WLS, I chose to explore the WLS' impact from the perspective of the *participants themselves*. Exploring the training impact from the perspective of learners illuminates an often-ignored, but critical aspect of leader development, namely the influence of leadership training on behavioral change through the transformation of habitual patterns of perceiving, thinking, feeling, and acting. While co-workers and other observers can describe the behavioral changes they observe after a trainee returns to work, they would not be able to describe how such changes occur and what they actually mean to the trainee. The learners' perspective is therefore important.

To understand the impact of the WLS from the learners' perspective, I explored three broad topics in my interviews: leadership experiences prior to the WLS, critical learning experiences during the WLS, and leadership experiences after the WLS. Interview responses were analyzed to address the following broad questions:

- Did the WLS training effect changes in participants' leadership behavior, and if so what were the nature of these changes?
- Did these changes enable alumnae to exercise leadership more effectively?
- What aspects of the WLS teaching and learning methodology facilitated learning and change, and why were these aspects important?

Two key themes emerged from the analysis of the interview data. The first is that of *leadership transformations*, and it addresses the first two questions. Specifically, I found that *four types of leadership transformations* contributed to greater leadership effectiveness of WLS participants. These are:

- Hidden to visible leadership
- Inflexible to receptive leadership
- Intuitive to deliberate leadership
- Depleted to inspired leadership

Each of these pairs pertains to pre-WLS and post-WLS leadership patterns, respectively.

The second theme is that of *creating a caring and safe learning environment for women*, and it addresses the third question. As it turns out, transformational learning was facilitated in the WLS by creating psychological safety for women learners in a caring environment that holistically affirmed women's experiences.

This book situates these empirical findings within a theoretical framework that I refer to as the *grounded, dual contingency framework of leader effectiveness*. For the sake of brevity, I refer to this framework as the *grounded, dual contingency framework*. This framework seeks to provide researchers and practitioners with a way to think about the transformation of habitual patterns of thinking and acting in a formal training environment to effect improvement in leadership practice. This framework will be developed here and in Chapter 2. Chapter 3 will primarily present empirical material but it will also elaborate on the notion of care, which will be introduced in Chapter 2. This chapter draws on three ideas from the leader effectiveness literature to establish the building blocks for the grounded, dual contingency framework and applies these to the idea of gendered organization. The next chapter will expand this conception by incorporating the idea of transformational learning and the four leadership transformations.

Approaches to Leader Effectiveness

Although definitions of leadership abound, there is agreement that, at its core, leadership is a relationship of influence involving two or more people (Stogdill, 1948, 1974; Yukl, 2009; Daft, 2011). While some see coercion as a valid influence tactic, others contend that coercion has no place in leadership (Daft, 2011). For this latter group, leadership is a relationship based on mutual influence, and it is exercised when an individual inspires others through his or her ideas, values, and actions (Yukl, 2009). In some cases followers might identify with and support the leader's goals and vision, while in other cases they may be inspired to pursue their own personal goals. In either case, followership is elicited by inspiration stemming from the leader's influence.

Researchers have spent decades attempting to understand the factors contributing to leader effectiveness. The *trait approach* was based on the assumption that effective leaders possessed certain attributes that differentiated them from non-leaders (Yukl, 2009; Daft, 2011). Although a wide range of traits have been associated with effective leadership (e.g., extraversion, agreeableness, conscientiousness, honesty, and charisma) and typologies providing conceptual order to the diverse findings have been proposed (Zaccaro, 2007; Zaccaro et al., 2004; Judge et al., 2009; Derue et al., 2011), the accumulated evidence does not support the idea that leaders possess a universal set of traits. In fact, the opposite appears to be the case: effective leaders not only exhibit a wide range of traits, but also seemingly incompatible ones such as extraversion and introversion.

Given the failure of trait research to explain effective leadership, attention turned to leader *behaviors*. Early work (e.g., Stogdill, 1950; Bowers & Seashore, 1966) laid the foundation for this research by identifying two mega-categories of leader behaviors: task-oriented and relationship-oriented. Although hundreds of studies have provided support for these two behavior categories, again the cumulative evidence failed to identify universally effective leader behaviors or to show that leader behaviors are direct predictors of leader effectiveness (Yukl, 2012; DeRue et al., 2011; Daft, 2011). In the end, behavioral research findings led to the conclusion that effective leaders employ a wide range of behaviors.

The inability to find the specific *traits* and *behaviors* of effective leaders led to a third approach to leader effectiveness. *Situational theories* or *contingency theories* posit that a leader's effectiveness depends on the interplay of three characteristics of *context*: leader, follower, and situation (Yukl, 2012; Daft, 2011). Some leader characteristics are presumed to be innate and stable (e.g., traits and style), while others are conferred by the formal organizational position. There are also dynamic follower attributes that have to do with growth and development (e.g., needs, motivation, maturity, training) or social influences (e.g., cohesion, cultural diversity). Finally, task characteristics relate to the technical requirements of the job and work and the structure and systems of the organization.

By highlighting the important role of context, contingency theories helped to explain why previous research failed to identify universal leadership traits and behaviors. Some contingency theories emphasize the "fit" between the leader and the context, suggesting that not all individuals will be able to lead in all contexts. Rather, an individual can be an effective leader when his or her innate tendencies are matched with the demands of the leadership context (Feidler, 1972; Singh, 1983). There are, however, contingency theories that have a more dynamic view of leadership effectiveness, where leaders acquire knowledge and skills to improve their capacity to exercise leadership effectively in whatever context they are embedded (Avolio, 2008).

While few leadership researchers would argue with the importance of crafting contextually appropriate and skillful behaviors, some have suggested that attention to context is not enough for leader effectiveness. A leader's ability to inspire others rests on his or her capacity for *authentic self-expression* (Bennis, 1989; George, 2003). That is, inspiration occurs when the leader infuses meaning into his or her behavior in a way that conveys enduring commitments—values, interests, vision, and passions (Bennis, 1989; Gardner et al., 2005; Harter, 2002). Unlike the other two leader attributes of trait and style, authenticity is not an innate and stable individual characteristic. Rather, becoming authentic is a learning process that is integral to maturity and the development of personal identity (Keagan, 1982, 1994; Baxter-Magolda, 2008, 2009). Identity development occurs in social relationships, and the capacity for authenticity in identity development involves choosing one's commitments on the basis of one's internal sense of self (Baxter-Magolda, 2009). Authentic leadership is built on this and involves the capacity to act on intrinsically resonant interests, values, and gifts while remaining connected to others to bring personal fulfillment and inspire and benefit others (Debebe, 2017a).

The Dual Contingencies of Leadership Effectiveness

The three lenses of leader effectiveness—behavior, context, and authenticity—were used to analyze and interpret the data from interviews with WLS alumnae to answer the question of whether the changes catalyzed by critical learning in the WLS enabled alumnae to become more effective as leaders. During this interpretive process, my perspective on the relationship of these three elements of leadership effectiveness began to shift slightly. The contingency theories suggest that effective leader behavior is attentive and calibrated to context. The grounded, dual contingency framework proposed in this book adds the element of authenticity to that of context. Thus, the dual contingency framework posits that effective leaders simultaneously look externally to understand their context and internally to understand themselves (Debebe, 2017b). In doing so, they craft behaviors that enable them to pursue their chosen interests, values, and goals in a particular setting.

Let's be more specific. Looking externally (context), the individual accounts for the cultural and political characteristics of the organization, including formal rules, informal norms, and group and political dynamics. Looking internally (authenticity), the individual accounts for their own interests, values, and beliefs to formulate an intention and respond to the context. In accounting for both context and authenticity, the person can be both inspired and inspiring and bonds can be formed between the leader and followers in which mutual influence is exercised in their relationship.

Although the three lenses on leaders' effectiveness—behavior, context, and authenticity—are applicable to both men and women, we need to consider how these come into play in the context of the varying social identity processes to which men and women are subjected. So we next need to consider how gender shapes the organizational context for women, how this affects women's efforts to become authentic, and the difficulties this poses for women's capacity to formulate action plans that are simultaneously aligned with their sense of self and sensitive to context.

Gendered Organizational Context

Although this book focuses on leadership as it is exercised within gendered organizational settings, it is important to recognize that organizations are also built on the foundation of other forms of difference and inequality (Acker, 1990). Individual identity is likewise multiple—women (and men) not only encounter gendered organizational expectations but also those based in race, nationality, sexuality, and social class (Bell & Nkomo, 2001; Debebe & Reinert, 2014; Moorosi, 2014; Crary, 2017). Therefore, a fuller exploration of women's leadership development would have to address the influence of multiple intersecting identities of different statuses, including subordinate (e.g., black and Muslim), dominant (e.g., upper class and white) and mixed (e.g., white woman). This intersectional analysis would undoubtedly be a very complex undertaking that would need to address not only the shared gendered experiences of women, but also the variations in women's experiences that stem from unique identity intersections. However, we should not forget that gender is a pervasive, inescapable, and fundamental influence in the experiences of all women. Therefore, a gender perspective is indispensable to understanding a very important aspect of women's experience in organizations, including in their efforts to lead.

Gendered Organization

Gender reflects a socialization process that begins at birth (Chodorow, 1978; Miller, 1976). The process of gender socialization is aimed at inculcating a masculine identity and worldview for men and a feminine one for women (Chodorow, 1978; Gilligan, 1982; Lorber, 1994). Gender schemas and practices are deeply embedded in every institution of a society such that the premises and assumptions related to sex differences are seen as natural rather than socially constructed and historically contingent (Lorber, 1994). While there are different types of masculinity and femininity, ideal types within both domains have a powerful influence on cultural narratives and individual understandings of how to be a man or a woman (Ashcraft & Mumby, 2004). The ideal feminine is associated with emotionality, fostering relationships, nurturing, and serving others (Miller, 1976). In contrast, the ideal masculine is associated with agency, assertiveness, aggression, and individual achievement (Miller, 1976; Gilligan, 1982). Men are taught and expected to exhibit masculine behaviors, while women are taught and expected to exhibit feminine ones (Miller, 1976; Gilligan, 1982). Although individuals rarely embody the ideal for their sex, they may seek to achieve it.

Work organizations mirror societal gender ideals in their structure and culture, and members of these organizations enact and maintain the gendered division of labor and hierarchy between men and women. Sociologists observe that, because organizations were designed by and for men, they are structures that reflect men's life situations and maintain men's dominant social status (Acker, 1990; West & Zimmerman, 1987). The dominant position reserved for men in organizations is evidenced in many of its features. These include the attributes, values and behaviors that are rewarded in organizations, the expectations placed upon employees, and the nature and assumptions underlying formal rules and procedures (Acker, 1990; West & Zimmerman, 1987; Bailyn, 1993; Ely & Meyerson, 2000; Fletcher, 1999). All these features have been shown to be aligned with, affirm, and normalize men's life situations and socialization as the norm for organizations (Bailyn, 1993; Ely & Meyerson, 2000; Fletcher, 1999).

The Double Bind

The gendered nature of organizations creates what is known as a *double bind* in many facets of women's work lives, including in leadership. I define a double bind as the stressful experience of feeling out-of-sync and without meaningful options for pursuing one's goals in a manner congruent with one's desires and preferences due to a persistent lack of fit between the demands of the environment, on the one hand, and one's life situation, values, and expectations, on the other. This broad definition does not include all situations in which there may be a lack of fit between the organization and the individual. It applies to situations where systematic institutional biases of organizations favor the worldview and life situation of a dominant social identity group over those of subordinate social identity groups. This book focuses on the double bind arising from hierarchies based in the gender binary. Some of the gendered features of organizations are out-of-sync with women's lives, and this can have significant negative impacts on women's career options and trajectories, women's efforts to exercise leadership, and women's inclusion in "masculine" jobs and professions. For this reason, we need to consider the double bind in some detail.

Two interrelated gendered norms within organizations, the ideal career and the ideal worker, converge in ways that significantly constrain women's career options and trajectories. The ideal career norm is based on the assumption that a successful career involves a steady upward advance in the organizational hierarchy (O'Neil & Bilimoria, 2008). The ideal worker norm relates to the organization's expectation that workers should assign priority to work over non-work obligations (Acker, 2006). From this perspective, the ideal worker is one who orients him/herself first and foremost to fulfilling the demands of their job and organization over those of family, friends, and even personal health and well-being (Correll et al., 2014).

Because women are biologically tied to childbearing and are central to child rearing, career interruption is inevitable. This puts women at a significant disadvantage in the face of the pervasive ideal career and ideal worker norms (Lorber, 1994; Correll et al., 2014). Given the dual priorities of women's lives and the gendered nature of organizations, women's careers are constructed in a fluid balance between personal and professional roles, resulting in career trajectories that are varied and depart from ideal norms (O'Neil & Bilimoria, 2008). Because organizations rarely recognize the gendered basis of formal career expectations, women who leave the workforce to care for their families accrue career penalties (O'Neil & Bilimoria, 2008). Women who decide to simultaneously attempt the dual endeavors of working and raising a family confront enormous challenges as they struggle to adequately meet the obligations at home and at work (Stone, 2007). The situation is particularly exacerbated for minority women who face additional biases, double standards, and structural barriers shaped by intersecting subordinate identities (Watts, 2008; Bradley et al., 2005). Thus, for many women, the idealized linear upward career trajectory expectations of organizations or the prioritization of work responsibilities over non-work ones are seen as neither realistic nor desirable in the context of women's dual commitments to home and work.

The masculine bias of organizations is also manifested in gendered expectations about organizational roles. In particular, the behavioral expectations for the roles of manager and leader favor men and are associated with masculine behaviors (Bailyn, 1993; Ely & Meyerson, 2000). These masculine role expectations are also rooted in the gendered, ideal worker norm. In addition to assumptions that workers should prioritize work over non-work obligations, the ideal worker norm also contains another evaluative criterion. High potential workers are assumed to be those that display stereotypically masculine behavior patterns (e.g., assertive, competitive, hard-driving) in contrast to feminine ones (e.g., nurturing, passivity, and receptivity). Yet when women attempt to meet these expectations, they soon discover that there is an unexpressed double standard that applies to them. Specifically, consistent with societal gender-role expectations, women managers and leaders are expected to exhibit feminine behaviors, but when they do, they violate organizational role expectations, which favor masculine behaviors (Eagly, 1987; Eagly & Carli, 2007; Bailyn, 1993; Ely & Meyerson, 2000). When they respond to this threat by adapting masculine behaviors, however, they violate gender-role expectations (Eagly, 1987; Eagly & Carli, 2007). In this dynamic, women encounter a no-win situation—seen as weak and incompetent or rendered invisible if they enact feminine behaviors, but seen as unfeminine or even unlikable if they enact masculine ones (Meyerson & Fletcher, 2000; Catalyst, 2004).

In addition to leadership and managerial roles, occupations and jobs are also gendered. Women's participation in the workforce, particularly within male-dominated professions, creates dissonance when inevitable tensions arise between espoused beliefs that women can do men's work and actual beliefs that they may not be suitable for them, or even more extreme, should not be doing "men's work." While studies on this issue are not exhaustive, they point to a repeated theme of conflicting expectations for women in male-dominated "masculine" professions and suggest that this is a key aspect of the context for women leaders.[1]

As women have joined the organizational ranks in ever growing numbers, advanced in their careers, and made headway in managerial roles and masculine jobs and occupations, the gendered nature of organizations has become more apparent. This has subjected the phenomenon to greater scrutiny. Despite greater attention, however, changes have been piecemeal and modest and, in some cases, remediation efforts may actually entrench the gendered nature of organizations (O'Neil & Bilimoria, 2008). Thus, while changes targeting organizational practices are necessary to address the double bind and other challenges faced by women, women cannot wait passively for these measures to take full effect. They must cope with the double bind as best they can and exercise leadership in their current jobs. Therefore, a key issue is: How do women leaders cope with the gendered context of organizations, and what are the implications of these coping strategies for their capacity to navigate the double bind and exercise leadership?

Behavioral Strategies for Coping With the Double Bind

Empirical studies of "doing gender" emphasize at least two strategies used by women to cope with gendered expectations, but neither of these enables them to overcome the double bind. The first strategy is to conform to organizational role expectations, either masculine or feminine. For example, in occupations such as engineering (Miller, 2004; Powell et al., 2009) or geology (van den Brink & Stobbe, 2009), where masculine norms and identities are associated with competence, women may seek to suppress values, ideas, and behaviors that are associated with femininity. In prototypically feminine professions such as nursing (Carvalho & Santiago, 2009) or clothing retail (Pettinger, 2005), where femininity is linked with competence, women managers may exaggerate their femininity. The second strategy of coping with the double bind involves resistance to societal gender norms. In contrast to conformity, resistance entails pushing back against problematic expectations and demands. Resistance strategies are adopted for a host of reasons, including to get work done (Nygren, 2010), reclaim avowed identities and guard against the imposition of ascribed ones (Tibabls, 2007; Kennelly, 2002), avoid harassment (Eveline & Booth, 2002), and fulfill the demands of work and life (Herman et al., 2012).

Unfortunately, neither conformity nor resistance resolves the double bind, and both may actually inhibit women's effectiveness as leaders. On the one hand, conforming to organizational expectations may lead to a degree of acceptance and professional success (Miller, 2004; Pilgeram, 2007; Powell et al., 2009), but this strategy can be precarious. For one thing, conformity can lead followers to perceive the leader as weak and lacking in integrity, damaging followers' trust and respect for the would-be female leader (Vosko, 2006). In addition, because acceptance gained from conformity is conditional, it undermines self-worth, breeding insecurity, hyper-vigilance, and anxiety. On the other hand, if resistance is the sole strategy, there is a risk of activating sexist stereotypes and engendering retaliation, which in turn inhibits leader effectiveness (van den Brink & Stobbe, 2009). Also, resistance is a reactive posture—enacted to limit the negative impacts of a force that is perceived to be overwhelming—rather than a proactive stance—carried out with an understanding of the context, from a sense of agency, and directed by chosen values and a sense of purpose. Because of their reactive nature, both conformity and resistance foster a downward spiral of powerlessness and counter-dependence, locking women's attention on external demands, while diverting attention from reflection on their internal sense of self—interests, values, and beliefs. Excessive external focus blocks women from gaining the self-awareness that is necessary to make inspired choices about what to do. Thus, both conformity and resistance strategies inhibit women's leadership effectiveness by ignoring the important element of attention to authenticity.

The literature on women in organizations has given us insight into the contradictory pressures women experience in many areas within the work setting. Given that these pressures stem from the gendered nature of organizations, it is not surprising that this literature has focused on external pressures that women encounter. While the repressiveness of gendered practices and structures and women's "reactive" responses to these have been well documented, the focus on context obscures the full range of women's coping strategies. With few exceptions, this literature sheds little light on how women learn over time from their experiences and exert greater agency with clarity of purpose within the gendered context of organizations (see: Madsen, 2008; Ruderman & Ohlott, 2002). By not placing sufficient focus on women's internal journey of cultivating an authentic identity, the women's leadership literature leads to the conclusion that the organizational context presents a double bind that cannot be overcome. However, when we take the component of authenticity into consideration, we recognize the space of maneuver that women can and do create to navigate the double bind and exercise leadership effectively. Although women's capacity to learn and craft an authentic way of being should give us all hope, the journey toward authenticity in the context of social identity ascription involving gender or other identities entails something akin to Joseph Campbell's (2008) hero's journey—a process of overcoming fear and uncertainty to understand oneself and exercise meaningful choices aligned with one's values and inner sense of self.

Becoming Authentic in Gendered Context

In her groundbreaking book, *Toward a New Psychology of Women*, psychologist and psychiatrist Jean Baker Miller (1976) wrote: "For women, as for certain other groups of people, being oneself—authenticity—was hardly spoken of seriously. . . . Authenticity and subordination are totally incompatible" (pp. 98). With this startling statement, Miller (1976) did not mean to suggest that the condition of political subordination made the task of becoming authentic impossible for women. Nor did she mean that becoming authentic was easier for men. In fact, one could argue that becoming authentic can be difficult for individuals when either dominant or subordinate identities are salient because the maintenance of the social order relies on the role-compliance of all involved. Miller's (1976) intriguing assertion is therefore intended to underscore the fact that the process of becoming authentic occurs in socio-cultural context and to remind us that this process is subject to historically contingent and culturally embedded social identity ascription processes whose function is to sustain meanings and hierarchies based on social identity categorization (Kemper, 1974). Thus, whether one is contending with the limits imposed by a dominant or subordinate social identity, the task of constructing an avowed and thereby authentic identity that resonates with one's sense of self necessarily involves engaging and resolving conflict between ascribed and avowed identity messages.

Ascribed vs. Avowed Identity

People are placed into social identity categories on the basis of physical attributes (e.g., sex and skin color), cultural characteristics (e.g., religion and nationality), or other social or biological factors (e.g., sexual orientation and physical ability). Sociologists use the term ascription to refer to the socialization process through which assumptions, beliefs, and expectations of members of social identity groups are transmitted (Kemper, 1974). Ascribed identity refers to others' expectations of a person's identity, and it is very important to understand that ascription is much more than the expectations people carry in their heads. The ascription of identity to others is guided by ingrained and taken-for-granted cultural schemas, which are viewed as natural and inevitable, confirming and legitimizing the social organization of a society (Kemper, 1974).

Ascription processes necessarily deny the multiplicity of individual social identities (e.g. male, Nigerian, African, Muslim, upper class, doctor, father, son, husband) through a process of reducing an individual's identity to a salient social identity category upon which stereotypical and limiting attributions are projected. Sen (2006) aptly referred to this process of identity shrinking and distortion as "miniaturization." Miniaturization involves the use of numerous social practices to induce individuals to conform to a salient socio-politically ascribed identity category that denies the richness and multiplicity of their identities and the avowed meanings of these identities (Debebe & Reinert, 2014). By this means, societies socialize individuals to internalize narrow identities and assume mindsets and behaviors that prepare them for social and occupational roles that conform to an ascribed division of labor.

Although social identity ascription results in the internalization and enactment of expected identities and roles, it is not full-proof. Individuals also have an avowed identity that not only includes multiple social identity categories, but also identity meanings that selectively embrace and challenge ascribed by society (Graziano et al., 2018; Trethewey, 1997). The exercise of choice in authentic identity construction is facilitated by greater awareness and ownership of one's internal sense of self, especially one's interests, values, and beliefs. These, as well as manifested areas of strength or giftedness, are better indicators of potentially appropriate foci for learning and occupational pursuits than those ascribed on the basis of social identity (Debebe, 2017a). These elements of avowed identity co-exist uneasily with internalized aspects of ascribed identity. While people might conform to ascribed expectations for some time, their inner sense of self cannot be fully contained. Each new experience has the potential of resonating with the individual's inner sense of self and thereby awakening a latent conflict between ascribed and avowed identities (Baxter-Magolda, 2009; Debebe, 2017a).

Identity Conflict and Constructing an Authentic Identity

Identity conflict occurs when an individual's evolving inner sense of self is incongruent with ascribed identity expectations (Miller, 1976). The conflict between ascribed and avowed identity can catalyze a learning process from which new identity meanings are constructed. The process of becoming authentic proceeds through the resolution of this conflict and the exercise of self-determination in the construction of an authentic identity (Miller, 1976; Baxter-Magolda, 2009; Debebe, 2017a).

Resolving this conflict may call cultural schemas into question and this might be seen by some as inappropriate and perhaps even morally questionable (Heritage, 1984). However, since every society is heterogeneous, there are often alternative cultural narratives that can be called upon to support efforts at self-determination and the construction of avowed identities (Graziano et al., 2018; Trethewey, 1997; Heritage, 1984). The efforts to craft an authentic identity by resolving the conflict between avowed and ascribed identity can elicit a range of responses from the environment—some positive and others negative. More importantly, the social environment likely contains alternative discourses and schemas that can be drawn upon to account for and legitimize the individuals' efforts to construct an authentic identity and role while also remaining connected and understood by others (Heritage, 1984).

While the manner in which an individual goes about resolving identity conflict may at times appear to be reactive and oppositional, reducing what is occurring in this process to mere reactivity would be a fundamental misunderstanding of the maturation process as well as the difficulties that arise in the process of transforming an internalized ascribed identity into a chosen and authentic one. Given that the chosen or avowed identity may be in some degree of conflict with ascribed identity expectations and roles, becoming authentic requires understanding that one needs to express the chosen self *skillfully and strategically*, with recognition that the social dynamics of the external environment are based in ascription processes. One must create space to express oneself authentically while building meaningful connections with others. This might require a number of different postures including: establishing and maintaining supportive relationships, seeking allies and mentors, asserting legitimacy of the chosen identity, finding common ground with others, educating others, and making one's contributions and accomplishments visible. It might also involve forming informal and formal identity-based affinity groups, or single identity training programs. It is by maintaining a delicate balance of being simultaneously attentive to one's sense of self and to the demands of context that leaders create the legitimacy they need to act on their chosen sense of self and bring others along as they learn from and influence others, creating a situation in which it is possible to forge new paths.

The Risks Women Confront in Resolving Identity Conflict

While the resolution of identity conflict is necessary for maturation and becoming authentic, undertaking this task can be experienced as psychologically and socially risky, especially for women and members of minority groups (Miller, 1976). Seeking to avoid these risks, many women (and men) suppress their internal desires and adopt expected roles with attendant mindsets, beliefs, and behavioral patterns. For many individuals, accepting to live within ascribed boundaries can be a lifelong posture (Miller, 1976). However, this does not mean that identity conflict is successfully suppressed. In various ways, at different points in time, and with differing degrees of urgency, the gap between expected roles and authentic desires creates on-going dissonance, discomfort, and even distress.

A critical psychological juncture in the process of becoming authentic for women (and men) is the *decision* to explore their inner desires (Miller, 1976). While this might seem benign, straightforward, and unproblematic, it actually involves a willingness to take social and psychological risks. When women decide to take these risks, they show a willingness to acknowledge that others' expectations of them are not the same as their desires for themselves and that suppressing the latter has become intolerable (Miller, 1976). At this point, consciously or unconsciously, women are prepared to cope with the risks and consequences that might ensue from the decision to understand themselves on their own terms (Miller, 1976). While the destination in this process cannot be known ahead of time, becoming authentic would require that women engage their inner conflict, propelled by a need to resolve the tension and turmoil they feel, and most importantly by the attractive possibility of finding a way to discover and express their intrinsic sense of self.

Engaging the confusing feelings that accompany self-examination is hard work, but the effort is typically rewarded by self-acceptance, clarity of intention, and greater capacity to craft and express an intrinsically resonant identity. According to Miller (1976), as women begin to explore their thoughts and feelings, they discover that they have internalized many of the ascribed expectations that conflict with their actual preferences and inner desires. The inner conflict therefore arises not only from a conflict between external pressure and internal desire, but also from a tension between internalized aspects of ascribed identity and the person's avowed sense of self (Steinem, 1993). According to Miller (1976), this is like being at war with oneself, and as such the process generates a range of confusing thoughts and negative emotions. Therefore, the initial period of self-examination and reflection is characterized by varying degrees of conflicting feelings that play out until new identity frameworks that provide meaning and direction are constructed (Miller, 1976).

There are also social dynamics and risks that may ensue from the decision to challenge ascribed identity expectations (Miller, 1976). These social dynamics can sometimes discourage an individual's efforts to understand his or her inner desires relative to societal expectations. More will be said about these dynamics in the next chapter, but a key issue will be foreshadowed here. When individuals attend to their own interests, values, and beliefs, they not only surface their own inner conflicts and contradictions, but also elicit those of others (Miller, 1976). In other words, as women redefine their identities and roles, other people are implicitly also being challenged to redefine theirs. This can have significant implications for relational partners and the relationships themselves.[2] Hence relationships are important to the process of becoming authentic both in terms of their potential to facilitate as well as hinder the process.

What is the implication of these considerations? Recall that the dual contingency framework suggests that an effective leadership behavior is one that is sensitive to the dual contingencies of context and authenticity. While this framework is seen as applicable to both men and women, for women, effective leadership entails the ability to read and navigate gendered expectations of the organizational context while also contending with internalized gender expectations in the process of constructing an authentic identity. The work of Jean Baker Miller (1976) suggests that this is not straightforward for women. Indeed, it is not too much of an exaggeration to say that becoming authentic involves some amount of courage. We will see how this courage comes into play in the remainder of this book.

Research Setting and Methodology

In this section I briefly introduce the WLS setting and my methodology. I refer readers interested in a more robust description of the methodology to the appendix. The women interviewed for this study were employed in the CGIAR, a global strategic alliance that creates and uses scientific knowledge to achieve sustainable food security in developing countries. The alliance is composed of private foundations that support 15 scientific research Centers. Launched in 1995, the WLS was one of several system-wide programs of the CGIAR's Gender and Diversity (G&D) program. Established in 1999, G&D's mission was to help the research Centers leverage their staff diversity to achieve research and management excellence. In addition to housing the WLS, the G&D program also provided thought leadership and strategic advice on gender and diversity to the 15 research centers of the CGIAR, maintained a global database of women scientists, created and disseminated research findings, and provided consultation to CGIAR Centers and National Agricultural Research Systems (Wilde, 2012).

The WLS was created in 1995 with the goal of working with senior international scientists in the CGIAR to build their leadership skills. The WLS courses included Women's Leadership and Management, Negotiation Skills for Women, and Advanced Leadership. While these courses were similar in content to their standard equivalents, they were designed with the unique needs of women in mind. Although the initial focus of the WLS was on international women scientists, the courses grew to include women in a variety of managerial and scientific jobs, at all hierarchical levels, and across all recruitment categories (international, national, and regional staff) within the CGIAR.

In 2012, the CGIAR underwent a reorganization in which system-wide programs such as G&D were consolidated in a Consortium Office in Montpelier, France. As part of this transition, all but one activity, the African Women in Agricultural Research and Development (AWARD) program, were transferred to the Consortium office. Located in the World Agroforestry Centre in Nairobi, Kenya, the AWARD program now delivers the WLS to women in the CGIAR as well as to some organizations in its network (Wilde, 2012).

Between 1995 and 2012, the WLS involved over 716 women (Wilde, 2012). Since the reorganization took place in 2012, approximately 500 women received leadership training through the WLS. The research carried out for this book focused on information from individuals who participated in the WLS training between 1995 and 2005 as well as G&D administrators and WLS instructors. Alumnae were initially contacted via a web-survey that asked general questions about the WLS as well as alumnae's assessment of it. Of the 76 alumnae who responded to the web-survey, 50 agreed to be interviewed; 24 of these followed through with signed consent forms and were interviewed for this book. Thus, approximately 8 percent of all alumnae that had completed at least one WLS training program between 1995 and 2005 were interviewed in-depth for this study. In addition, two instructors and two G&D administrators were interviewed. This book draws on information from the 24 alumnae that were interviewed.

Interviewees represented many nationalities from six regions of the world: East Asia and Pacific (25%), North America (20.8%), Europe and Central Asia (25%), Sub-Saharan Africa (12.5%), South Asia (4.2%), and Latin America and the Caribbean (12.5%). Research Centers in the Middle East and North Africa were not represented due to non-response from those regions of the world. On average, these interviewees worked for nine years within their research Centers, with a range from two to 29 years. The interviewees came to their current roles having had a variety of experiences, including working in other CGIAR Centers, war zones, villages, and community organizing. Interviewees' job titles were: program leader/theme leader, scientist/researcher, and manager/administrator. Program and theme leaders have a Ph.D. and a minimum of 20 years' experience, including significant management and leadership experience.

I used a semi-structured interview protocol to explore three broad topical areas during the interviewing process. These topics were: participants' pre-WLS leadership experiences, post-WLS leadership experiences, and critical learning within the WLS. One alumnae interview took place in person and lasted for five and a half hours. The remainder of the interviews were conducted by telephone and lasted between one hour and three and a half hours with an average interview length of two hours. All interviews were taped and transcribed. Data analysis and data collection were concurrent processes but focused analysis of the data as a whole occurred once interviewing had come to an end. As previously indicated, the data analysis process produced two core themes: transformational learning and creating a caring and safe learning environment for women.

Looking Ahead

This chapter introduced the basic elements of the dual contingency framework suggesting that effective leader behavior is attentive to the contingencies of context and authenticity. Chapter 2 will further develop this framework, applying it to the applying it to the CGIAR's WLS program. This expanded framework will incorporate the transformational learning process and conditions necessary for transformational learning for women. It will also ground these theoretical ideas in the four leadership transformations produced in the WLS.

The bulk of this book is devoted to providing an interpretive analysis of the two core themes resulting from my data analysis, namely, leadership transformations and creating a caring and safe learning environment for women. These chapters illustrate and show the usefulness of the grounded, dual contingency framework. Chapter 3 describes the core theme of creating a caring and safe learning environment for women. The interpretive analysis of this chapter confirms what has been well documented by relational psychologists and feminist care researchers, namely, that transformation and growth for women occur in relationships among women characterized by mutual enactment of care-giving practice. The analysis of this chapter builds on this basic idea and underscores that, for women in leadership training, safety is created in a women-only environment in which gender-sensitive teaching and learning practices are used.

Chapters 4 through 7 describe the core theme of leadership transformations. Each of these chapters describes a unique pre-WLS leadership pattern that reflects a particular type of leadership dilemma. These chapters also describe critical learning experiences that occurred in the WLS and the changes that these effected in participants' leadership behavior after the WLS. Taken together, these chapters show that, while the WLS alumnae brought differing leadership difficulties to their training, the learning experiences they had contributed to shifts in unhelpful habitual patterns of thinking and acting that fostered greater leadership effectiveness after the WLS. The improvements in leadership effectiveness, in turn, were accomplished by enhancing participants' capacity to attend to the dual contingencies of context and authenticity. To protect the anonymity and confidentiality of the interviewees, the descriptive accounts of these chapters use fictitious names and alter identifying information. These include names of participants, organizations, programs, and countries of origin or countries in which alumnae work. The book concludes with Chapter 8, the key findings and take-aways of the book.

Notes

1. For example, Lahiri-Dutt and Macintyre (2006) examined women's participation in mining in several Asian, African, and Latin American countries and found that one way women were allowed to work in this nontraditional

occupation was by means of policies that barred them from "masculine" jobs (e.g. disallowing women from doing underground work). While such policies opened some doors for women in mining, they also created job segregation based on societal gender-role divisions and helped affirm the idea that women are fragile and not suitable for "masculine" work. A study in Sweden examined how early career professionals in two masters-level programs, psychology and political science, navigated gender to gain legitimacy in relation to their colleagues and clients (Nyström, 2010). This study identified differing strategies among men and women and concluded that these differences reflected responses to gendered expectations within the two professions.

2. For some relational partners this may be unproblematic; others might initially resist but eventually accept and explore their own discomforts and support the learner's developmental struggles (Miller, 1976). If this occurs, relational partners create an accepting environment that mitigates the learner's concerns of rejection and grants the learner with a safe space in which to explore her inner desires. However, there are also times when relational partners are too threatened and react negatively in an effort to control the woman. In such instances, the learner may choose to bring an end to these old relationships and forge new ones that support her continued self-exploration (Miller, 1976). However, there are also times when the learner finds external resistance too extreme or threatening and she may decide to abandon her efforts to resolve identity conflict in exchange for others' approval. If this occurs, the learner may revert to suppressing her discomforts and resort to enacting ascribed roles, making it less likely that she will engage identity conflict again (Miller, 1976).

References

Acker, J. (1990). Hierarchies, jobs, bodies: A theory of gendered organizations. *Gender & Society, 4*(2), 139–158.

Acker, J. (2006). Inequality regimes gender, class, and race in organizations. *Gender & Society, 20*(4), 441–464.

Ashcraft, K., & Mumby, D. (2004). *Reworking gender: A feminist communicology of organization.* Thousand Oaks, CA: Sage Publications.

Avolio, B. (2008). *Leadership development in balance: Born/made.* Mahwah, NJ: Taylor & Francis.

Bailyn, L. (1993). *Breaking the mold: Women, men and time in the new corporate world.* New York, NY: Free Press.

Baxter-Magolda, M. B. (2008). Three elements of self-authorship. *Journal of College Student Development, 49*(4), 269–284.

Baxter-Magolda, M. B. (2009). *Authoring your life: Developing your internal voice to navigate life's challenges.* Sterling, VA: Stylus Publishing.

Bell, L. J., & Nkomo, S. M. (2001). *Our separate ways: Black and white women and the struggle for professional identity.* Boston, MA: Harvard Business School Press.

Bennis, W. (1989). *On becoming a leader.* New York, NY: Basic Books.

Bowers, D., & Seashore, S. (1966). Predicting organizational effectiveness with a four-factor theory of leadership. *Administrative Science Quarterly, 11*(2), 238–263.

Bradley, H., Healy, G., & Mukherjee, N. (2005). Multiple burdens: Problems of work-life balance for ethnic minority trade union activist women. In D.

Houston (Ed.), *Work-life balance in the 21st century* (pp. 211–229). New York, NY: Palgrave McMillan.

Campbell, J. (2008). *The hero with a thousand faces*. Novato, CA: New World Library.

Carvalho, T., & Santiago, R. (2009). Gender as a "strategic action". *Equal Opportunities International, 28*(7), 609–622.

Catalyst. (2004). *Women and men in U.S. corporate leadership: Same workplace, different realities?* New York, NY: Author.

Chodorow, N. J. (1978). *The reproduction of mothering: Psychoanalysis and the sociology of gender*. Berkeley, CA: University of California Press.

Correll, S. J., Kelly, E. L., O'Connor, L. T., & Williams, J. C. (2014). Redesigning, redefining work. *Work & Occupations, 41*(1), 3–17.

Crary, M. (2017). Working from dominant identity positions: Reflections from "diversity aware" white people about their cross-race work relationships. *Journal of Applied Behavioral Sciences, 53*(2), 290–316.

Daft, R. L. (2011). *The leadership experience*. Stamford, CT: Cengage.

Debebe, G. (2017a). Authentic leadership and talent development: Fulfilling individual potential in sociocultural context. *Advances in Developing Human Resources, 19*(4), 420–438.

Debebe, G. (2017b). Navigating the double bind: Transformations to balance contextual responsiveness and authenticity in women's leadership development. *Cogent Business & Management, 4*, 1–28.

Debebe, G., Anderson, D., Bilimoria, D., & Vinnicombe, S. (2017). Women's leadership development programs: Lessons learned and new frontiers. *Journal of Management Education, 40*(3), 231–252.

Debebe, G., & Reinert, K. A. (2014). Leading with our whole selves: A multiple identity approach to leadership development. In M. Miville & A. Ferguson (Eds.), *Handbook of race, ethnicity, and gender in psychology* (pp. 271–293). New York, NY: Springer.

Derue, D. S., Nahrgang, J. D., Wellman, N., & Humphrey, S. E. (2011). Trait and behavioral theories of leadership: An integration and meta-analytic test of their relative validity. *Personnel Psychology, 64*(1), 7–52.

Eagly, A. H. (1987). *Sex differences in social behavior: A social role interpretation*. Hillsdale, NJ: Lawrence Erlbaum.

Eagly, A. H., & Carli, L. L. (2007). *Through the labyrinth: The truth about how women become leaders*. Boston, MA: Harvard Business School Press.

Ely, R. J., & Meyerson, D. E. (2000). Theories of gender in organizations: A new approach to organizational analysis and change. *Research in Organizational Behavior, 22*, 103–151.

Eveline, J., & Booth, M. (2002). Gender and sexuality in discourses of managerial control: The case of women miners. *Gender, Work & Organization, 9*(5), 556–578.

Feidler, F. (1972). The effects of leadership training and experience: A contingency model interpretation. *Administrative Science Quarterly, 17*(4), 453–470.

Fletcher, J. K. (1999). *Disappearing acts: Gender, power, and relational practice at work*. Boston, MA: MIT Press.

Gardner, W. L., Avolio, B. J., Luthans, F., May, D. R., & Walumba, F. (2005). Can you see the real me? A self-based model of authentic leader and follower development. *The Leadership Quarterly, 16*(3), 343–372.

George, B. (2003). *Authentic leadership: Rediscovering the secrets to creating lasting value.* San Francisco, CA: Jossey-Bass.

Gilligan, C. (1982). *In a different voice: Psychological theory and women's development.* Cambridge, MA: Harvard University Press.

Graziano, M. J., Okazaki, S., Chung, G. H., & Barnes, S. P. (2018). Identities of accommodation; identities of resistance: Korean American women and meaning making during post-college. *Narrative Inquiry, 28*(1), 75–93.

Harter, S. (2002). Authenticity. In C. R. Snyder & S. Lopez (Eds.), *Handbook of positive psychology* (pp. 382–394). Oxford, UK: Oxford University Press.

Heritage, J. (1984). *Garfinkel and ethnomethodology.* Cambridge, UK: Polity Press.

Herman, C., Lewis, S., & Humbert, A. L. (2012). Women scientists and engineers in European companies: Putting motherhood under the microscope. *Gender, Work & Organization, 20*(5), 467–478.

Judge, T. A., Piccolo, R. F., & Kosalka, T. (2009). The bright and dark sides of leader traits, a review and theoretical extension of the leader trait paradigm. *The Leadership Quarterly, 20*(6), 855–875.

Keagan, R. (1982). *The evolving self.* Boston, MA: Harvard University Press.

Kegan, R. (1994). *In over our heads: The mental demands of modern life.* Cambridge, MA: Harvard University Press.

Kemper, T. (1974). On the nature and purpose of ascription. *American Sociological Review, 39*(6), 844–853.

Kennelly, I. (2002). "I would never be a secretary": Reinforcing gender in segregated and integrated occupations. *Gender & Society, 16*(5), 603–624.

Lahiri-Dutt, K., & Macintyre, M. (2006). *Women miners in developing countries: Pit women and others.* Burlington, VT: Ashgate.

Lorber, J. (1994). *Paradoxes of gender.* New York, NY: Yale University Press.

Madsen, S. (2008). *On becoming a woman leader: Learning from the experiences of university presidents.* San Francisco, CA: Jossey-Bass.

Meyerson, D. E., & Fletcher, J. K. (2000). A modest manifesto for shattering the glass ceiling. *Harvard Business Review, 78*(1), 126–136.

Miller, G. E. (2004). Frontier masculinity in the oil industry: The experiences of women engineers. *Gender, Work & Organization, 11*(1), 47–73.

Miller, J. B. (1976). *Toward a new psychology of women.* Boston, MA: Beacon Press.

Moorosi, P. (2014). Constructing a leader's identity through a leadership development programme: An intersectional analysis. *Educational Management Administration & Leadership, 42*(6), 792–807.

Nygren, K. G. (2010). Narratives of ICT and organizational change in public administration. *Gender, Work & Organization, 19*(6), 615–630.

Nyström, S. (2010). Graduates "doing gender" as early career professionals. *Career Development International, 15*(4), 324–337.

O'Neil, D. A., & Bilimoria, D. (2008). Women's career development phases: Idealism, endurance, and reinvention. *Career Development International, 10*(3), 168–189.

Pettinger, L. (2005). Gendered work meets gendered goods: Selling and service in clothing retail. *Gender, Work & Organization, 12*(5), 460–478.

Pilgeram, R. (2007). Ass-kicking women: Doing and undoing gender in a US livestock auction. *Gender, Work & Organization, 14*(6), 572–595.

Powell, A., Bagilhole, B., & Dainty, A. (2009). How women engineers do and undo gender: Consequences for gender equality. *Gender, Work & Organization, 16*(4), 411–428.

Ruderman, M. N., & Ohlott, P. J. (2002). *Standing at the crossroads: Next steps for high achieving women.* San Francisco, CA: Jossey-Bass.

Schein, V. E., & Davidson, M. J. (1993). Think manager, think male. *Management Development Review, 6*(3), 24–29.

Schein, V. E., Mueller, R., Lituchy, T., & Liu, J. (1996). Think manager: Think male: A global phenomenon? *Journal of Organizational Behavior, 17*(1), 33–41.

Sen, A. (2006). *Identity and violence: The illusion of destiny.* New York, NY: Norton.

Singh, R. (1983). Leadership style and reward allocation: Does least preferred co-worker scale measure task and relation orientation? *Organizational Behavior and Human Performance, 32*(2), 178–197.

Steinem, G. (1993). *Revolution from within: A book of self esteem.* Boston, MA: Little Brown & Co.

Stogdill, R. M. (1948). Personal factors associated with leadership: A survey of the literature. *Journal of Applied Psychology, 25*(1), 35–71.

Stogdill, R. M. (1950). Leadership, membership and organization. *Psychological Bulletin, 47*(1), 1–14.

Stogdill, R. M. (1974). *Handbook of leadership: A survey of the literature.* New York: Free Press.

Stone, P. (2007). *Opting out? Why women really quit careers and head home.* Berkeley, CA: University of California Press.

Tidball, M. E. (1973). Perspectives on academic women and affirmative action. *Educational Record, 54*(15), 130–135.

Trethewey, A. (1997). Resistance, identity, and empowerment: A postmodern feminist analysis of clients in a human service organization. *Communication Monographs, 64*(4), 281–301.

van den Brink, M., & Stobbe, L. (2009). Doing gender in academic education: The paradox of visibility. *Gender, Work & Organization, 16*(4), 451–470.

Vosko, L. F. (2006). *Precarious employment: Understanding labour market insecurity in Canada.* Montreal, Canada: McGill University Press.

Watts, J. H. (2008). Allowed into a man's world' meanings of work: Life balance: Perspectives of women civil engineers as "minority" workers in construction. *Gender, Work & Organization, 16*(1), 37–57.

West, C., & Zimmerman, D. H. (1987). Doing gender. *Gender & Society, 1*(2), 125–151.

Wilde, V. (2012). CGIAR gender & diversity program progress report: 2010–2012. In *Consultative Group for International Agricultural Research.* https://cgspace. cgiar.org/bitstream/handle/10947/2709/CGIAR_Gender_Diversity_Program_ Progress_Report_2010-2012.pdf?sequence=1&isAllowed=y

Yukl, G. A. (2009). *Leadership in organizations.* Upper Saddle River, NJ, London & New Delhi: Pearson Prentice Hall.

Yukl, G. A. (2012). Effective leadership behavior: What we know and what questions need more attention. *Academy of Management Executive, 26*(4), 66–85.

Zaccaro, S. J. (2007). Trait-based perspectives of leadership. *American Psychologist, 62*(1), 6–16.

Zaccaro, S. J., Kemp, C., & Bader, P. (2004). Leader traits and attributes. In J. Antonakis, A. T. Cianciolo, & R. J. Sternberg (Eds.), *The nature of leadership* (pp. 101–124). Thousand Oaks, CA: Sage Publications.

2 Grounded Dual Contingency Model of Leadership Effectiveness

In the previous chapter, I identified four types of leadership transformations resulting from participation in the WLS. These were:

- Hidden to visible leadership
- Inflexible to receptive leadership
- Intuitive to deliberate leadership
- Depleted to inspired leadership

An interesting feature of these transformations is that each involved change in *habitual patterns* of perceiving, thinking, and feeling about context and authenticity. While we often think of habits as unconscious patterns of behavior, the research has a broader view of habits as learned predispositions to perceive, think, feel, and act in certain ways in response to experienced situations (Dewey, 1922; Garrison, 2002; Cohn et al., 2012). Habits are learned from repetition and are indispensable if people are to conduct themselves competently in daily life. However, not all habits are helpful and, while difficult, habit change is not only possible but is an inescapable and lifelong aspect of development and maturation.

In this chapter, I will expand the dual contingency framework introduced in Chapter 1. In doing so, I will incorporate three additional elements: transformational learning, creating psychological safety through care-practices, and leadership transformations. Subsequent chapters illustrate this framework in detail, using data from the WLS. The crucial insight that these chapters offer is that a shift in habitual patterns of perception, thought, and feeling is the subtle but powerful change that we want to effect to bring about sustainable transformation and improvement in leadership practice. Further, such shifts were effected in the WLS by the use of caring teaching and learning practices that fostered psychological safety, creating the conditions needed for transformational learning. Before moving directly to the presentation of the grounded dual contingency framework, I begin in the next section by briefly discussing the idea of habits.

What Are Habits and How Do They Change?

The automatic, subtle, and ephemeral nature of habitual patterns of thinking is illustrated in a story told by Claudia, one WLS participant. Throughout this chapter I will return to Claudia's story to illustrate and enliven various theoretical points. Before the WLS, Claudia felt that she was "a nobody." Despite positive performance feedback from her boss, it was difficult for her to see the importance of her role in the program she supported. "I got very good feedback, but I saw it as: 'It's not me. I'm not doing this. It's my good boss. And I'm just supporting.'" Despite maintaining this diminished self-conception, Claudia regularly had good ideas that she wanted to share. Claudia described her maneuvering to shield herself from the risk of self-expression:

> Before the course, I would hide behind people. If I had a good idea, or if I thought we should do something, I would not come out alone as the one suggesting it. Instead I would ask somebody else, "What do you think? Should we do this?" And then I would step back. I wouldn't want the idea to come from me.

Let's consider this statement. The construct of habit refers to taken-for-granted *predispositions* of perceiving, feeling, thinking, and acting that inform how people approach the tasks involved in carrying out the myriad activities of daily life (Dewey, 1922). In Claudia's case, when she reflected on how she got others to voice her thoughts, she came to the realization that she played it safe in many situations, asking for permission to do even the smallest of things, instead of taking the risk and acting on her own ideas and judgments. She recognized her general predisposition to hide and avoid taking responsibility for her own thoughts and actions.

Our current understanding of habits has been informed by two complementary theoretical approaches. First, neurologists and psychologists have developed a decontextualized approach that focuses on changes in the brain resulting from repetition of behaviors, the storage of past learning in memory, and the internalization and activation of habitual routines in response to contextual cues. Second, sociologists, philosophers, and educational theorists articulate a context-sensitive perspective of habits. Context-sensitive perspectives focus on the shared nature of habits within societies, as well as the habitual patterns through which distinct social groups emerge. Shared habits arise from socialization processes and have the very important function of preparing new members to enact roles that sustain social customs and hierarchies. While this ensures stability and contributes to social cohesion, the cultivation of shared habits also reproduces societal inequalities, tension, and social conflict. Although having different foci, these two approaches to habit research converge on some important points and, taken together, their distinctive insights complement one another and provide a richer understanding of habits.

One key difference between decontextualized and context-sensitive approaches relates to where habits are located—in a person's brain or in the social environment. Decontextualized theories of habit formation and change seek to understand how learning something new changes the structure of the brain. Using experiments and brain scanning technology, neurologists have shown that, when people learn new behaviors or ways of thinking, neural circuits (communication between nerve cells in the brain facilitated by connectors called synapses) are created (Wood & Rünger, 2016; Davidson & Begley, 2012; Duhigg, 2012; Dunn, 2000). As the behavior or thought is repeated, these connections are strengthened and become durable, committing what has been learned to memory. When triggering context cues are present, the learned habit pattern is automatically recalled from memory and unconsciously performed (Wood & Rünger, 2016; Dunn, 2000). Another important point is that permanent changes to the brain take place in the process of habit formation, a process likened to grooves carved into a vinyl LP. Because of the permanence of the neural circuitry in the process of habit formation, learning a new habit does not proceed by eliminating the established brain structure. Rather, it requires learning something new, a potentially difficult process (e.g., stopping smoking or drinking). Nevertheless, change is not only possible, but is in fact a common occurrence, the vehicle through which human development and growth takes place (Mustafa et al., 2012; Bubolz & Simi, 2015; Cohn et al., 2012; Brockelman, 2002). Thus, the potential to change unhelpful habits is available for any individual who is willing to engage in lifelong learning.

While context-sensitive conceptions of habit formation acknowledge the neurological dimensions of habits, they focus on their social and shared nature. As Cutchin (2007) succinctly stated, "shared situations bring out shared predispositions" (p. 525). Context-sensitive approaches draw attention to the idea that the mind (thoughts, feelings, perception) emerges from society or, to put it another way, the habits of mind are the outcome of socialization. For example, Dewey (1922) comments on the social and shared nature of habit:

> The family into which one is born a village or city interacts with other more or less integrated systems of activity, and includes a diversity of groupings within itself, say, churches, political parties, clubs, cliques, partnerships, trade unions, corporations, etc. If we start with the traditional notion of mind as something complete in itself, then we may well be perplexed by the problem of how a common mind, common ways of feeling and believing and purposing, comes into existence and then forms these groups.
>
> (p. 58)

In these ways, shared habits are a result of socialization and some shared habits potentially include nearly all members of a society (e.g., standing in line at a grocery store and stopping at a red traffic light). Other shared habits are developed within culturally distinct social groups (e.g., religious practices). Thus, individuals develop both widely shared social habits, as well as habits that distinguish them as members of the various sub-cultures within a society (Bordieux, 1984). Furthermore, these contexts of habit formation can interact in dynamic ways, sometimes in synchrony and other times in contradiction and conflict with one another (Gibson, 1979; Bickenbach, 1993; Berlyne, 1966; Dyck, 2002). These dynamics are not only felt at the societal level but also at the individual level, and in some cases, the unique manifestation of the societal tensions and contradictions initiate learning and change in the lives of individuals (Brockelman, 2002).

Individuals can self-select into some social groups, but they are assigned to others based on social identity ascription. While self-selection does not necessarily have inherent implications for an individual's role in society, ascribed identities can be deeply implicated in the maintenance of cultural practices and societal hierarchies (Kemper, 1974). Indeed, social identity ascription processes can involve the development of self-concepts and habit patterns deemed appropriate for their distinct social identity group. For example, as described in Chapter 1, gender socialization processes are means through which men and women internalize masculine and feminine patterns of thought and feeling and use these to navigate in socially endorsed roles and ways as members of a society. The habit of enacting masculinity or femininity therefore becomes internalized and implicated in identity. By enacting internalized and habituated gender identities, men and women help to reproduce the gender differences and hierarchies that characterize a society (Pedwell, 2017).

Functional and helpful habits are indispensable to crafting productive and fulfilling lives. William James (1890, 1950; cited in Garrison, 2002, p. 11S) aptly described this:

> The great thing in all education is to make our nervous system our ally instead of our enemy. For this we must make automatic and habitual, as early as possible as many useful actions as we can. The more of the details of our daily life we can hand over to the effortless custody of automatism, the more our higher powers of mind will be set free for their own proper work.
>
> (Vol. 1, p. 122)

The preceding quote is clearly about the importance of developing good habits but it can also be read as a warning to guard against developing bad ones. Implicit in the preceding quote is a recognition that while good habits are indispensable, bad habits are easy to develop. While some of these bad habits may just be a nuisance, others can be quite harmful and can inhibit growth, damage relationships, derail and undermine hard-won accomplishments, and produce and reproduce a range of social problems. The principle challenge in the process of human development and maturation is not only cultivating and maintaining functional and helpful habits but also changing unhelpful and destructive ones.

Although the learning of formative years is deeply ingrained, new habit patterns can be established, replacing dysfunctional and limiting ones (Mustafa et al., 2012; Bubolz & Simi, 2015; Cohn et al., 2012; Brockelman, 2002). As anyone who has attempted to change a habit knows, however, the process can be difficult. As previously stated, decontextualized perspectives suggest that the difficulty lies in the fact that the cues that trigger a habitual response, as well as the automaticity of the habit response, operate outside of conscious awareness and resist a person's conscious change intentions (Wood & Rünger, 2016; Davidson & Begley, 2012; Duhigg, 2012; Dunn, 2000). Context-sensitive perspectives add that the problem of habit change goes deeper than merely changing how brains are wired. Efforts to change habits must also include an appreciation of how the brain's "wiring" arises from an individual's environment (Dewey, 1922; Cutchin, 2007; Garrison, 2002; Pedwell, 2017). Despite the resulting complexity, the process of shedding old habits and creating new ones is relatively common. Understanding how habits change requires seeing decontextualized and context-sensitive approaches as complimentary rather than at odds with one another.

Decontextualized perspectives focus on the deliberative nature of cognitive processes in the habit-change process. Here the process of change involves learning to recognize habit-triggering contextual cues, catching oneself when automatic habitual patterns are activated, consciously experimenting with new behaviors, and reflecting on the effects of one's experimentation with new ways of thinking and acting (Wood & Rünger, 2016; Davidson & Begley, 2012; Duhigg, 2012; Dunn, 2000). Through such a process, a person begins to learn new ways of perceiving, thinking and acting and slowly creates desired habits that can be activated to override prior and undesirable conditioning.

By contrast, context-sensitive approaches are suspicious of a purely cognitive approach to habit change because of their failure to acknowledge the powerful norms, practices, and social relations that reinforce a habitual pattern. Context-sensitive approaches therefore focus on the learners' capacity to critically reflect on the role and influence of social norms on habitual patterns of thought and action (Dewey, 1922; Garrison, 2002; Cutchin, 2007; Swartz, 2002). Context-sensitive approaches suggest that efforts to change habits often involve examining and critically appraising social influences, especially ascribed identity expectations, on one's conditioned patterns of behavior relative to one's interests, desires, and goals (Pedwell, 2017; Garrison, 2002). Furthermore, if a person's desires run counter to ascribed expectations, attempts to act on new insights might engender social resistance. As will be suggested in what follows, this is where creating a caring and safe environment for exploration becomes very helpful to habit change. The grounded dual contingency model does not create an artificial duality between creating a safe and caring environment for critical reflection and learning and deliberate processes of change. Rather, through this framework I seek to convey the complementarity of decontextualized and context-sensitive approaches to effect lasting habit change.

The Elements of the Grounded, Dual Contingency Framework of Leader Effectiveness

Habits are acquired and changed through a process of learning. As posited by philosopher and educational reformer John Dewey (1938), the learning process is catalyzed by a problematic situation. In the context of this book, a problematic situation can arise from difficulties encountered in navigating context and constructing an authentic identity. A problematic situation is critical to the initiation of learning, but learning is not an automatic response to it. For example, people sometimes ignore the discomforts arising from a problematic situation, preferring evasive coping strategies that inhibit the resolution of the underlying conditions that perpetuate the problematic situation. This was the case in the example of Claudia, who preferred to engage in a complicated behavioral routine to avoid the possibility of failure and displeasing others. The motivation to engage the discomforts and tensions associated with a problematic situation, which initiates learning, is heightened when the situation is no longer acceptable or tolerable or when an individual believes that resolution may be possible. At this point, people may decide to confront their discomforts and initiate the learning process.

Learning may occur at different levels and depths—cognitive, emotional, and behavioral—with different implications for change (Kegan, 2000). Transformational learning is a process that engages all three levels and results in insights that are deep and meaningful, producing a paradigm shift that substantially alters how a person perceives, thinks, feels, and behaves (Mezirow, 2000; Kegan, 2000). Transformational change in the context of leadership entails a shift in habitual patterns of thinking regarding the dual contingencies of context and authenticity. Although subtle, such shifts can be very significant. Ingrained schemas, beliefs, and unconscious assumptions that are socially reinforced are habitually used to frame and act on experiences about the self and context. When habitual patterns are disrupted and schemas modified, sometimes radically, individuals tend to approach a previously problematic situation in an entirely new way.

The grounded, dual contingency framework offers a theoretical perspective on the process of disrupting habitual patterns of thinking about context and/or authenticity through transformational learning within leadership training programs. Figure 2.1, depicted on the next page, pictorially represents this framework. The boxes in the far-left column pertain to habitual patterns of thinking prior to the WLS, while those on the far right pertain to changed patterns of thinking after the WLS. There are also two sets of arrows moving towards the right. The first set of arrows connects the left-column boxes, pertaining to habitual pre-WLS patterns, to the top-middle box labeled "cycle of transformational learning." The second set of arrows connects this top-middle box to the right-column boxes, pertaining to post-WLS patterns. The directionality of both sets of arrows, toward the right, signifies movement and transformation from an unhelpful, habitual pattern towards a new one by means of a transformational learning process. Below the top-middle box is another one labeled, "creating safety through care practices." This box pertains to the characteristics of the WLS learning environment that fostered psychological safety and catalyzed transformational learning in the WLS. The upward-pointing arrow from this box to the one labeled "cycle of transformational learning" signifies that the conditions for psychological safety were created in the WLS by enacting caring teaching and learning practices.

The remainder of this chapter I will elaborate on each of these aspects of the grounded, dual contingency framework. The concept of care-practices will be taken up in Chapter 3 where it will be used to frame the interpretive analysis of that chapter. We begin in the next section with the transformational learning process.

Transformational Learning Process

Mezirow (2000) describes transformational learning as a "movement through time of reformulating reified structures of meaning by reconstructing (a) dominant narrative" (p. 19). The idea of "reified structures" refers to the deep, cognitive frameworks through which we perceive, organize, interpret, and act on stimuli from the environment. Mezirow (2000) calls these frames of reference or "habits of mind." Habits of mind are learned through socialization processes that begin at birth and are reinforced throughout life. Eventually, they become entrenched as beliefs and schemas that are automatically and unconsciously consulted in interpreting situations and acting in response to them. The term "dominant narrative" refers to the idea that these reified, cognitive structures legitimize *a* version of reality and thereby sustain a social order based on an institutionalized, therefore dominant, socio-cultural practice. The final concept in the definition is "reformulating" and has to do with both the re-evaluation of internalized schemas and the construction of new ideas that make change in reified structures possible.

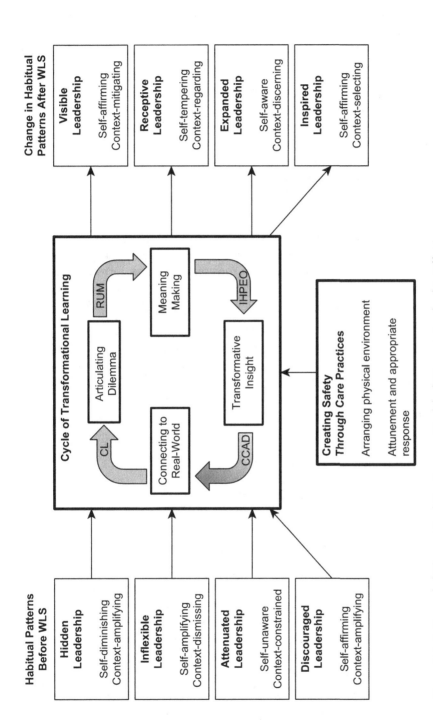

Figure 2.1 A Grounded Theory, Dual Contingency Model of Women's Leadership Effectiveness

Mezirow (1991) articulated *ten stages* in the transformational learning process:

- Disorienting dilemma
- Self-examination of feelings
- Critical assessment of socio-cultural and psychic assumptions
- Recognizing and sharing one's discontent with similar others
- Exploring new roles and relationships
- Planning a course of action
- Acquiring action-relevant knowledge and skills
- Experimenting with new roles
- Building competence and self-confidence
- Reintegrating into one's life

While these ideas have been very influential, they have also been criticized. Taylor (1997) notes that, while Mezirow's stages have been confirmed in some studies, the stages are presented as occurring in linear progression and the boundaries between the steps are not always clearly defined. Studies of transformational learning have shown, however, that the process may be evolving and recursive, and that not all of the stages necessarily apply to all transformative learning experiences. Others criticized Mezirow's (1991) emphasis on rationality, suggesting that learning also includes intuition (van Woerkom, 2010), emotions (Taylor, 1994), and affect (Clark & Wilson, 1991). Each of these critiques has added nuance and complexity to Mezirow's formulation.

In this book and drawing on Debebe (2011), I significantly simplify Mezirow's (1991) ten-stage process, collapsing it to three and adding a new stage. As seen in the box in Figure 2.1 labeled "cycle of transformational learning," the four stages of transformational learning are:

- Encountering a disorienting dilemma
- Meaning-making
- Achieving a transformative insight
- Connecting insight to real-world practice

These four stages best fit the interview data gathered from WLS participants. In addition to these four stages, there are also four preconditions of stage progression (Debebe, 2011). These refer to the shifts in learner focus and attention that occur when the tasks of one stage of transformational learning are completed, and the individual is ready to move on to the task of the next stage. These preconditions are represented by the acronyms embedded within the block arrows that indicate the flow from one stage to the other in the transformational learning process.

- Recognition, uncertainty, and motivation (RUM)
- Interrupting habitual patterns and expanding options (IHPEO)

- Conviction and confidence to act differently (CCAD)
- Continual learning

I will describe these stages and preconditions in some detail next. It is important to recognize, however, that while the stages are presented as conceptually distinct, in practice, there may be blurring between them. For example, issues identified in earlier stages can recur in subsequent stages in the recursive dynamic suggested by some scholars. The discussion will suggest that a linear movement in stages of transformational learning can co-exist with a more dynamic recursive process.

Articulating a Disorienting Dilemma

As described earlier, habit patterns are automatically triggered by a context-cue and carried out unconsciously, without deliberation, reflection, or even meaningful choice. A disconfirming event is a situation that has the potential to interrupt the unconscious enactment of a habitual pattern of thought, feeling, and action. In the example of Claudia, introduced earlier, a disconfirming event was created by 360-degree feedback which revealed to her that her co-workers "saw" how she impacted the program she supported despite her efforts to go unnoticed. As signals from the environment, disconfirming events are often discounted or ignored. Claudia might have been unable and/or unwilling to explore her feelings about the surprising feedback that she had been given. But in some cases, the event grabs an individual's attention and temporarily pauses automaticity, fostering reflection on habitual patterns. Such was the impact of feedback on Claudia.

Reflection is critical in transformational learning and provides some psychological distance from what was previously assumed to be natural and incontrovertible (Mezirow, 1990). If reflection ensues from a disconfirming event, the individual may surface a wide range of issues— concerns, fears, contradictions, and motivations—that can help to reveal the complex considerations involved in a habitual pattern. It can also provide insight into the problem the habitual patterns were developed to address. Claudia was aware that she hid her ideas and justified this behavior by telling herself that she did not have good ideas, while others did. At the same time, however, she offered ideas indirectly by making suggestions to her colleagues who would then voice her thoughts as if the ideas were their own. Reflecting on this apparent contradiction, she pointed out that she hid because she was insecure about how others might react if they did not like her ideas and realized that she tended to play it safe in many other situations.

Claudia's story reveals how people can develop a complicated habitual routine to deal with uncertainty and avoid risk. Surfacing and critically reflecting on the issues that maintain a habitual pattern is necessary if the learner is to articulate a disorienting dilemma. This, in turn, is critical for the person to understand what they need to learn (Mezirow, 1990). Fear of rejection was a critical concern for Claudia and understanding this was important to her being able to articulate her leadership dilemma, namely, how it might be possible to voice her thoughts and work through differences, if they arise, in a manner that preserves relationships. Without articulating a dilemma, the learner does not know what problem they need to find new ways of addressing.

As indicated in the first block arrow in Figure 2.1, and as mentioned previously, there are three preconditions of stage progression. In the case of the movement from encountering a disorienting dilemma to meaning-making, the precondition is recognition, uncertainty, and motivation (RUM). First, the learner *recognizes* that a habitual pattern exists and that it contributes to a problematic situation. Second, although the learner understands that the habitual pattern is inspired by an effort to manage a complex problem, he/she is *uncertain* about how to handle the problem in a more productive manner. Third, the learner must be *motivated* to learn a new way of managing the problem.

The idea of disorientation relates to the situation where a person has gained insight into the issues underlying a problematic habitual pattern, but the way forward is not immediately apparent. The disorientation around the dilemma can produce fear of the unknown and/or concerns of losing control. If these concerns are overpowering, a person will not feel safe enough to examine the issues a habitual pattern seeks to address (Winnicott, 1991; Edmondson, 1999; Argyris, 1986).

Learning is possible if the uncomfortable feelings accompanying disorientation are coupled with curiosity and a motivation to find answers. Relaxing the instinctive defensive posture in the face of the unknown is necessary for learning of any type to take place. In cases where meaning-making commences, the fear of losing control is likely to be present, but apprehensions are mitigated by support from others who can provide a safe space for working through the ambiguities and risks that come with deep examination of habitual patterns (Winnicott, 1991).

Meaning-Making

Mezirow defined learning as "the process of making a new or revised interpretation of the meaning of an experience" (Mezirow & Associates, 1990, p. 1). Meaning-making, the second stage of transformational learning, is the central mechanism in crafting a revised interpretation. It is an activity that unfolds in routine circumstances, as well as in those circumstances where new experiences call into question taken-for-granted constructs. While meaning-making involves crafting an interpretation of events, how it is enacted in routine circumstances differs from how it is enacted in transformational learning processes. As stated by Mezirow and Associates (1990), in routine situations, "when we learn something we attribute an old meaning to a new experience" (p. 11). However, in transformational learning, typically initiated by non-routine circumstances where old meanings cannot render a new experience meaningful, meaning-making involves developing a *new* set of ideas and assumptions (Mezirow & Associates, 1990). Similarly, Daloz (1986) emphasizes the creative nature of the meaning-making process as "taking apart and putting together the structures that give our lives meaning" (p. 236).

Meanings are constructed in social interactions in a collaborative process of working through the ambiguity presented by a novel situation and searching for new input (Mezirow, 2000). We interact with others through texts, theory, conversations, or observations in order to learn new things, test out our ideas, and arrive at some sense of the reasonableness of those ideas, all activities that are integral in leadership train-ing (Velsor, 1998; McCauley & Hughes-James, 1994; Young & Dixon, 1996; Markus, 2001; Zimmerman-Oster & Burkhardt, 2002). Abstract theories as well as the experiences of other learners in the learning environment provide the input necessary for gaining this broader perspective (Mezirow, 1991). The meaning-making process requires that learners maintain a posture of openness in the presence of ambiguity in order to develop an interpretive framework to handle themselves differently in their environment in a manner that resolves the disorientation. Practicing and experimenting with new skills beyond the training setting enable learners to continually explore and refine alternative ways of thinking and acting, and these experiments allow the learner to envision new ways of handling previous dilemmas (Mezirow, 1991).

Numerous studies have used Mezirow's framework to conceptualize how people construct new meanings when faced with disruptive events. While these studies have offered some support to Mezirow's formulation, they have also critiqued and further elaborated it. For example, van Woerkom (2010) critiqued the rationalistic and normative bias of Mezirow's conceptualization of transformational learning and the meaning-making process. He argued that, in addition to cognitive processes, the transformational learning process needs to also explore how emotions and intuition are involved in meaning-making. Moreover, the tendency to distinguish and characterize reflective activities as "good" and "bad" obscures the messy nature of the meaning-making processes.

Clark and Wilson (1991) offered a different critique, arguing that Mezirow's conception of transformational learning and meaning-making ignores how the meaning-making process itself reflects the immediate and historical social conditions to which a learner is subjected. Although they acknowledge that context is *implicitly* considered in the characteristics of the stages that Mezirow developed, his presentation of these stages as *universal* obscures how contextual pressures may necessitate slightly different learning processes for learners, reflecting their social situatedness and standpoint.[1]

Given these critiques, it would be reasonable to think about how learners proceed through the ambiguities of the meaning-making process. That is, what are the emotional and cognitive processes involved in taking in and evaluating new information? What conditions within the meaning-making process thwart the learner's capacity to resolve the disorienting dilemma? What conditions facilitate resolution? The discussion of care-practice in Chapter 3 will provide some possible answers to these questions in the context of women learners.

When meaning-making proceeds in such a manner that learners consider and reflect upon new inputs, they inevitably do what Daloz (1986) described as "taking apart . . . the structures that give our lives meaning" (p. 236). When one has discovered and evaluated one's assumptions and beliefs, it is difficult to pretend that all is as it was before. New knowledge, when deeply considered for its relevance to the dilemma, inherently alters how the dilemma is perceived and disrupts the learner's habitual patterns. This leads to the second precondition of transformational learning, interrupting habitual patterns and expanding options (IHPEO). This precondition is identified in Figure 2.1 by its acronym in the block arrow, indicating movement to the third stage of transformational learning: achieving transformative insight. The learner's next task is to, using Daloz's (1986) language, "put together" what has been learned into new structures that resolve the dilemma in a meaningful way. This is the transformative insight.

Achieving Transformative Insight

A transformative insight is the outcome of meaning-making. It is treated as a separate stage because it marks a significant turning point in meaning construction. It can be thought of as the recognizable "Aha" moment that comes from the exploration and processing of information to resolve a dilemma. Let us return to the example of Claudia. As described previously, Claudia came to the WLS with a habitual pattern of thinking that distorted the value of her contribution to the organization, as well as her capacity for agency relative to those of others. She had developed this pattern of thinking and acting to avoid the discomforts of failure and displeasing others. After receiving 360-degree feedback as part of the activities of the WLS, she understood that her hiding was problematic. This motivated her to find a more functional way of dealing with the potential of others' disapproval. Claudia's "Aha" moment came from written feedback provided by WLS alumnae with whom she had worked on a team during the one-week program. The feedback was part of an exercise in which alumnae were asked to write a letter addressed to each member of their team on what they thought were their strengths and weaknesses. These letters were read out loud by the authors with all team members present. Claudia recalled the positive feedback as follows: "If everyone in the course saw something of value in me, then there must be something in me that I'm not seeing, and I need to be more aware of it."

A transformative insight resolves the disorientation. It is often experienced as that moment of recognition when a person finally "gets it," where confusion lifts, contradictions make sense, and there is a shift in perception. The resulting insight reinstates meaningfulness and provides clarity and relief from the tension created by a disorienting dilemma. The "Aha" moment provides clarity and elicits a "conviction and confidence to act differently" (CCAD), a precondition indicated by the third block arrow in Figure 2.1. This leads to the final stage of transformational learning, connecting insight to real-world practice.

Connecting Insight to Real-World Practice

A transformative insight matures in the fourth stage of transformational learning, namely, connecting insight to real-world practice. Even if it may be some time before a learner manifests a new pattern of behavior, the transformative insight allows her to glimpse an alternative way of thinking and feeling that is deeply compelling and powerfully motivating. In fact, the entire learning experience that takes place in each stage of transformational learning sensitizes the learner to the habitual patterns that are triggered when certain contextual cues are present. This sensitivity, coupled with the new possibilities glimpsed in the transformative insight, heightens learner self-awareness and alters the learner's perception upon returning to work after a transformative formal training experience (Clark, 1993).

Although meaning-making may result in a transformative insight, this is not assurance that the individual can translate the insight into practice automatically. Sometimes, what is required is deliberate learning. That is, applying insights to real-world practice settings entails discipline and the hard work of changing unhelpful and habitual patterns of the past. The insights gleamed from this recursive and on-going process of reflection and learning provides the learner with greater self-understanding, skill, refinement, and confidence as she practices and develops new habits.

Initially the transformative insight will facilitate noticing when habitual patterns are activated. This recognition may create the capacity to pause and reflect on habitual responses. Reflection on habitual patterns requires "catching oneself" engaging in the habitual pattern that may have remained unnoticed if it weren't for the transformative insights. Because of the conditioned and ingrained nature of habit, the learner's challenge is to repeatedly engage in "catching oneself" and "reflecting" in recursive cycles of deepening insight into their underlying assumptions about context and self (authenticity). The maturation of a transformative insight therefore evolves over time to provide the learner with firmer footing in a new and desired behavior. At some point in this iterative process, a new habit or set of habits emerges, and the learner's habitual patterns shift in a consistent way.

Claudia described how she made sure that she applied the insights from the WLS training upon returning to work. Claudia said she repeatedly returned to the feedback from a senior woman on her team, encouraging her not to discount herself because she was young. Claudia said: "I think she got it all right. She really hit it on the head. She told me not to look at my being young as a constraint. I should have more confidence—that is so true. Even now, I still read her notes." Claudia would also think more objectively about her contributions to the organization and focus on the positive impact she was making: "I was able to see how well things have worked out. I saw that I am the one who is doing this and this and that. I have some leadership skills, but I need to appreciate them more." Because earlier patterns are already deeply entrenched, "catching oneself" can be facilitated by a recall tool—an object or thought—to help interrupt the habitual pattern and engage in learning. Claudia's tools were the feedback letters that had been given to her by her team as well as her recall of the encouraging verbal feedback from them. When Claudia became aware of when her fears of displeasing others would arise, she would read the letter or reflect on the verbal feedback and proceed to tell herself: "I have to stop being afraid. The worst is that they won't like it or they'll say 'no,' but I won't die." In these ways, Claudia developed a new way of perceiving how she suppressed her capacity for authentic self-expression and felt overwhelmed by context. She cultivated a new habit pattern that she had only glimpsed as a possibility in the WLS.

Cultivating Conditions for Transformational Learning for Women

The leadership development literature identifies four learning outcomes from training: knowledge acquisition, skill acquisition, self-awareness, and perspective change (Velsor, 1998; McCauley & Hughes-James, 1994; Young & Dixon, 1996; Markus, 2001; Zimmerman-Oster & Burkhardt, 2002). These are essential aspects of meaning-making. However, a purely cognitive understanding can leave habitual patterns of thinking and acting unchanged. An interruption of habitual thought patterns is likely where all four learning outcomes come to bear on a disorienting dilemma, thereby cultivating deep reflection, increased self-awareness, and change of perception.

As emphasized several times, habit change involves transformational learning, which unfolds when a learner feels safe. One key question of this book is: Given the pervasiveness of gender norms that discount women's life experiences and values, how might it be possible to create psychological safety for women learners in a classroom setting? In this section, I frame the discussion of this issue by drawing on Donald Winnicott's idea of *holding environment* (Winnicott, 1991). This idea is a powerful lens through which to view how learners might be encouraged to put down their defenses and trust the learning process and fellow learners as they explore their taken-for-granted assumptions, beliefs, and motivations.[2] In Chapter 3, I go into more depth regarding the activities that occur in a holding environment and through the lens of care-practice.

The Holding Environment and Psychological Safety

The transformational learning process requires that learners maintain a posture of openness in the face of ambiguity and uncertainty. It is particularly difficult for learners to accomplish this when they are faced with a disconfirming event where their deeply conditioned assumptions, ideas, and beliefs come into question. Under these circumstances, the common response is knee-jerk defensiveness (Argyris, 1986), but the opposite reaction is required to learn in the context of a disconfirming event. Winnicott (1991) describes the necessary, receptive learning posture as a *transitional state*. This refers to a posture of curiosity and receptiveness that emerges when a person relaxes his or her defensive routines and suspends habitual patterns of perceiving, thinking, and acting. This state must be sustained to some degree in a robust way throughout the transformational learning process.

A transitional state emerges when a person feels *safe*, but safety cannot be engineered or guaranteed. It can only be *invited* when individuals in a relationship—learners and others—interact in ways that allow the learner freedom to explore his or her thoughts and feelings without fear of judgment. When defenses are lowered, a transitional state emerges (Winnicott, 1991; Edmondson, 1999; Argyris, 1986). The need for self-protection and control wane, and learners become willing to explore uncomfortable thoughts and feelings without hurt or fear of rejection. This supports the transformational learning process.

Winnicott's notion of the holding environment and transitional object help us understand the dynamics that contribute to the creation of psychological safety. The holding environment refers to the social interactions and learning resources assembled in a particular place to support learning (Rogers, 1970; Winnicott, 1991). A holding environment can be thought of as a relational space that is simultaneously a part of and apart from the larger contexts in which the learner is embedded (e.g., family within a community, work group within a division, a classroom within a school). A holding environment is a space in which learners are granted acceptance, respect, support, and challenge to persist in working through conflicting emotions, confusion, and ambivalence that arise when surfacing assumptions upon which habitual patterns are based (Van Buskir & McGrath, 1999; Reinstein, 2006).

The notion of transitional object refers to the individual(s) to whom a learner connects as she works through the ambiguities created by the decision to engage with new and novel ideas in the process of meaning-making (Winnicott, 1991). Such a person essentially "holds" the learner or provides a sense of security despite the ambiguities and uncertainties generated by exploration. This individual can play a crucial role in helping the learner remain calm, open, and focused as she navigates the uncertainties and the social and psychological risks of transformational learning. As it turns out, the holding environment is crucial to providing this realm of support at each step of the transformational learning process.

Given these considerations, we need to explore the requirements to put these learning elements in place within a classroom setting, especially for women.

Barriers to Psychological Safety for Women in Mixed-Sex Groups

Research suggests that, to create safety in a classroom setting, learners must feel accepted and respected, challenged and supported, and have the resources they need to work through a disorienting dilemma (Kolb & Kolb, 2005). Inclusive classroom and training settings encourage learners to engage with texts from the point of view of their unique personal experiences. Challenge is necessary to foster critical thinking and to expand perspectives, but this needs to be coupled with support to resolve a disorienting dilemma. Supportive relationships are built on conversational practices that convey mutual respect and acceptance in the context of differences (Baker, 2002). The goal is to create conditions in which learners are willing to put down their defenses, suspend habitual patterns of perceiving, thinking and acting, and become receptive to new possibilities.

While these general guidelines for creating psychological safety in the classroom resonate with the characteristics of Winnicott's (1991) idea of the holding environment and are applicable to all learners, creating psychological safety for women in the classroom deserves special consideration. One of these is the fact that classrooms, like all other institutions, are embedded within and reflect the broader society. Hence, societal norms and practices relating to gender and other social identities seep into and influence classroom norms and dynamics, undermining the conditions necessary for creating psychological safety. For example, Tanton (1992) evaluated the impact of three types of groups—all male, majority male, and sex-balanced—on classroom safety for women. Although women were not physically present in the all-male group, male bonding was partly achieved through what Tanton (1992) called the "debasement" of women. In the majority male group, both males and females denied gender differences. Although women participants acquired knowledge and skill in this setting, they also felt that there were risks associated with sharing their experiences and values when these departed from the ideal worker norm discussed in Chapter 1. Some commonly suppressed concerns include women's differing career paths (Hopkins et al., 2008), emphasis on instrumental goals and rationality, the associated lack of attention to ethical issues, and narrow definitions of success (Vinnicombe & Singh, 2003).

Balanced groups are rare in management training but seem more promising in terms of the inclusion of women's experience. For example, Tanton (1992) found that, in sex-balanced groups, men and women expressed their differing experiences, there was intergroup dialogue, and little tolerance for dishonoring women's experience. Baker (2002) describes a similar dynamic in conversations about diversity in a classroom balanced in terms of social identity dimensions (race, gender, nationality, and ethnicity). Although demographic balance can contribute to inclusion of women's experience, this may not be sufficient to facilitate transformational learning for women. Specifically, although female participants in gender-balanced groups were able to share their experiences and perspectives without fear of ridicule and in an accepting environment, much of this sharing was focused on others' learning. That is, women in the sex-balanced group setting shared their experiences in an effort to educate men. While this is likely helpful for both men and women, it also serves a purpose which is different than that of fostering self-awareness and transformational learning for women.

Conditions for Psychological Safety for Women in Single-Sex Classrooms

As it turns out, fostering relationships that grow out of a shared gender experience may be promising for the purpose of creating a safe learning environment for women's transformational learning. Some researchers advocate women-only training (WOT) where participants can be free from gender-related constraints to fully explore their experiences without feeling the need for suppression or explanation (Limerick & Heywood, 1993). For many women, being in an all-female environment is both rare and affirming, immediately putting them at ease. For example, when Willis and Daisley (1997) asked women to describe their experiences within WOT, the majority said they felt more able to express their views freely, felt confident and trusting, and were willing to take risks and speak up in a large group. Participants in WOT also described the invaluable lessons gleamed from the collective wisdom and experience of other women.

Effective WOT programs are designed with an understanding of women's preference for collaborative and relationally oriented teaching and learning methods (Vinnicombe & Singh, 2002, 2003). The instructor and other participants can serve as "midwives," eliciting women's experience and offering their resources to facilitate self-discovery in supportive and challenging relations (Vinnicombe & Singh, 2003). Women are also encouraged to discuss issues that are salient and relevant to their lives and organizational experiences. Such issues include work-life balance, authentic self-expression, competition and conflict, and managing gender in these and other aspects of women's organizational lives (Vinnicombe & Singh, 2002, 2003). In addition, attention can be given to exploring how the gendered structures of organizations impact women's work and leadership experience (Hopkins et al., 2008). Like in most other leadership training settings, WOT programs use a variety of self-assessment tools to increase self-knowledge, but these are interpreted with sensitivity to women's experiences and relational-orientation and values (Vinnicombe & Singh, 2002, 2003).

Although the WOT literature does not explain *how* these programs engender the conditions that foster safety for learners, the single-sex education literature proposes the outlines of an interesting explanation. The research suggests that creating a safe learning environment for women requires a *holistic* approach. This means that every aspect of the environment, including the content of learning, teaching methods, values, and the norms of interpersonal relationships, affirm and reflect women's experiences and values (Tidball, 1973; Meehan, 2007). This environment does not rely on negating or denigrating other experiences. Rather, its defining feature is the recognition that acknowledging and validating women's life experiences and values is important to making education relevant, meaningful, and transformative. The relatedness of identity to education has been well documented elsewhere (Stacey, 1974; Spender, 1997; Belenky & Clinchy, 1986; Sefa Dei & Simmons, 2010). This literature addresses the damaging effects of education that suppresses, rejects, or disappears learner experiences, as well as the liberating and empowering effects of education that affirms and celebrates learners' lived experiences.

A key insight from the literature on single-sex education is that creating an environment for girls and women requires taking a holistic approach, validating and affirming women's values and experiences. Such an environment creates the subjective experience of belonging, of shared experiences and the likelihood of being understood by others, and thereby has the potential of relaxing the anxieties learners bring into the classroom. In addition to harkening back to Winnicott's (1991) notion of holding environment, both the WOT and single-sex education literatures underscore the importance of the quality of interactions in the creation of safety for participants.

Despite the promise of WOT programs, however, there are some limitations that should be noted. For example, the single-sex nature of WOT is a necessary but insufficient condition for creating a holding environment for women learners. Some researchers caution that WOT programs can inhibit psychological safety for women if they are designed on the premise that, for women to be taken seriously and succeed as leaders, they must abide by the rules of the game, which is aligned with the ideal worker norm discussed in Chapter 1. This often translates into an unchallenged assumption that women must try to emulate the masculine characteristics of their male colleagues (Gray, 1994). Such program characteristics can undermine psychological safety for women by reducing women's confidence, devaluing their experiences, values, and aspirations, and reinforcing the gendered pressures women already face (Gray, 1994; Reavley, 1989). Therefore, the key takeaway from the single-sex research, is that WOT programs create the conditions for transformational learning when they are designed to holistically affirm women's experiences.

The Four Leader Transformations of the WLS

The final component of the grounded, dual contingency framework relates to the four transformations of the WLS. These transformations were the result of transformative learning experiences, which were catalyzed by the safety created within the WLS. Each of the four transformations contributed to improved leadership effectiveness among WLS alumnae by effecting shifts in participants' habitual patterns of perceiving and responding to their context and sense of themselves (authenticity).

The first transformation facilitated by the WLS was from *hidden* to *visible* leadership. Hidden leadership is associated with behaviors whose function is to make attributes or characteristics of the leader blend in, go unnoticed, become obscured, and be easily overlooked. Hidden leadership stories were about how individuals suppressed key aspects of themselves (ideas, values, identities) that could be important to task performance. This reflected a habitual pattern of self-diminishing and context-amplifying thinking in which individuals constructed the self as weak relative to a robust external context. In contrast, visible leadership behaviors were aimed at owning one's views, ideas, and beliefs. Visible leadership involved self-expression and connecting with others in order to make a contribution. In contrast to hidden leadership stories, visible leadership stories reflected a different pattern of thinking that I refer to as self-affirming and context-mitigating. Visible leaders acknowledged their strengths and realistically assessed the context relative to obstacles and opportunities for taking action, a significant shift from the pre-WLS habitual thought pattern.

The second transformation facilitated by the WLS was from *inflexible* to *receptive* leadership. Inflexible leader behaviors are characterized by bewilderment about the context and rigidity in the face of uncertain and ambiguous situations. Bewilderment about context often caused anxiety and trepidation, and inflexible leaders responded by clinging to what they knew or believed, or what had worked in the past. A habitual pattern of self-amplifying and context-dismissing thinking shaped inflexible behaviors. This thought process involved providing justification for one's actions, while expressing indignation and negative judgment about the unwanted behavior of others. Whereas inflexible leaders anxiously relied on their ideas, values, and beliefs when faced with uncertainty, the transformation to receptive leadership involved a willingness to relax prior beliefs or assumptions so as to learn from and be influenced by others, while also having a clear sense of one's views and preferences. In stories of receptive leadership, alumnae described self-amplifying and context-dismissing thought processes being replaced by self-tempering and context-regarding thought processes. These new thought patterns were characterized by acknowledgment of the validity of and need to account for both one's own and others' views, and this granted receptive leaders the opportunity to learn and more fully account for context.

The third transformation facilitated by the WLS was from *intuitive* to *deliberate* leadership. Based on their experiences of leading others, intuitive leaders felt they were effective as leaders, but they could not explain their successes. Their leadership capacity came from their ability to listen, observe, and interpret their environment and their own thoughts and feelings by drawing on tacit knowledge. Stories of intuitive leadership were characterized by self-unaware and context-constrained thinking. While the capacity to access and use intuitive knowledge contributed to their attunement and responsiveness to their environment, their inability to consciously access this knowledge proved to be a stumbling block when they encountered resistance. Thus, context-constrained thinking was manifested in a struggle to read the environment and discern and understand what others needed. It was precisely when they encountered resistance that they needed to be conscious of what they did, why it worked, and when it worked. Without being mindful of the basis or grounds for their actions, they could not identify what was missing in the circumstances when they met with resistance. The shift to deliberate leadership entailed just this type of conscious application of knowledge. Deliberate leadership was evidenced in greater self-awareness and regulation of intuitive processes that guide behavior and the capacity to choose new approaches attuned to the situation and to the self. Thus the shift to deliberate leadership was characterized by a new pattern of thinking that I call self-aware and context-discerning.

The fourth and final transformation facilitated by the WLS was from *depleted* to *inspired* leadership. The notion of depletion suggests a lack of optimism and energy due to encountering seemingly persistent structural and cultural obstacles to goal achievement. Depleted leaders told stories of overcoming such obstacles only to encounter them repeatedly in subsequent efforts. This left them drained and disinclined to "play-the-game." A habitual pattern of self-affirming, context-obliged thinking shaped leadership behaviors. This thought process is characterized by an individual's commitment to consistently act in accordance with one's values despite the lack of support for one's efforts. The notion of being inspired pertains to a sense of becoming energized, encouraged, and excited to do something. While the context had not changed, inspired leaders had. Instead of thinking of themselves as marginal and unappreciated, they focused on how they could feel fully engaged in carrying out organizational goals by selectively cultivating supportive contexts. Post-WLS leadership stories reflected transformation to inspired leadership in which self-affirming and context-aligned thought processes replaced the earlier self-affirming and context-obliged ones. These latter thought processes are characterized by recognizing the value of one's contributions and being committed to honor them but doing so selectively with inspired leaders' well-being in mind.

Summary

In this chapter, I built on the dual contingency framework laid out in Chapter 1 by incorporating insights from the transformational learning and women's learning literatures. I grounded these theoretical perspectives by incorporating the four leadership transformations resulting from the WLS training as well as the notion of creating a caring and safe environment. This chapter has also focused on habit change, suggesting that the four transformations of the WLS were accomplished by shifts in habitual patterns of thinking and feeling about context and authenticity that enabled WLS alumnae to better attend to the dual contingencies of context and authenticity. Chapters 3 to 7 will draw on the WLS data to illustrate the model. I begin in the next chapter by describing the core theme of creating a caring and safe environment for women leaders. Chapters 4 to 7 will consider each transformation type in some detail.

While the single-sex education and women-only-training literatures provide valuable insights into the question of how psychological safety might be created for women in a classroom setting, these insights are largely descriptive. The next chapter builds on these descriptive insights and provides a theoretical explanation that illuminates the conditions and processes needed within women-only programs to foster safety. In particular, Chapter 3 will consider the concept of care-practice to provide a more general understanding of how psychological safety is fostered in relationships, bounded within a holding environment. The concept of care-practice offers a theoretical explanation for the "midwife" metaphor that has been used to describe how learning is facilitated in WOT.

Notes

1. Some of these issues were partially addressed by Debebe (2011).
2. The idea of the holding environment has also been applied to the classroom setting by other scholars (e.g. Ely et al., 2011; Kisfalvi & Oliver, 2015; Garran & Rasmussen, 2014).

References

Argyris, C. (1986). Reinforcing organizational defensive routines: An unintended human resources activity. *Human Resource Management*, 25(4), 541–555.

Baker, A. C. (2002). Receptive spaces for conversational learning. In A. C. Baker, P. J. Jensen, & D. A. Kolb (Eds.), *Conversational learning: An experiential approach to knowledge creation* (pp. 101–124). Westport, CT: Quorum Books.

Belenky, M. F., Clinchy, B. M., Goldberger, N. R., & Tarule, J. M. (1986). *Women's ways of knowing: The development of self, voice, and mind.* New York, NY: Basic Books.

Berlyne, D. (1966). Curiosity and exploration. *Science, 153*(3731), 25–33.

Bickenbach, J. (1993). *Physical disability and social policy.* Toronto, Canada: University of Toronto Press.

Bordieux, P. (1984). *Distinctions. A social critique of the judgment of taste.* Cambridge, MA: Harvard University Press.

Brockelman, P. T. (2002). Habits and personal growth: The art of the possible. *Occupation, Participation and Health, 22*(Suppl. 1), 18S–30S.

Bubolz, B., & Simi, P. (2015). Leaving the world of hate: Life-course transitions and self-change. *American Behavioral Scientist, 59*(12), 1588–1608.

Clark, C. M. (1993). Transformational learning. In S. B. Merriam (Ed.), *New directions for adult and continuing education: No. 7. An update on adult learning theory* (pp. 47–56). San Francisco, CA: Jossey-Bass.

Clark, C. M., & Wilson, A. L. (1991). Context and rationality in Mezirow's theory of transformational learning. *Adult Education Quarterly, 41*(2), 75–91.

Cohn, E. S., Cortes, D. E., Fix, G., & Mueller, N. (2012). Habits and routines in the daily management of hypertension. *Journal of Health Psychology, 17*(6), 845–855.

Cutchin, M. P. (2007). From society to self (and back) through place: Habit in transactional context. *Occupation, Participation and Health, 27*(Suppl. 1), 50S–59S.

Daloz, L. A. (1986). *Effective teaching and mentoring: Realizing the transformational power of adult learning experience.* San Francisco, CA: Jossey-Bass.

Davidson, R. J., & Begley, S. (2012). *The emotional life of your brain: How its unique patterns affect the way you think, feel, and live: And how you can change them.* New York, NY: Penguin Group.

Debebe, G. (2011). Creating a safe environment for women's leadership transformation. *Journal of Management Education, 35*(5), 679–712.

Dewey, J. (1922). *Human nature and conduct.* New York: Modern Library.

Dewey, J. (1938). *Experience and education.* New York, NY: Touchstone Rockefeller Center.

Duhigg, C. (2012). *The power of habit: Why we do what we do in life and business.* New York: Random House.

Dunn, W. W. (2000). Habit: What's the brain got to do with it? *Occupation, Participation and Health, Occupational Therapy Journal of Research, 20*(Suppl. 1), 6S–20S.

Dyck, I. (2002). Beyond the clinic: Restructuring the environment in chronic illness experience. *OTJR: Occupation, Participation and Health, 22*(Suppl. 1), 52S–60S.

Edmondson, A. (1999). Psychological safety and learning behavior in teams. *Administrative Science Quarterly, 44*(2), 350–383.

Ely, R. J., Ibarra, H., & Kolb, D. M. (2011). Taking gender into account: Theory and design for women's leadership development programs. *Academy of Management Learning & Education, 10*(3), 474–493.

Garran, A. M., Rasmussen, B. M. (2014). Safety in the classroom: Reconsidered. *Journal of Teaching in Social Work, 34*(4), 401–412.

Garrison, J. W. (2002). Habits as social tools in context. *The Occupational Therapy Journal of Research: Occupation, Participation, and Health, 22*(1), 11S–17S.

Gibson, J. (1979). *The ecological approach to visual perception.* Boston: Houghton Mifflin.

Gray, B. (1994). Women-only management training: A past and present. In M. Tanton (Ed.), *Women in management: A developing presence* (pp. 202–228). London, UK: Routledge.

Hopkins, M. M., O'Neil, D., Passarelli, A., & Bilimoria, D. (2008). Women's leadership development: Strategic practices for women in organizations. *Consulting Psychology Journal: Practice and Research, 60*(4), 348–365.

James, W. (1890). *The principles of psychology.* New York: Henry Holt and Company.

James, W. (1950). *The principles of psychology.* New York: Dover Publications.

Kegan, R. (2000). What "form" transforms? A constructive-developmental approach to transformative learning. In J. Mezirow, & Associates (Eds.), *Learning as transformation* (pp. 3–34). San Francisco, CA: Jossey-Bass.

Kemper, T. (1974). On the nature and purpose of ascription. *American Sociological Review, 39*(6), 844–853.

Kisfalvi, V., & Oliver, D. (2015). Creating and maintaining a safe space in experiential learning. *Journal of Management Education, 39*(6), 713–740.

Kolb, A. Y., & Kolb, D. A. (2005). Learning styles and learning spaces: Enhancing experiential learning in higher education. *Academy of Management Learning & Education, 4*(2), 193–212.

Limerick, B., & Heywood, E. (1993). Training for women in management: The Australian context. *Women in Management Review, 8*(3), 23–30.

Markus, G. B. (2001). *Building leadership: Findings from a longitudinal evaluation of the kellogg fellowship program.* Battle Creek, MI: W.K. Kellogg Foundation.

McCauley, C. D., & Hughes-James, M. W. (1994). *An evaluation of the outcomes of leadership development program.* Greensboro, NC: Center for Creative Leadership.

Meehan, D. (2007). *Learning like a girl.* New York, NY: Public Affairs.

Mezirow, J. (1991). *Transformative dimensions of adult learning.* San Francisco, CA: Jossey-Bass.

Mezirow, J. (2000). Learning to think like an adult: Core concepts of transformation theory. In J. Mezirow (Ed.), *Learning as transformation: Critical perspectives on a theory in progress* (pp. 3–34). San Francisco, CA: Jossey-Bass.

Mezirow, J., & Associates. (1990). How critical reflection triggers transformative learning. In J. Mezirow (Ed.), *Fostering critical reflection in adulthood* (pp. 1–20). San Francisco, CA: Jossey-Bass.

Mustafa, N., Ahearn, T., Waiter, G., Murray, A., Whalley, L., & Staff, R. (2012). Brain structural complexity and life course cognitive change. *NeuroImage, 61*(3), 694–701.

Pedwell, C. (2017). Transforming habit: Revolution, routine and social change. *Cultural Studies, 31*(1), 93–120.

Reavley, M. (1989). Who needs training: Women or organizations? *Journal of Management Development, 8*(6), 55–60.

Rogers, C. (1970). *On becoming a person.* New York, NY: Houghton Mifflin.

Sefa Dei, G., & Simmons, M. (2010). *Fanon and education: Thinking through pedagogical possibilities.* New York, NY: Peter Lang Publishing Inc.

Spender, D. (1997). *Invisible women: The schooling scandal.* London, UK: Women's Press, Ltd.

Stacey, J. (1974). *And Jill came tumbling after: Sexism in American education.* New York, NY: Dell Publishing Co.

Swartz, D. L. (2002). The sociology of habit: The perspective of Pierre Bourdieu. *OTJR: Occupation, Participation and Health, 22*(Suppl. 1), 61S–69S.

Tanton, M. (1992). Developing authenticity in management development programmes. *Women in Management Review, 7*(4), 20–27.

Taylor, E. W. (1994). Intercultural competency: A transformative learning process. *Adult Education Quarterly, 44*(3), 154–174.

Taylor, E. W. (1997). Building upon the theoretical debate: A critical review of the empirical literature. *Adult Education Quarterly, 48*(1), 34–59.

Tibbals, C. A. (2007). Doing gender as resistance: Waitresses and servers in contemporary table service. *Journal of Contemporary Ethnography, 36*(6), 731–751.

Tidball, M. E. (1973). Perspectives on academic women and affirmative action. *Educational Record, 54,* 130–135.

Van Buskir, W., & McGrath, M. C. (1999). Organizational cultures as holding environments: A psychodynamic look at organizational symbolism. *Human Relations, 52*(6), 805–832.

van Woerkom, M. (2010). Critical reflection as a rationalistic ideal. *Adult Education Quarterly, 60*(4), 339–356.

Velsor, E. (1998). Assessing the impact of development experiences. In C. D McCauley, R. S. Moxley, & E. V. Velsor (Eds.), *The center for creative leadership handbook of leadership development* (pp. 262–288). San Francisco, CA: Jossey-Bass.

Vinnicombe, S., & Singh, V. (2002). Developing tomorrow's women business leaders. In R. J. Burke & D. L. Nelson (Eds.), *Advancing women's careers: Research and practice* (pp. 206–219). Malden, MA: Blackwell.

Vinnicombe, S., & Singh, V. (2003). Women-only management training: An essential part of women's leadership development. *Journal of Change Management, 3*(4), 294–306.

Willis, L., & Daisley, J. (1997). Women's reactions to women-only training. *Women in Management Review, 12*(2), 56–60.

Winnicott, D. W. (1991). *Playing and reality.* New York, NY: Routledge.

Wood, W., & Rünger, D. (2016). The psychology of habits. *Annual Review of Psychology, 67*(11.1), 289–314.

Young, D. P., & Dixon, N. M. (1996). *Helping leaders take effective action: A program evaluation.* Greensboro, NC: Center for Creative Leadership.

Zimmerman-Oster, K., & Burkhardt, J. C. (2002). *Leadership in the making: Impact and insight from leadership development programs in U.S. colleges and universities.* Battle Creek, MI: W.K. Kellogg Foundation.

3   Creating a Caring and Safe Environment

They immediately said, we want to take care of you this week. We've got a lot to do and we're going to work hard, but this is also about taking care of you guys and thinking about the work-life balance and taking care of yourself.

WLS participant

A large part of the transformation that happens for women is actually at a psychological and emotional level. And you need to create a safe place for that exposure.

WLS Participant

Chapter 1 identified two core themes resulting from analysis of data obtained from interviews with WLS alumnae. These themes were: *leadership transformations* and *creating a caring and safe environment for women learners*. The first theme will be illustrated in Chapters 4 through 7. This chapter will illustrate the second of these core themes and, in doing so, address one of the three research questions explored in this book. The question is: What aspects of the WLS teaching and learning methodology facilitated women's leadership transformation and why were these aspects important? The interpretive analysis of this chapter will seek to answer this question, and in the process, it will also illustrate one aspect of the dual contingency framework: fostering psychological safety by creating a safe learning environment.

Recall the claim, in the previous chapter, that the four leadership transformations of the WLS were effected by shifts in habitual patterns of thinking and feeling about context and authenticity. In this chapter, we will see that creating a caring environment in the WLS fostered psychological safety for participants. Specifically, the chapter will argue that, in the WLS, the competitive behavioral norms prevalent within the CGIAR centers were kept at bay, and a caring environment was created by means of caring teaching and learning practices. WLS alumnae responded to this by putting down their defenses and allowing themselves to be vulnerable.

This, in turn, facilitated the expression and exploration of participants' real concerns about their work and life experiences, and this led to greater self-awareness, particularly with regards to the habitual patterns of thinking, feeling, and acting that limited their effectiveness as leaders.

The previous chapter identified contrasting approaches to conceptualizing habit formation and change. A decontextualized perspective emphasizes how habits are formed through the repetition of behavior. Repetition results in permanent changes to the brain, a process likened to grooves carved into a vinyl LP. Once a habit pattern is created, the habit routine is triggered unconsciously and automatically in the presence of habit-activating cues. Although the neural networks created in the habit formation process are permanent, habit change is an inescapable part of human maturation and development. From the perspective of decontextualized theories, new habits are established through deliberate learning.[1] Context-sensitive perspectives, on the other hand, view habits as socially generated and shared. Habits are created and sustained by the confluence of multilayered influences operating on an individual in the workplace setting. Thus, ignoring context and assuming that mere repetition of new behaviors is sufficient to change habits is tantamount to paying attention to the image in the foreground and ignoring the background. Context-sensitive approaches put less emphasis on the repetition of new behaviors and focus on the creation of transformative contexts, for the purpose of fostering critical reflection and learning in the habit change process.

The WLS was one such context, simultaneously a part of the CGIAR and apart from it. This chapter will focus on how the conditions for transformational learning and shifts in unhelpful habitual patterns were created in the WLS by means of caring teaching and learning practices. I begin in the next section by elaborating on the idea of care-practice, introduced in the previous chapter. The remainder of the chapter will draw on data from my interviews to elucidate five caring and teaching practices related to creating a caring and safe environment. These are: *disruptive physical cues, building an inclusive and accepting environment, caring norms, relaxed learning,* and *staying in touch.* Safety is created through care practices by *arranging the physical features of a holding environment and attuement to care recipient's verbal and non-verbal cues.* The concept of care-practice was crucial to understanding how these teaching and learning practices fostered psychological safety, learner willingness to be vulnerable, and encouraged exploration and eventually shifts in learners' habitual patterns.

Relationships of Care and Human Development

In a groundbreaking article and book, Carol Gilligan (1977, 1982) challenged the prevailing understanding of human moral development proposed by her mentor Lawrence Kohlberg (1971). Kohlberg presented boys of different ages with hypothetical scenarios that entailed a moral dilemma and asked them to explain their moral evaluation of the scenario. Analyzing the boys' rationale, he proposed a theory of stages of moral development. Empirical studies measuring moral development using Kohlberg's model found that boys were more morally mature than girls. Gilligan (1977) argued that Kohlberg's framework privileged a masculine perspective on morality and was therefore biased, incomplete and unable to account for women's moral development. She stated:

> The very traits that have traditionally defined the goodness of women, their care for and sensitivity to the needs of others, are those that mark them as deficient in moral development. The infusion of feeling into their judgments keeps them from developing a more independent and abstract ethical conception in which concern for others derives from principles of justice rather than from compassion and care.
>
> (p. 484)

Gilligan (1977, 1982) proposed an alternative perspective on morality, stemming from women's social experiences, an ethic of care. Although she did not discount Kohlberg's theory, she argued that justice concerns co-existed with those of care, the latter emphasizing relationships, as well as the needs and wants of particular people. Gilligan's work made seminal contributions to feminist scholarship on the care ethic. This literature also intersects with humanistic relational psychologists' conceptualization of care by elaborating on the activities that take place in Winnicott's (1991) holding environment discussed in Chapter 2. Considered together, these streams of care research offer a glimpse into the vital, complex, and subtle phenomenon of care and especially its role in human learning and growth.

Care is a multidimensional construct, and its different features become salient depending on the context to which the concept is applied (Abel & Nelson, 1990). Drawing on women's stories, Gilligan incorporated the notion of care in moral reasoning. Building on her work, other feminist scholars explored the role of care in human development, bringing particular attention to what mothers do to foster growth and development in their infants and children. For example, Ruddick (1998) conceptualized care as a relationship and explored care-practice as a particular type of labor within the relationship. Held (2006) also viewed care as a type of labor and added the notion of inspirational ideal to her conception of care. In this work, care is a form of labor that is guided by an inspiring image of what is desired. Finally, without losing the focus on the ethical, inspirational, and practice components of care, Tronto (2013) expanded the notion of care from the private sphere of the home to the public spheres of organizations, institutional arrangements, and policy formulation. Fischer and Tronto (1990) offered one of the most popular and helpful definitions of care as: "a species of activity that includes everything we do to maintain, contain, and repair our 'world' so that we can live in it as well as possible. That world includes our bodies, ourselves, and our environment" (p. 103). It is worth noting here that, to the three functions of care proposed in this definition—maintaining, containing, and repairing—there is also the function of fostering growth, a crucial concern for both feminist scholars of care and humanistic relational psychologists (Miller & Stiver, 1997; Winnicott, 1991; Bowlby, 1988; Ruddick, 1980).

Referring to the work of pediatrician and relational psychologist Donald Winnocott, Davis and Wallbridge (1981) note that Winnicott believed that, "every human being, given a facilitating environment intrinsically contains the momentum for growth towards emotional as well as physical maturity, towards a positive contribution to society" (p. 88). Opportunities for continued growth present themselves throughout life with new developmental tasks and challenges. Growth requires meeting these challenges with new learning—acquisition of knowledge, skills, mindsets, confidence—that enable the individual to take on new roles in ever-widening contexts.

Learning is initiated by a problematic situation, characterized by an unrealized need and a goal, however vaguely conceived by the learner. The effort to resolve the problem gives rise to uncertainty and risk (Dewey, 1938). How the learner perceives and responds to uncertainty has significant bearing on whether growth occurs or if it is blocked. Fear of failure can foster risk aversion and uncertainty avoidance. Avoidant behaviors temporarily reduce anxiety but if these are relied upon, they become habits that block long-term growth. The natural inclination toward learning and growth is supported in a growth-fostering relationship between care-recipient and care-giver. The absence of such a relationship or dysfunction within it impedes learning, blocks growth, and fosters helplessness. Therefore, important questions concern the care-giver and care-recipient interaction when uncertainty is encountered: What do care-givers do in relation to care-recipients to encourage the latter to engage with uncertainty and learn and grow? Alternatively, what do care-givers do relative to care-recipients in situations where the latter shrink from risk and withdraw to their comfort zone?

Ruddick (1980) used the term care-practice to refer to what care-givers do to foster growth in another person. Care-practice is not an emotion, although it is motivated and sustained by the energy of love (Kittay, 1999). But love alone is insufficient to foster growth. Providing care requires skill. This skill has been obscured because care-practice has been primarily reserved for cultural subordinates—women and ethnic and racial minorities. It has also been regarded as natural for these groups (e.g., mother's instinct) rather than a learned and skilled practice. However, care-practice requires knowledge and skill which must be continually refined to enable the care-giver to respond appropriately to the care-recipient's changing needs and capacities (Ruddick, 1980). Because it involves lifelong learning, care-giving can also contribute to care-givers' learning and growth (Miller & Stiver, 1997). Care-practice is therefore an active, evolving, and committed exertion of mental, emotional, and physical energy on the part of the care-giver to foster learning and growth in the care-recipient.

Ruddick (1980, 1998) encapsulated care-practice in the concept of maternal thinking. According to Ruddick (1980), maternal thinking refers to intellectual practices that co-exist in "unity" with feeling, judgment, reflection, metaphysical attitudes, and values. These elements work together to foster the care-giver's attunement to the care-recipient's emotional needs and moods and to guide care-giver responses to the care-recipient. The attitudes of the care-giver, humility being a chief one, allow him or her to respond to the care-recipient with a recognition that opening to the unknown is necessary for learning and growth, despite there being no assurances that things will turn out as desired and intended. The care-giver persists with acceptance of this fact and responds to the emerging needs of the care-recipient, hoping that these efforts will propel the care-recipient to engage with uncertainty, learn, and grow.

Instead of using the term care-practice, Winnicott (1991) prefers the term "holding" to describe the nature of skilled care-giving. According to him, holding occurs in a physically and psychologically bounded, safe space that is simultaneously part of and apart from the larger environment in which the care-recipient and care-giver interact (Ruddick, 1980; Winnicott, 1964). Although Ruddick (1980) does not specifically cite the notion of holding environment, she too envisions caring as taking place in a physically and psychologically bounded environment. One aspect of care-practice involves arranging the physical features of a holding environment to respond to all aspects of the care-recipient's needs so as to foster physical and emotional comfort and contentment. Another aspect of care-practice is attunement and appropriate response to care recipient's verbal and non-verbal cues. (Ruddick, 1980; Winnicott, 1964). This entails the capacity to sense, recognize, and interpret the care-recipient's emotional needs and moods and respond appropriately. The goal is to elicit alertness and interest rather than defensive withdrawal. An engaged and alert care-recipient is more likely to respond to the care-giver's encouragement to engage and explore the unknown than one who maintains a distance.[2]

Through arranging the physical environment with the needs of the care-recipient in mind and through attunement to the care-recipient's cues, the skilled care-giver seeks to, on the one hand, shield the care-recipient from environmental demands that could be overwhelming and, on the other hand, encourage the care-recipient to explore new things in order to learn and develop comfort and competence in new domains (Bowlby, 1988). By letting go, the care-giver grants freedom and autonomy, but by keeping a watchful eye and being there, the care-giver provides reassurance that the care-recipient has a safe space to which to retreat and regain equilibrium. This delicate balance fosters psychological safety and the willingness of the learner to engage uncertainty and take risks (Bowlby, 1988). The capacity to calm oneself when faced with unsettling experiences fosters the care recipient's continued willingness to engage uncertainty, learn, and grow throughout life.[3]

Even in the best of circumstances, care-practice may fail or not follow this idealized trajectory. Sometimes care-givers are not attuned to the needs of the care-recipient and are unable to respond to the care-recipients' distress cues in ways that promote a sense of safety and willingness to engage uncertainty (Ruddick, 1980; Bowlby, 1988). In other cases, the problem may lie in inconsistency or disunity of care-practice within the network of care-givers (e.g., parents, teachers, co-workers, friends). Or trouble may arise from an inhospitable environment that undermines the care-giver's efforts. When such threats to the efficacy of care-giving are unmanaged, the care-recipient is flooded by the demands and uncertainties of the environment without the buffer and the resources provided by the care-giver to manage them. Under these conditions, taking risks may feel intolerable, and the care-recipient will avoid risk, retreat from the unknown, and temporarily reduce stress (Winnicott, 1991; Bowlby, 1988).

The establishment of a care relationship is essential to changing habits. This is where the reparative and growth-producing modes of care-practice comes into play and work together to foster learning, forward movement, and growth. Care relationships provide a safe space in which the learner can explore habitual coping strategies. As will be shown in the remainder of the chapter, the WLS created such a safe environment for participants by means of five care practices: disruptive physical cues, building an inclusive and accepting environment, caring norms, relaxed learning, and staying in touch.[4]

Disruptive Physical Cues

Upon entering the WLS setting, participants noticed various curious items laid out on the conference room tables. The following quote identifies a few of these items and characterizes the interviewee's first impression:

> There were all kinds of things in the middle of the table, stickers and toys and rubber thingies. So it was colorful. It was playful. You immediately knew you weren't in a normal conference, you know? It just had an entirely different feeling, right away. And that immediately makes you loosen up, makes you a little more open.

Several WLS alumnae described the moment of entry to the workshop where they were caught by surprise by these "toys" and paused to decipher their meaning. I use the term "disruptive physical cues" to refer to the intentional use of objects to startle and interrupt expectations and to bring people to a state of curious alertness. Disruptive physical cues interrupt or disturb prior assumptions about what a place will look like, what people will do or not do, and by extension what one will be expected to do. Encountering disruptive cues did indeed startle participants. Their senses were heightened, and they became attentive to what might come next. Had the trainers defined what the WLS was about instead of invited curiosity through disruptive cues, participants might have thought the matter settled, and slumped into habitual patterns. Leaving the characteristics of the WLS open, to be discovered through direct experience, caused participants to remain alert and open.

As the previous quote suggested, the toys on the tables signified fun and invited risk-taking and creativity. In addition to the objects on the tables, there were also objects that were held back and brought out periodically. These latter objects served a second function of disruptive cues, that of carrying meanings.[5] In later chapters, I will offer several examples of how these objects were used to recall critical meanings learned in the WLS and to serve as sources of inspiration and motivation for engaging in new behavior. In the following quote, a WLS participant describes how bracelets signified and anchored a key lesson of women's strength:

> The bracelet came around the fourth day of the course. All the things they had weren't given out at once. The bracelet was about courage and strength, and I think those were given out when we were reviewing the challenges women typically face in organizations. So we talked about, you know, twenty years ago, the challenges women typically faced and now what they face. So we got these bracelets on courage and strength.

The same person also went on to describe the extent to which the trainers went to provide for the comfort and needs of participants through the way they arranged the physical environment of the WLS. She said:

> Every chair had a 10th anniversary T-shirt draped over it, which G&D had produced, and the front said, "Powerful and Healthy" and the back said "10th Anniversary." And every chair had a G&D bag hanging from it full of our materials and brochures and background information packages. But then they also had a wrapped present that was a kanga, a Kenyan cloth that you tie around—you can use it as a shawl, you can use it as a skirt, you can use it as a towel, but they're very beautiful colors and very African. On the table also were the workshop materials, which included a copy of some books and included a special women's journal, a very beautiful journal with quotes on every page and very nice pens and pencils and things. And

then in the middle of the table were all these toys, all these colored pencils and rubber things and metal things and paper things, because some people learn better when they're doing things with their hands, especially scientific types. They need to be doing something with their hands when they're listening.

As stated here, objects were not only used to create an environment of fun and carrying meanings, but to ensure participants comfort—physical (e.g. Kenyan cloth), practical (e.g., "workshop materials," "nice pens and pencils"), aesthetic ("beautiful" Kenyan cloth and "beautiful" journal), and intellectual (e.g. objects that cater to different learning styles).

Finally, some participants reflected on how it felt to be cared for in this way, and they drew some important lessons from the experience. The following participant described a moment when remarks by the trainers gave her a glimpse into what the physical cues signified. As she explained, there was a sense of authentic congruence between the disruptive physical cues and the message that the WLS was going to be an experience of learning in a caring environment, something that stood in sharp contrast to her prior experiences in conferences and in organizations:

Right from the outset, it was unbelievable. You go into this room of women. You've got these women greeting you. They've got toys on the table. And it was great—little things to play with. They immediately said, we want to take care of you this week. We've got a lot to do and we're going to work hard, but this is also about taking care of you guys and thinking about the work-life balance and taking care of yourself. And I went up to the trainer immediately after their opening, and I said, "You just taught me something huge. It's about atmosphere as much as anything, and the fact that you immediately said, 'We care about you and we want to take care of you this week,' I've never heard a man open a meeting saying that." Never in my life. It's always about, "We've got to do this, we've got so much to do, and sorry, I don't want to work you too hard, but we really have a lot of work to do." There's none of this, "We care about you and want to take care of you."

Disruptive physical cues were used in creating an environment of care in the WLS in much the same way described by care researchers. Arrangement of the physical environment required reflection on and anticipation of learners' intellectual, emotional, physical, and aesthetic needs. Although the exact needs cannot be known ahead of time, some of them can be known based on the task-at-hand. The goal of this aspect of care-practice is to put learners at ease. In the case of disruptive cues, however, putting women at ease required sensitivity to the fact that gender pressures are pervasive. Thus, the arrangement of the physical environment in the WLS put alumnae at ease by signaling that the WLS is a space that is designed to intentionally keep the competitive gender pressures of the organization at bay.

Building an Inclusive and Accepting Community

Setting up the physical environment to give care is just one part of care-practice. Another crucial dimension is the quality of attunement in inter-actions between the care-giver and care-recipient in the setting of the holding environment. In the WLS, the foundation for encouraging high-quality interactions amongst participants was building an inclusive and accepting community that fostered a sense of belonging and connection. This took place in a few different ways.

Story telling was a powerful tool for this endeavor. Ice-breaking life stories allowed participants to share details about their lives in their own words. They allowed participants to claim their chosen identities and left nothing up to the imagination or assumptions of their listeners. There-fore, stories helped to break the ice by breaking down organizationally and socially reinforced categories, humanizing participants and honoring their complexities beyond socially ascribed categories. Stories allowed participants to feel safe, remove the masks they felt obliged to wear at work, and feel like they were on equal ground with other participants. In the following quote, one participant describes how telling stories broke down generational and hierarchical boundaries:

> The first thing we did was to draw something that represents our life, our personal history, or us. That was very peaceful—to meet everybody and learn from their experience. Like, to break the ice in the beginning. And that helped to put myself in the same level as everybody, because again, I was the youngest of the group. But I didn't feel as intimidated as when I came to work at my center. It was very good. It felt like there were other people that you could relate to and get support from.

Through stories, participants learned about their shared experience of struggling with gender expectations throughout their lives. They also learned about their differences. Two practices, finding commonality and solidarity through their shared gender experience and talking about diverse experi-ences to dissolve familiar categorical differentiations, helped WLS partici-pants to build an inclusive and accepting community.

Finding Commonality and Solidarity

Sharing stories forged a sense of solidarity through recognition of shared experiences. One participant recounted that, although gender pressure was not an explicit topic on the agenda, it was a burning issue for participants and the topic naturally came out in the life stories:

> When I say that gender wasn't a focus, it's that it wasn't a *deliberate* focus. It was very natural. So, I think that we will understand our challenges that are unique to women leaders and managers, because of gender or because of culture, things like this. So, when we're sharing this, you know that somebody will be able to identify with it much better.

As WLS participants shared life stories, there was a dawning recognition that gender had been a pervasive and powerful force in the personal and professional lives of each participant. As the stories were told, many WLS alumnae described having "Me Too!" moments. Some described being surprised about the global nature of gender issues as they heard their concerns echoed by other women who lived and worked all over the world. The following participant recounts surprise when she realized this:

> A similarity that I see is that a lot of us do face discrimination—not so much in the family because I remember hearing a lot of them say that they don't have this problem in the family. Their parents encouraged them. But when they go out into the work world, they do have that kind of problem. Somehow, there's still kind of a glass ceiling limiting where they can go. The thing that surprised me is that gender discrimination is quite universal. Of course, we have gender issues in Asian culture, or the Middle East, but we also heard from people that work in Europe. So I started to think that maybe what we are dealing with here is the degree or a different kind of gender issue. For example, some of them have to prove themselves much harder than male colleagues. Some of them are not given the opportunity to excel or to do more. Some may say they don't have gender discrimination, but there is was.

Along with challenges to the assumption that gender pressures were relegated to only some parts of the world, there were challenges also to the assumption that gender pressures lessen as one moves up the organizational hierarchy. More junior participants were surprised to hear senior women struggling with similar issues as themselves. The participant quoted next describes being amazed to learn that, not only was her assumption about seniority incorrect, but so too was her assumption that English-speaking women were exempt from gender bias:

> The advanced course was very focused on senior women, and we talked about how difficult it is to get through the different walls or impediments: being the only woman, being the only minority, and being whatever. And I thought I was the only one dealing with these

issues, and that it was because I was young, that I came from Argentina, my English is not perfect. I thought that was the issue, but it's not.

WLS alumnae identified many gender-related issues. These included marginalization, restriction of opportunity, different evaluation criteria, age discrimination, work-life balance, being a minority or token, stereotype threat, isolation, turnover, mistreatment, access to line positions, access to professional networks, and non-prescribed career trajectories. Although each of these problems was taxing and difficult to deal with, they paled in comparison to the trauma resulting from sexual harassment. In the following quote, one participant described how her experience of sexual harassment and the indifference of her center had been devastating. In the WLS, she met others who had similar experiences. She also finally had the discussion she needed, namely what a victim might do when harassment occurs. She recounted the following:

> Within moments, people open up about common experiences that they've had, especially in what tends to be male-dominated centers. So it's helpful to know that other people are having the same experiences and to say, well, what do you do about it? What can we do about it? Can we come to some common conclusions about what we should be thinking about? For example, I had this terrible experience years ago with sexual harassment. It was absolutely devastating to me, and I reported it. There was no policy, and no experience, and nobody knew what to do. So, essentially, they didn't do anything. I was devastated by that experience. I just felt like nobody thought my experience was believable or important or anything else. So then going out and having conversations with other people who had had similar experiences and had it dealt with, or not—I mean, that was very helpful because I felt like I wasn't completely alone in having this type of issue come up in a center which had mostly men. We actually could gain something from other peoples' experiences and feel like you're not the only one and you weren't hysterical and you weren't overreacting, and in fact your reactions were fair and justified.

Finally sharing stories not only informed individual women about the shared nature of their struggles, but the shared struggles were also a basis for solidarity. One woman said, "We all came up with stories and realized that we all were suffering here, some more than the others, but there was none of us who hadn't suffered because of gender issues." Another participant commented on the sense of solidarity and the feeling of buoyancy from the collective resilience of the group:

> I think it was important for everybody to say, "Oh my god, I've got the same problem. It's not just me!" Then you can build a bit of

solidarity around an issue and get a bit of strength about it and have a little bit of courage to say, "This isn't just me!" It helped me a lot, and I think it helped other people as well—it was just this group of women surrounded in all this confidence in themselves, it felt like people you can trust.

Different Like Me

Life stories also revealed the differences in experience among WLS participants. A common narrative trajectory involving differences is where individuals who are positioned as cultural dominants take themselves as the norm and take those who are unlike them as the "difference" or the "other." Another common narrative trajectory, told from the perspective of individuals who are positioned as cultural subordinates, is characterizing the self as the "difference" and members of the culturally dominant group as the "norm." For the most part, the ways in which WLS participants described their differences were nuanced and generally unencumbered by these characterizations. This was somewhat surprising, because the dualistic narratives of difference are quite common (e.g., Western vs. non-Western, national staff vs. international staff, developed country vs. developing country, management vs. staff, men vs. women, white vs. people of color) and to some extent reflect the material inequalitie encountered in most societies and organizations. But the absence of caricatures of difference is instructive for understanding how an inclusive and accepting community was created in the WLS courses.

Even when there were hints of the familiar "us" vs. "them" in accounts of difference in the WLS, these threw up less-rigid boundaries than we typically hear. Consider the following quote. While the account of learning about differences retains the familiar dualistic thinking pattern by assuming within-group homogeneity for "developed country" or "international staff" on the one hand and "developing country" and "national staff" on the other, the quote also suggests that something new was learned and some barriers had relaxed:

> There are these voices we don't hear from. They're developing world women with very different backgrounds, different experiences than a lot of the international staff have. The diversity in the course was really, hugely informative to me. I learned a lot from these diverse women.

Consider also the next quote in which the participant characterizes diversity in terms of the issues important to the story tellers and entirely avoids categorical thinking. The participant speaks about the differences in upbringing between herself and another WLS colleague:

> There was a woman from another center, way high up, and she was sitting across the table from me and we had to talk about some formative

experience from our youth and how that affected us. And I described how my mother had five children and was always the peacemaker. Always keeping things quiet, peaceful, making sure we're all happy. And how I see myself similarly when I'm on a team, doing the exact same thing. I always worry that everyone's happy, that they're not upset, that they are not getting something they need. And the woman described to me how, when she was a small girl, about five years old, she got knocked down by a bully in the school grounds, and she came home and told her mother about it and her mother said to her, "You go back and you knock that guy over." And it was like an epiphany to me. You can't imagine two more different upbringings than this woman and me. And here we are, we're trying to solve a problem together. Of course we're going to solve it differently. We're going to approach it differently, you know, think differently. It just was so clear to me, and it was just a wonderful moment.

While learning about common experiences fostered solidarity, learning about differences built another type of bond: the recognition of interdependence. In the following quote, one participant describes how learning about the different experiences of her colleagues impressed upon her the importance of partnering with others in ways that can lead to synergies:

There was a comprehension that not everybody's like me and that I need to be acutely aware of the different qualities that people are bringing to the table and appreciate them. And appreciate the fact that, just because I may be in charge of a particular activity doesn't mean that it's my way or the highway. There are an awful lot of opinions that need to be on the table, and I need to appreciate them and nurture those views.

While the life story exercise helped break the ice, it also began building the foundation for cultivating caring interactions. Recognizing their commonalities, WLS participants felt a sense of solidarity, and few felt the need to wear the masks they put on at work. Recognizing their differences further tore down caricatures and masks. Participants simply appreciated hearing fascinating stories that affirmed the inherent humanity and vulnerability of all present. This encouraged mutual attunement in interactions as they began to engage the many activities of the WLS.

Promoting Caring Norms

The recognition of shared humanity and vulnerability confirmed that all WLS participants deserved the same level of consideration and regard, and this was the foundation for the cultivation of caring behavioral norms within the WLS. As will be described next, participants described how they put aside the competitive paradigm informed by instrumental and transactional workplace norms. Instead, they interacted in ways that suggested that they placed priority on providing care to one another to foster learning and growth. This involved two-way sensitivity and attunement to others' needs but also awareness of one's own needs. Given that this was a group of women whose socialization would have presumably emphasized care-practice, a prototypical feminine attribute, the encouragement of care was likely both a welcome and familiar change from the competitive norms of the organization. Let's consider this further.

Deliberately Disrupting Dominant Social Norms

Social norms are taken-for-granted, shared understandings and expectations about the types of behaviors that are viewed as appropriate or inappropriate for members of a group. Although not formal and explicit, norms are ubiquitous, learned in the course of socialization into a community. Through socialization, certain assumptions, values, and beliefs become internalized. And behaviors stemming from them become habituated and maintained by repetition and social reinforcement through rewards and punishment. Norms provide an automatic and efficient means of conducting oneself in ways that are expected in organizations, and in doing this, norms help interdependent people communicate and coordinate their activities (Heritage, 1984).

As described in Chapter 1, women face contradictory norms: one set of norms rooted in their organizational roles and the other set of norms rooted in societal gender-role expectations. Like many other cultural subordinates, women have acquired and internalized at least two systems of meaning based in the dominant and subordinate cultures in which they are embedded. Women understand the individualistic and competitive masculine norms dominant in organizations and have learned to survive in these contexts, but they also understand feminine norms that have been inculcated into them at birth.[6] Because of this, women and members of culturally subordinated groups tend to be highly attuned to the norms at play in their environments and are particularly sensitive when the dominant cultural norm is disrupted. The WLS participants were aware that the norms of the WLS were different from the norms they were accustomed to within their workplaces. More specifically, some aspects of organizational masculine norms were viewed as inappropriate in the WLS.

The majority of WLS participants credited the absence of the competitive norms in the WLS to the absence of men. One participant stated, "I think that the fact that there are no men there is huge. I'm not a sociologist, so I can't explain that phenomena very well, but it's there. It's definitely there." Such statements were extremely common in the interviews. The next quote goes farther, naming and explaining why the absence of men contributed to psychological safety within the WLS:

I've been through lots of management courses with women and with men and the sorts of lessons they teach are similar in terms of how you encourage teamwork and that sort of thing. The lessons aren't particularly different, but because we're a minority and have issues that men don't have in terms of family and stuff like that. I think that you can create an environment of trust and understanding—with women, it happens almost immediately, which is interesting. That's the thing about women. You know, these things—people start sharing things almost immediately, and I think that when you're in a situation also with men, you don't have that kind of environment where you can share things. The course was an easier environment for learning things and sharing things more quickly and more honestly than you would if you were in a situation with men. We can learn a lot of things in a training course with men, but you're not going to be dealing with issues that are specific to your gender and you're not going to be as open to sharing.

While there was widespread agreement, even consensus, on the value of an all-women setting, there was nuance as well. Some individuals suggested that what mattered was not just that the WLS setting was all-female, but also that the trainers had set a tone and expectation for caring interactions. By doing this, the trainers disrupted a pattern of competitive and individualistic thinking and behavior that WLS participants were accustomed to within their centers. One participant suggested that the WLS discouraged competitive behaviors that might otherwise have been present within the WLS: "I think it's that degree of skepticism, the protection that men bring in. But it's not that there aren't skeptical and cynical women out there, but something about this atmosphere keeps them quiet."

Some Caring Practices of the WLS

As previously stated, WLS participants noted the contrasting norms between their workplaces and the WLS. As one person put it, "there is no tension or stress" in the WLS. Another person echoed the same feeling, and specifically identified the source of stress at work, namely a singular focus on task over people. She stated:

I've been to so many bad meetings and bad courses, and the reason is that we try to do too much in too short a time. The stress is there, the tension is there, and the competitiveness is there. I mean, how many meetings have you sat through where they forget about the coffee break because they're so caught up in getting everything done, and you're sitting for four hours without moving?

Competitive norms, also cited in the previous quote, produced a win-lose dynamic. Win-lose dynamics are rooted zero-sum beliefs rooted in fear and deprivation. This belief fosters the norm of trying to dominate, tear others down, and come out on top. One participant expressed surprise in the absence of win-lose dynamics in the WLS. She noted the expectation that participants would be of mutual support to one another and stated: "I think, basically, women being with other women, they are more supportive. When you have a male, like in the office, I'm feeling that they always want to win."[7]

Unlike what they were accustomed to in interactions within their workplaces, WLS participants noted the *absence of ridicule*. Given norms of professionalism, ridiculing and bulling behavior in organizations is often tolerated or even accepted.[8] One participant described one subtle form of ridicule—making jokes—that minimizes or discounts a person's views. In her account, she noted how this dynamic was absent in the WLS: "Again, what was absent, I think was the competitiveness. Things like 'Oh, this is stupid, this is goofy.' You don't have that kind of thing in the courses. So you really open yourself up."

Competitive behaviors in the workplace were also enacted through skepticism, often disguised as objectivity, rigor, or realism. Skepticism is often valued and rewarded in organizations, but it fosters timidity, stifles ideas, and kills creativity. In the next quote, one interviewee noted that, instead of the usual skepticism, individuals in the WLS expressed appreciation and curiosity about one another's experiences and views:

> Men always have a sort of protective thing around them, so they have to act skeptical. They have to act tough, they have to act sort of competitive. They have to show that they know things. It's just not there at all in these groups of women. It's a very interesting question, to tell you the truth. That level of comfort is just gone when the men enter the room. You've seen it—in any group of a bunch of men, there's always that one guy who's completely skeptical and cynical.

Participants also said that because they did not feel the familiar competitive dynamics within the WLS, the need to be vigilant and ready to defend oneself did not seem necessary. The respect and consideration expressed when they shared thoughts helped them relax and express sensitive topics without fear of ridicule or denigration. One person specifically cited how acceptance from others allowed her to feel that she could be herself: "There was no tension or stress or feeling like you should be something you're not." Another WLS participant described how being heard without confronting competitive dynamics helped her open up:

> There are certain things you might be inhibited about saying. I think the way a woman would react to something that you say is quite different from how a man would. If a man asks a question, it's asked in a very confrontational way. It's like throwing a challenge at you—they

can fight across the table, but there's nothing serious in it for them. They treat it as just very objective. But, they like throwing this challenge. They like getting into a fight kind of thing. A woman doesn't do that. And so, you're totally off-guard when you're with women. You're relaxed. I somehow find that I am much more myself, and much more relaxed and I let my hair down, talking about certain issues when it's just women only. Oh my goodness, it was critical, absolutely critical! Because you start opening up.

Thus far, I have described some WLS norms that were cited in contrast to competitive workplace behaviors. WLS participants were surprised by the absence of business-as-usual as much as they were surprised by the care that was present. There were also other norms that were described as helpful but not posited as contrasts. For example, *listening to others* is a cornerstone to attunement and care-giving. Being heard and understood is a powerful and affirming experience. As one participant recounted, the listening norm was initiated and established almost immediately:

Even before the course started, we had lunch together. The way the women approached everybody was so great—nobody was shy. You just introduce yourself and everybody *listens* to you and appreciates your story.

All the norms described here are built on the foundation of listening. One of the most frequently cited norms was that of *being supportive of others*. Sometimes the supportiveness was exhibited by offering resources to gain insight into and find possible solutions to a practical problem. One of the most valuable resources within the WLS was the collective experience of participants. WLS participants listened carefully to a colleague's work-related challenges. They asked questions to understand the problem deeply, the dynamics around the problem, and the participant's feelings, assumptions, and goals. Accounting for these details of their colleague's view of the situation, WLS alumnae offered their insights, experience, and knowledge of the organizational culture, generated ideas for addressing the problem, strategized, and offered advice. As described by one participant, "They support each other, and they talk among themselves and they strategize, and they know the context of each other and they can advise on what they've seen that works."

Support can also relate to *emotional backing* and *affirmation*. Others' willingness to listen and be there was one way that emotional support was offered. Supporting others emotionally involved the willingness to make space for another person to express their emotions, no matter how contradictory or raw. It also involved affirming another person's feelings without judgment and inviting exploration and the search for self-insight.

As one participant described: "I could feel their sense of willingness to help me. I had that feeling of actually looking up to them—they were approachable." Another participant described how people opened up and allowed themselves to be vulnerable:

> You can lay out all your cards. You can open up your heart. You can be emotional, you can cry, you can do anything—it doesn't matter. All you get is support. I mean that happens at some of these courses. I mean, even at this last leadership course, some people were crying, but it's okay. It's safe to do that. It's okay to show your most vulnerable self.

Another commonly cited norm was *encouragement*. Encouragement involves pushing someone to take action and apply their strengths to address problems. Encouragement is associated with ideas that involve forward movement. As one participant reported:

> I shared all my experiences with all these senior women. And I learned from their experiences as well. And they even told me, "You are a good problem-solver." And it was just receiving all this positive energy from them—that I am in the right track, wherever I want to go, whatever my dream is, things like that. I can see that in them as well. That helped me a lot. You know, this inspired me. It was all the inspiration and motivation I got out of both courses that made a huge difference.

Another participant described the impact of encouragement in the form of positive feedback: "All this positive feedback you get in these courses, this interaction with these very senior people, these women. I don't think they themselves quite realize what a huge impact it can have on people."

Two final norms were *non-judgmental receptivity* and *learning from others' experiences*, and these went hand in hand. No topic was prohibited, and no question was dumb. One younger participant describes how she felt she could finally ask the questions that had nagged her for some time. In the next quote, she described feeling comfortable to pose some very personal questions to other senior participants:

> All the participants were so open, so frank about their feelings. I had many good conversations with many people who listened to my stories, and they told me, you know, "I relate to you. When I was young, this is what happened to me. This is how and why I solved the problem as I did." I got many, many good experiences from other people, and in all aspects—the professional aspects, the personal aspects— because I wanted to know. I asked all the ladies there, "So, are you married? How do you deal with that? Did your husband follow you? Did you have to follow him? How did that happen? How are you

now in this top position? Are you happy?" And I asked almost everybody these questions, and I got a really good grasp of what it is like to be on the top, being a professional, being a mother, everything. If I want to follow that life or not, very useful.

In the preceding quote, the participant described deliberately posing questions, but learning from others also occurs vicariously from attentive listening. As the interviewee below recounts, by listening to other women's stories, she began to gain insights into the internal politics and dynamics of the CGIAR, something she had not been able to decipher before. This insight helped her make sense of past events in her organization and possibly informed her understanding of ones she encountered after the WLS:

> Now we have many women around us that are higher-level and proficient. And one definitely has a better understanding of what's going on. Also, experiences they were offering in this very open exchange simply help you to handle issues at work, particularly human issues rather than facts and scientific figures. To deal with them much better, to do them in a way that works for you as a woman because women do things differently, we see things differently, and we should be proud of it and build on our strengths.

In other instances, learning from one another was part of the design of the course. One vehicle for this, "feedback-buddies," was a formal course mechanism for encouraging sharing of information and experiences among participants themselves. As will be discussed later, this feedback-buddy system was very useful, and its use by participants outlasted the actual training itself. Conversations that took place amongst feedback-buddies were both wide-ranging and specific. In the following quote, the interviewee describes recognizing the value of the feedback-buddy relationship:

> You have a problem or issue. You take advantage of the presence of these women in this course, in smaller groups, to present your issue. In my case, I presented the IT issue, and not only got input from the facilitators but from the group.

Another woman addressed the relevance of feedback and coaching from other participants whose experiences and settings were similar to her own. Although feedback from facilitators was useful and appreciated, it was feedback from peers that was attuned to the concrete realities of the CGIAR. One participant described this, saying:

> To get input from them would make a difference. So you're not only in exercises together where you simulate hypothetical things, but really talking about issues that you're burning to resolve in this

context because you are getting so many ideas during this stage of the course. And you don't want only to talk to the facilitators because they're not your peers.

Relaxed Learning and Willingness to Be Vulnerable

Deliberately cultivating a caring environment through the practices described here paid off with participants' willingness to put down their defenses, relax, and open up. The experience of being cared for by others put WLS participants at ease. They were willing to examine unacknowledged fears (e.g. unworthiness, insignificance, weakness, inadequacy, and confusion) instead of expending their energy managing the impression they made on others. WLS participants were willing to put aside the inauthentic and defensive masks of independence, competence, control, and mastery that they felt were necessary to command respect in the workplace. Instead they chose to expose their soft sides to others and share their struggles and uncertainties as well as their confidence and strength. By allowing themselves to be vulnerable, they examined how they coped with uncertainties and thereby became aware of their habitual patterns and how these impacted their growth as leaders.

WLS participants were willing to be vulnerable, because they felt confident that they would be safe. One participant used the term "relaxed learning" to describe the effect of learning in a caring environment:

> I remember being so relaxed. The feeling of relaxed learning was so unbelievable. So this is my strong memory of the program. I have a lot of emotional and strong memories of that course. It was such an atmosphere of non-competitiveness that I never experienced before. It was a perfect atmosphere.

The relaxation response cited in the previous quote is crucial to transformational learning. The willingness to be vulnerable is potentially one of the most important first steps in being able to explore, understand, and change unhelpful habitual patterns. According to Brown (2012), to be vulnerable is to feel uncertainty, risk, and emotional exposure. Because vulnerability is culturally associated with weakness, Brown (2012) argues it is avoided with the unfortunate consequence that we fail to learn how to use our feelings to gain clarity, insight, and resolution. Brown (2012) suggested a helpful reframing of vulnerability. Instead of seeing it as a weakness, she suggests it is much more useful to accept that uncertainty, risk, and emotional exposure are unavoidable experiences in life, and can be resources to draw upon to make everyday choices.

The narratives of the WLS participants strongly suggest that participants engaged uncertainties they faced in their work and personal lives by opening up to others who they trusted would respond with care. Relational psychologists have long recognized the crucial role of relationships in growth and maturation.[9] The WLS participant's accounts suggest that their interactions with peers were characterized by the "five good" attributes that Miller and Stiver (1997) argued were present in "growth-fostering" relationships. These are: increased sense of zest or energy, increased self-worth, clarity or greater knowledge of self and the other person in the relationship, productivity or the ability and motivation to take action both within the relationship itself as well as outside of it, and a desire for more connection with the relational partner.

Brown (2012) also acknowledged the importance of relationships in helping individuals approach uncertainty with curiosity rather than fear and avoidance. However, she cautioned that vulnerability can be rewarding when one shares one's feelings with trustworthy people and in appropriate ways. She stated that "vulnerability is based on mutuality and requires boundaries and trust. It's not oversharing, it's not purging, and it's not indiscriminate disclosure. Vulnerability is about sharing our feelings and experiences with people who have earned the right to hear them" (p. 45). She goes on to suggest that oversharing without appropriate boundaries leads to disconnection and can actually be a strategy of avoiding vulnerability. Vulnerability is sharing feelings appropriately, with discernment, and in a manner that fosters trust and connection.

Given that the WLS courses were only one week in length, a reasonable question would be, how can trust be developed amongst a group of women in this short time? Without digressing into the dynamics of trust building and maintenance in interpersonal relationships, we can draw some preliminary conclusions about the importance of care-practice in making this possible. One participant aptly described the deeply impactful change care-practice can produce in a short timeframe:

> A large part of the transformation that happens for women is actually at a psychological and emotional level, so that needs to be totally explored if the transformation is supposed to happen. And you need to create a safe place for that exposure. To expose yourself emotionally and psychologically so that you get real feedback that is relevant to you. You need to see your true psychological state so that you get the right feedback.

Staying Connected

One of Miller and Stiver's (1997) five good attributes in growth-fostering relationships is the desire for more connection. This desire comes from the energy of mutual attraction fostered through caring relationships. In light of this, the last day of the program was very emotional for WLS participants. Consider these two accounts:

> One thing that is quite unique for this course is on the last day, when we share our learning experiences, it became very emotional, which I

think is very unique for a women's leadership course. I know there is one person, she admitted she is a very logical person and is not somebody who is emotional. She said, "This is supposed to be a professional management and leadership course, but here we are, all of us, getting so emotional about the whole thing." Even then, I was thinking that it really is a very unique experience for a leadership and management course.

And:

That moment was on the last day—it was a day that was filled with emotion. People expressed their minds about what they feel about women, what they think women are, what women can achieve, notwithstanding our organizations and the society, and how we can cross the hurdles.

Caring interactions fostered strong bonds that, for many participants, lasted well beyond the WLS course. One woman said:

It was excellent: the issues, the tools, and the network. I came out of that course with sisters. And I learned so much about our organization through these other women, and I came out with support. These are women I still communicate with today, and we can still speak in a certain way with each other because we were in that course together.

Given that the participants dispersed after the course, staying connected took many forms. Sometimes it was achieved passively, through participants' imagination of their colleagues' presence. Some participants expressed the feeling that they were no longer isolated and alone and that they had the examples of strong and capable women to continue to inspire them. Further, in case consultation was needed, the community was just a phone call or an email away. As suggested in the following quote, knowledge of others' presence provided a sense of security:

What you learn from the course is relationships that you make with other women in the system are important. Given the fact that we're still a minority in the system, I think that's important—to recognize that there are other women in the system and that they're doing important work and it's important to know what they're doing. That certainly gives you a sense of solidarity, and that you're not just kind of like on your own.

WLS participants also actively sought one another for assistance, sustaining the feedback-buddy vehicle of the course upon their return to work.

Numerous instances of this were cited, and some of these instances will be described in the post-WLS stories contained in Chapters 4 through 7. Here is one case:

> When I encountered a particular problem in a research study, I said, "Okay, let's think who can help me or who can I have as an ally?" So I talked with several persons: "What do you think of this? I'm sure this is a good methodology; I think this is a serious study. What do you think?" And I talked to several allies just to get more feedback on it and more ideas on how to handle it. There were several women to whom I talked.

WLS participants not only stayed connected with other members of their cohort but also found that their network expanded *beyond* their cohort. One vehicle for this was the G&D program's newsletter. Because WLS participants were automatically subscribed, they received information on what was going on in the G&D program. Beyond this, the newsletter specifically contained information of interest to participants. According to a G&D administrator of the WLS:

> The newsletter includes the best articles, the latest thinking, the latest controversies on women and science. We also put our alumni on the top of the mailing list for the follow-up courses, like the negotiation course and so on. We make sure they're first in line to attend another opportunity.

The annual, week-long CGIAR meeting also brought participants together. These formal G&D events not only included participants from multiple years but also other women in the CGIAR system. It also included men. Through this vehicle the WLS participants expanded their networks further, connected with other women, and also cultivated allies with senior management, especially male allies. One thing that was noted, however, was that because of the hierarchy existing between international staff and national staff, the annual meetings only benefited the international women who were funded to attend. Nevertheless, one participant (also the G&D administrator) stated that the annual gatherings were a pivotal means of staying connected:

> There's about a thousand of us all together and I always organize a women's networking event, and the alumni of our courses are invited, and also the female donor representatives. All the women who are attending the annual meeting are invited, but many of them are alumni of our leadership courses, and this is the only all-female event of the annual meeting of the week. And it has become one of the most popular things that happen the entire week. Last year, for

the first time ever, men crashed the party. We had a Vice President of the World Bank, the head of Science Council, eight of the Director Generals all crashing the party and joining the women's network because they said, "We hear this is the best thing that happens." And it was great because my speakers last year were speaking about work-life balance, and I had these women who were running global programs with one hand and raising children with the other, talking about how they do it. It's very informal. It's just women speaking from the heart and sharing strategies and stories. Oh, we never have one of these events where we're not crying, where we're not laughing, and for many of us it's the only time we see each other because we're so far-flung around the world, and this is the one time we can see each other in the room. However, this is only the most senior women. Because only the most senior members of management attend the annual meeting, so that means a lot of alumni are not there, but we have several alumni who are there every year. It's really fun.

Impromptu or accidental meetings were also opportunities to share information, express appreciation, re-ignite solidarity, and strategize. Consider the following story of an accidental meeting:

I felt wonderful when, during the annual meeting in Mexico City last year, I was in the women's bathroom. And you know, all the women are in there because we're so few. And I'm in one of the stalls and one of the women saw me going in and she's yelling at me over the door, called my name excitedly and said: "I've been using what I learned in the negotiations course every single day since." Then you could hear the other women in the stalls saying, "Me, too. Yeah, me, too." And then other women that had not yet attended, who also happened to be in the bathroom, were saying, "I want to come next year." It was so funny. It was classic. It was like a scene out of a movie in the women's toilet. So it's having an impact.

Summary

Encouraging caring norms generated interactions characterized by attunement and skillful response. This allowed WLS participants to explore a wide range of issues from the very personal and sometimes painful to the practical and political. Caring interactions fostered psychological safety and elicited relaxation and openness. Participants felt they could be vulnerable and open up. By allowing themselves to be vulnerable, participants examined how they coped with uncertainty and thereby gained insight into the unhelpful, habitual patterns through which they coped. They also learned from one another in the process of exploring their experiences and seeking to envision new and more helpful habits. The four chapters that follow will describe the *specific types of changes* that emerged from the transformative learning experiences in the WLS. As will be described in these chapters, WLS interactions fostered transformational change by producing insight into unhelpful, habitual patterns and committed practice to change them.

Notes

1. This is where an individual intends to change a habit pattern, envisions the desired behaviors, and goes about practicing these new behaviors. Because the old habit pattern will arise unconsciously and automatically, the individual must be vigilant and catch her/himself when this happens, deliberately interrupt the unwanted pattern, and replace it with the desired behavior. The deliberate learning process eventually results in changes to the brain, laying down new neural pathways that weaken the expression of old patterns, while strengthening the new and more desirable ones. Eventually, the desired new patterns become habitual, unconscious, and automatically enacted.
2. Tronto (2013) offers a related view of care-practice, specifying some of the elements of care implicit in Ruddick's account of care-practice. These aspects of care are: (1) attentiveness, a proclivity to become aware of need; (2) responsibility, a willingness to respond and take care of need; (3) competence, the skill of providing good and successful care; and (4) responsiveness, consideration of the position of others as they see it and recognition of the potential for abuse in care.
3. Learning to "hold" oneself is a very important indicator of learning and growth. However, throughout their lives, human beings continue to be confronted with many a variety of situations that entail uncertainty and risk challenges. They will therefore continue to need to forge growth-fostering relationships at each stage of life.
4. In the following account, all identifying information has been either altered or left out.
5. See MacGregor (2013) for an interesting and insightful historical analysis of the ancient roots of this practice.
6. Miller's (1976) book has a highly insightful chapter entitled "Domination and Subordination" that has a detailed analysis of the challenges posed to subordinates of understanding the norm (defined by the dominant), while also recognizing both the damaging nature of the norm and the existence of alternative systems of meaning that question the prevailing masculine norms. See also the concept of double consciousness, first coined by W.E.B. Du Bois (1968, orig. 1903) to bring attention to the fact that Black Americans need to develop a consciousness of their own identities within the prevailing dominant norms of White American culture. While DuBois was describing the experience of a particular dominate-subordinate relationship, his insights apply to many types of identity conflict produced by competing social definitions with dominate-subordinate aspects.
7. Mary Parker Follett coined the terms "power-over" and "power-with" to contrast these differing behavioral postures (Follett, 1995). Miller and Stiver (1997) explored these dynamics in the context of growth-fostering interactions between women. Debebe (2012) examined these dynamics in cross-cultural coordination.
8. See Collinson (1988) for a discussion of the affirmative as well as destructive use of humor in organizations. Collinson's (1988) analysis is particularly apt

here because of his attention to the gendered nature of joking and humor in organizations and to their role in controlling workers.
9. See Rogers (1951), Winnicott (1965), Miller and Stiver (1997), Miller (2004), and Robb (2006).

References

Abel, E. K., & Nelson, M. K. (1990). *Circles of care: Work and identity in women's lives.* Albany, NY: Sate University of New York Press.

Bowlby, J. (1988). *A secure base: Parent-child attachment and healthy human development.* London, UK: Routledge.

Brown, B. (2012). *Daring greatly: How the courage to be vulnerable transforms the way we live, love, parent, and lead.* New York, NY: Penguin Random House.

Collinson, D. L. (1988). Engineering humour: Masculinity, joking and conflict in shop-floor relations. *Organization Studies, 9*(2), 181–199.

Davis, M., & Wallbridge, D. (1981). *Boundary and space: An introduction to the work of D.W. Winnicott.* New York, NY: Routledge.

Debebe, G. (2012). *Navigating power: Cross-cultural competence and coordination in Navajoland.* Lanham, MD: Lexington Books.

Dewey, J. (1938). *Experience and education.* New York, NY: Touchstone Rockefeller Center.

Du Bois, W. E. B. (1968). *The souls of black folk; essays and sketches.* Chicago, A. G. McClurg, 1903. New York, NY: Johnson Reprint Corp.

Fischer, B., & Tronto, J. C. (1990). Toward a feminist theory of caring. In E. Abel & M. Nelson (Eds.), *Circles of care: Work and identity in women's lives* (pp. 36–54). Albany, NY: Sate University of New York Press.

Follett, M. P. (1995). Power. In P. Graham (Ed.), *Mary Parker Follett: Prophet of management* (pp. 97–120). Boston, MA: Harvard Business School Press.

Gilligan, C. (1977). In a different voice: Women's conceptions of self and of morality. *Harvard Educational Review, 47*, 481–517.

Gilligan, C. (1982). *In a different voice: Psychological theory and women's development.* Boston, MA: Harvard University Press.

Held, V. (2006). *The ethics of care.* New York, NY: Oxford University Press.

Heritage, J. (1984). *Garfinkle and ethnomethodology.* Cambridge, UK: Polity Press.

Kittay, E. F. (1999). *Love's labor: Essays on women, equality and dependency.* New York, NY: Routledge.

Kohlberg, L. (1971). *From is to ought: How to commit the naturalistic fallacy and get away with it in the study of moral development.* New York, NY: Academic Press.

MacGregor, N. (2013). *A history of the world in 100 objects.* New York, NY: Viking Group.

Miller, G. E. (2004). Frontier masculinity in the oil industry: The experiences of women engineers. *Gender, Work & Organization, 11*(1), 47–73.

Miller, J. B. (1976). *Toward a new psychology of women.* Boston, MA: Beacon Press.

Miller, J. B., & Stiver, I. P. (1997). *The healing connection: How women form relationships in therapy and in life.* Boston, MA: Beacon Press.

Reinstein, D. K. (2006). *To hold and be held.* New York, NY: Routledge.

Robb, C. (2006). *This changes everything: The relational revolution in psychology*. New York, NY: Picador.

Rogers, C. R. (1951). *Client-centered therapy: Its current practice, implications and theory*. Boston, MA: Houghton Mifflin.

Ruddick, S. (1980). Maternal thinking. *Feminist Studies, 6*(2), 342–367.

Ruddick, S. (1998). Care as labor and relationship. In M. S. Haflon & J. C. Haber (Eds.), *Norms and values: Essays on the work of Virginia Held* (pp. 3–26). Lanham, MD: Rowman & Littlefield.

Tronto, J. S. (2013). *Caring democracy: Markets, equality, and justice*. New York, NY: New York University Press.

Winnicott, D. W. (1964). *The child, the family, and the outside world*. Harmondsworth, Middlesex: Penguin Books.

Winnicott, D. W. (1965). *Maturational processes and the facilitating environment: Studies in the theory of emotional development*. London, UK: Hogarth Press.

Winnicott, D. W. (1991). *Playing and reality*. New York, NY: Routledge.

4 Transformation From Hidden to Visible Leadership

If I say something, how would it be taken?

Ayana, Hidden Leader

Our next task in this book is to turn to the *first two* of the three research questions introduced in Chapter 1. To remind the reader, these questions are:

- Did the WLS training effect changes in participants' leadership behavior, and if so what were the nature of these changes?
- Did these changes enable alumnae to exercise leadership more effectively?

In this chapter and the three that follow it, I will draw upon the leadership stories of WLS alumnae to illustrate the core theme of leadership transformations. In doing so, I will affirmatively address both questions posed here. This chapter explores the first leadership transformation produced by the WLS, from *hidden* to *visible* leadership. The analysis will show that the WLS fostered greater leadership effectiveness through this transformation by effecting a shift in a habitual, self-diminishing and context-amplifying pattern of thinking that was at the root of hiding behavior. As implied by these adjectives, this pattern of thinking was characterized by disproportionate attention to contextual demands at the expense of authenticity. The transformation to visible leadership, evidenced in a self-affirming and context-mitigating pattern of thinking addressed this imbalance, restoring both a more realistic view of the context and the value of the leader's suppressed knowledge, ideas, and values.

Twenty-two percent of the WLS interviewees told stories about the transformation from hidden to visible leadership. Hidden leadership stories pertained to leadership experiences prior to the WLS, while visible leadership stories pertained to leadership experiences after the WLS. Hidden/visible leaders held a variety of positions at different levels of the hierarchy. The position classification distributions among hidden leaders were as follows: 20 percent program leaders, 40 percent scientists/researchers, 20 percent managers, and 20 percent technician/administrator. None of those classified as hidden/visible leaders held the "theme leader" position. They were also represented in all recruitment categories with 60 percent recruited internationally, 20 percent recruited regionally, and 20 percent recruited nationally.

Hidden leadership stories focused on how aspects of the self were a liability to be concealed in the organizational context. For example, Angela, shared:

> I had grown up in (Southeast Asian country), so I had been raised with this idea that women shouldn't speak too much. But not just women—tooting your own horn was not a good thing. In (Southeast Asian country) the culture is very much that the teacher—or really anyone—should be modest, and other people should praise.

The problem for Angela was that these attributes were devalued within her research center. In fact, she observed that individuals who were respected and rewarded with professional recognition displayed the *opposite* attributes: assertiveness, competition, and individual achievement. Recognizing that her proclivity to be humble and modest could become a liability to her career prospects, Angela decided that she had to learn how to play the game:

> I made myself argue with (my boss) and found that he enjoyed engaging, but also found that a lot of the economists, because that's the dominant discipline at (my center) are trained that way. And so, okay, if that's their training. And that's not the way I was trained, I needed to learn to respond similarly. It took me quite a bit to get to that point where I could, but once I did, then I got taken much more seriously. I realized that I couldn't just wait for my boss to discover that I was brilliant; I had to periodically tell him that I was a respected authority in my area. I needed to speak up in meetings and things like that.

At first blush, Angela's story might appear to be a story of gaining visibility, not hiding. This is an undeniable aspect of it, but it came at a price. To be appreciated and recognized for her professional capacities, she felt that she had to suppress her modesty. While this did earn her increased professional success, she was also uncomfortable with the culture of intolerance for differences within her center. Angela's story therefore had the quintessential quality of hidden leadership, namely a dualistic and distorted perception of herself and the context. For Angela, to be successful one had to exhibit prototypical Western and masculine attributes and hide attributes of modesty, relational-orientation, and harmony-seeking behaviors.

The dualistic view of self was that you either had to hide your humility and play the game or lose respect as well as your job. The tenacity with which she held to this duality came into sharp focus during the WLS role play exercise when her formula for success was challenged, eliciting an almost panicked and indignant response:

> The interesting thing was that—in the training, we were doing some kind of a role play of a woman who had a new boss that wanted her to go back to being in a kind of a secretarial position. And she had rather grown beyond that and felt that she had other things to offer besides fetching his coffee. And I was supposed to role-play her part in conveying this to the new boss. And when I was going through it, everybody just started, the woman who was role-playing the boss just started coming down on me really hard. Even pretty aggressive women said that I was being too aggressive, too assertive And I finally just said, "okay, if we need to have somebody play doormat, then I really have to have somebody else play doormat because it has taken me a lot to get to the point where I feel like I can talk, I can say what's on my mind. I need that as a survival strategy at (my center), and if I go back to playing doormat, I will not survive at (my center)."

Angela's story, as well as the stories of hidden leaders told throughout this chapter, share a common habitual thought pattern that I describe as self-diminishing and context-amplifying. This pattern of thinking produces a distorted construction of context and self. Specifically, the work setting is perceived as all-powerful and demanding and in order to survive in such a context, aspects of the self need to be suppressed. The following sections draw upon these stories to illuminate these habitual patterns of thought and action, how these patterns shifted from critical learning experiences in the WLS, and how these changes were manifested in new patterns of visible leadership characterized by self-affirming and context-mitigating thought processes. The chapter will return to Angela's story, concluding with an extended account of it.

Behaviors of Hidden Leadership

Hidden leaders' stories were not necessarily about the lack of agency but rather its curbing. Hidden leaders told stories about self-doubt and the cloaking of self-aspects they believed would not be valued in their centers. Despite their skills and contributions (and their awareness of these), they tended to see themselves as weak or deficient in some way, bestowing agency to others. Hidden leaders described three types of behaviors: self-censorship, rare and controlled speech, and obstructed visibility. *Self-censorship* involves intentional withholding of one's ideas, values, or expertise out of fear of generating negative reactions from others. Self-censorship sometimes involved an unwillingness to voice one's thoughts publicly or privately. For example, if Ayana was called into a last-minute meeting, she kept silent, thinking: "If I say something, how would it be taken?" Rosaria, another person who self-censored said:

> Whenever I have an idea, I just keep it to myself. I don't spread it; I don't articulate it. I have a tendency to keep quiet. And I think it's because, whenever there's a new idea, I'm too careful to really think about it and plan about it. I'm afraid it might not be a popular idea.

Rosaria had been promoted from a national to a regional position within her research center, and she and her family had moved to a neighboring country for her new job. She attributed her hiding to stress created by cross-cultural adjustment. While she saw the move as an opportunity for professional growth, it also brought the pressures that accompany taking a new job and making a cross-cultural sojourn with family in tow. Given her limited managerial experience, she worried whether she could meet the demands of her job. In her previous job, she had only interacted with her fellow national citizens, but in her new workplace, she regularly interacted with people from all over the world. While these workplace interactions posed new challenges, she found that interactions with individuals from a particular country were uniquely fraught with conflict, leaving her feeling hurt and angry. Her response to these sources of pressure was to withdraw into self-censorship. She recalled that, one time, her boss asked why she was silent, and she told him that she was observing and learning about the new culture. In reality, she was very stressed:

> It was not helping me to be silent, in the sense that I was raising stress in myself. I kept thinking about it, and the tension was building inside me. This affected my performance, my dealings with others, and because I had tension that I had not released, it showed in my actions.

Although almost all the hidden leaders in my interviews self-censored, not all individuals that engaged in this behavior remained completely silent. Some did find ways to express themselves, although when they did so, they showed a great deal of self-restraint and caution. In Chapter 2, I described the case of Claudia. Recall that Claudia went to great pains to have others voice her thoughts for her. She could not withstand the gaze of others especially if there was a possibility that they might not like her ideas.

Some hidden leaders also engaged in what I call *rare and controlled speech*. This form of hiding may appear to be similar to self-censorship because it involves being silent, but with rare and controlled speech, the silence is a precursor to self-expression. Those who engage in rare and controlled speech spoke *very infrequently* because, for them, speech was a planned event involving a lot of pre-work, calculation, and careful thought. Spontaneous speech was often confusing and too chaotic.

Ayana was one of those individuals who engaged in rare and controlled speech. We saw that Ayana's silence was not because she had nothing to offer but because she wanted to make sure that before she uttered a word she had done her homework, anticipated every potential criticism, and come prepared with a clear sense of her recommendations and their pros and cons. Ayana described a memorable team meeting in which the group was discussing how to develop a web-based communication strategy. Ayana had been working to develop such a strategy without anyone's knowledge and had some well-formed ideas. However, when she spoke up, she found herself drowned out (made invisible) by a more assertive speaker who was able to inspire confidence in her ability to take on the task. Ayana described this scenario, stating:

> The topic of communication strategy came to the table and I thought, "Oh, I'm doing these things already." I tried to push myself to speak about my work, what I'm doing, what I'm finding on the web. Then, I felt intimidated when another colleague, she's a very strong communicator, came out with absolutely the same ideas, but she said them loudly. So when my boss said, "Oh, that's wonderful," I spoke up and said, "Well, isn't that what I just said? I thought I had communicated this." And then he got very confused.

Ayana's experience is very revealing about the impact of lack of spontaneity and the need to exercise control when speaking. In the eyes of co-workers Ayana's tendency to be silent led to her being seen as someone who had nothing to offer. Thus, while she was physically in the room with her teammates during the meeting, she might as well have been invisible. In the story, Ayana shared the rare pattern-breaking act of controlled speech, but this was no match for the entrenched expectations that others had of her. Therefore, Ayana's inability to establish presence in that meeting may have been a discouraging factor, reinforcing the need for greater control in future speech. Repeated experiences such as this might even produce self-censorship.

Obstructed visibility refers to the reliance on meritorious contribution as a strategy of gaining visibility. Those who engaged in obstructed visibility were not passive—they worked very hard and assumed that this would be sufficient to receive appreciation and recognition for their contributions. However, structural and/or normative barriers obscured the visibility of their skill and work. Unlike those who self-censored or engaged in rare and controlled speech, those that engaged in obstructed effort did not feel insecure about what they could offer the organization.[1] Quite the opposite—they felt confident in their abilities, and they sought to become visible. However, they were unable to formulate a productive and effective strategy to circumvent the entrenched barriers that obstructed the visibility of their capacities and contributions.

Eva is an example of a leader whose leadership effectiveness was obstructed. One of Eva's main leadership challenges was gaining independence and visibility in her center. Even though she headed a unit and her job had components that required leadership, she felt that her job was treated as merely operational. As she explains, while she was encouraged and credited for her performance of culturally feminine roles (e.g., note taking in meetings), she was discouraged from visibly performing and taking credit for culturally male roles such as strategy formulation and participating in policy making processes:

> I was very good at taking notes and minutes in the meetings and I still like to do it. The only thing they saw about my work was, "Oh, she's very good about taking notes" and not my other skills in strategizing. But part of my job also involved policy making. One time I helped produce, policies and wrote a detailed report outlining shipping costs for the senior staff and making recommendations (which, by the way, were accepted), but my name did not appear anywhere on the report, and I did not get to present it. Now, if the DG wants to present the report to the board, I don't expect my name to be there. But if my boss wants to present any report that I produce, in his name, there I see the problem. But because he was the member of the management team, he did it. And it was awful, terrible. Initially I was not quite sure if I should have this ability, but then I said later on, "Well, why not? I did the work. If I took my time, if that was my idea, and I had to work hard on making a proposal, why shouldn't I present it?"

The opportunity to break from this pattern of obstructed visibility arose when Eva was presented with the task of developing criteria for salary increases for international staff. Because her immediate boss was classified as international staff, she decided to take her recommendations to the head of the division (her boss's boss) and not follow the customary chain of command. When her immediate boss found out that she had not consulted him, he was furious and said that he did not want to be responsible for her office if she planned to continue taking things directly to the division head. Eva argued that, in this particular instance, she felt that it would have been inappropriate to go directly to him because she was making recommendations on international staff salary increases, and he was in that category. He saw things differently. Because he was very angry, she proposed that they discuss the issue with their mutual boss. This meeting resulted in a clear articulation of the situations under which it was appropriate for her to go to her immediate boss and the situations when it was appropriate for her to go to the head of the division.

Although the meeting with her angry boss and the division head had been uncomfortable, it was also the first time that Eva had gained the opportunity to break free of the cloak imposed over her competence by the structural arrangement and norms of the organization. She had essentially created a structural hole through which some of her previously obstructed capabilities could be made visible to decisionmakers. While this was a narrow window of visibility, it proved to be sufficient for others to observe her capabilities beyond the specific case of international staff salaries. Over time, her positive track record led to the recognition of her skills and this contributed to an expansion of her professional opportunities in her center.

Eva commented that an important factor in her gaining recognition for her meritorious efforts was "support from the top," and in particular from her center's Director General (DG). As she explained:

> The main obstacle was precisely the structure that I had. I couldn't go above my boss, so—any idea, any proposal, couldn't go further. The DG not only supported women, but also really believed that the role of women in the institution is really important. He was one of those people who didn't want to go to meetings if there was not a woman there to give her opinion about what was being discussed.

Although Eva had some success in gaining visibility by the time she came to the WLS course, she continued to encounter a subtle, yet more pervasive barrier. The trouble was that she was ill-equipped to handle these new challenges. Therefore, when she came to the WLS, she hoped to gain the tools she needed. What Eva did not realize was that the WLS would offer her much more than ideas and tools and she would come to recognize that the barriers to her visibility were not only external, they were also internal.

Discovery and Transformation of Habitual Patterns of Thinking

The behaviors of hidden leaders were fueled by a habitual pattern of self-diminishing and context-amplifying thinking, in which individuals constructed the self as weak relative to a robust external context. Hidden leaders attributed their self-diminishing and context-amplifying thought processes to issues within themselves, their organizational contexts, or to both. Critical learning experiences within the WLS led hidden leaders to gain insight into their habitual thought processes and to examine and challenge their assumptions.

Self-diminishing and context-amplifying thought processes were manifested in the descriptions that hidden leaders gave of hiding behaviors. Self-diminishing thoughts emphasized a perceived deficiency of some aspect of the self. This self-aspect was not seen as deficient universally but as a liability in the specific context of the workplace. Context-amplifying thoughts emphasized the idea that workplace norms and expectations and demands were uncompromising and intolerant. Given their perception of the context and themselves hiding behaviors were crafted to allow hidden leaders to lay low and not bring attention to self-aspects that were perceived as liabilities in the organizational setting.

Although all the hidden leaders emphasized the power of context and the relative powerlessness of the self, there were differences in the degree to which they emphasized these two elements. Some hidden leaders emphasized self-diminishing thoughts over context-amplifying ones. These individuals generally constructed themselves as having nothing of value to offer, or at least having very little of value. To justify their perceptions, they cited concerns such as age-related insecurity or the belief that others were smarter and more capable than themselves. Fearing that visibility would lead others to lose respect for them or dislike and reject them, they traded being authentic for being acceptable to others. This led to a hyper-sensitivity to others' reactions and to hiding parts of themselves they feared could raise others' ire.

Rosaria's story illustrates the habitual thinking pattern of this type. Recall that Rosaria attributed her self-censoring to cross-cultural adjustment and adjustment to a new regional job. Although these were relevant factors, it was not until the WLS that she would become more aware of the full nature of her leadership dilemma, which surfaced when she received contradictory feedback from WLS teammates and work colleagues. In the next quote, she describes receiving feedback from WLS teammates:

> Toward the end of the course, we had to give feedback to every member of our team on general behavior and performance during the training. I really spent time the night before writing feedback to every one of the team members. Trying hard to recall their faces, their actions, which struck me most, and then the words that they told me that struck me most. They found my feedback to be the most insightful. It was a surprise to me because I had been concerned: "Would they appreciate it?" But I also felt I deserved appreciation. I spent time thinking about this feedback. It turned out that a number of them found me quiet, and they had a hard time writing feedback for me. They couldn't find anything to say about me. One of them told me: "Actually, your being quiet is your strength"—I was struck by that phrase—"because your quietness actually gives you the time to really think through things, in making insightful comments." They said, "You have all those thoughts inside you. You just have to bring them forward."

360 degree feedback from work colleagues stood in contrast to this. A comment from a work colleague that Rosaria was "unimaginative"

grabbed her attention and made her feel misunderstood. But, reflection on this feedback led to insight into the habitual thought patterns stemming from Rosaria's insecurity had produced the social outcome that she wanted to avoid in the first place:

> I consider myself imaginative, but apparently, it doesn't show to others. The reason, I think, is because when I have an idea, I keep it to myself. I don't spread it. I don't articulate it. I keep quiet. I'm too careful, I think about it, plan about it. I'm afraid it might not be a popular idea.

Sorting out the implications of the contradictory feedback from WLS teammates, on the one hand, and work colleagues on the other, shifted Rosaria's perspective of both herself and her work setting. With respect to herself, the appreciative feedback from WLS teammates affirmed the value of her ideas. With respect to her work context, although feedback from co-workers was less positive, it revealed that people at work wanted to hear her ideas. This challenged her belief that that her environment was unreceptive, judgmental, and unforgiving. Critically, Rosaria recognized that her silence was misunderstood as lacking imagination, and this was a wake-up call for her. The awareness that she had something to offer, that others wanted what she had to offer, and the desire not to be misunderstood led to a transformative insight and recognition that she needed to change how she habitually thought about herself and her context. She said: "It was a good feeling, because it gave me the confidence that what I'm thinking is right. I just need to express it. I just need to articulate it."

Whereas Rosaria and some other hidden leaders emphasized self-diminishing thoughts, there were also hidden leaders like Angela (opening story) and Eva who emphasized context-amplifying thoughts. Unlike the hidden leaders who emphasized the former types of thoughts, those who emphasized the latter had confidence in their ideas and work and wanted these to be recognized, respected, and appreciated for their work. There were some differences between Angela and Eva. While Angela's story contained both self-diminishing and context-amplifying dimensions at least initially, Eva focused on context-amplifying thoughts. Angela was very conscious that she had suppressed valued self-aspects (e.g., modesty) so as to be respected by her colleagues. Eva, on the other hand, discovered in the WLS how self-diminishing thoughts silently crept into her thoughts and behavior at work. For example, she had developed the habit of being very cautious and conservative in what she displayed about her thoughts so as not to be discounted by her colleagues.

Since Angela's story is described in the extended story at the end of this Chapter, here I illustrate and describe Eva's story of critical learning in the WLS to illustrate both the nature of emphasis on context-amplifying thought as well as its transformation. During a 360-degree feedback exercise, Eva recalled receiving two surprising comments from co-workers. The first focused on her strengths and the second on her weaknesses.

> I was perceived as being very inflexible and a perfectionist. That was a perception that others had of me and I didn't have of myself. Maybe I keep doing the perfectionist person thing—inflexible with others and I want to do things my way and things like that. People who were working with me also said that I was very supportive, and I have many, many ideas, and that I helped them to develop their own ideas. So I also found some strengths that I didn't know I had. They also said: "You have many things to offer to us, but you don't think they are very valuable." Another thing was: "Don't be insecure, don't be shy."

Combined, these two pieces of feedback gave Eva a sense of what she might do more of and what she might do less of. But more importantly, she realized that over time, her response to the relentless pressure of external scrutiny had led her to be careful, conservative, and less willing to try out new ideas, experiment, make mistakes, and learn. Eva's story illustrates a common dilemma encountered by individuals trying to cope with stereotype threat where her behavior is motivated by a desire to avoid conforming to stereotypes.[2] This reactive posture likely stifles spontaneity, experimentation, and the opportunity to learn from mistakes. But, as we will see in the next section, Eva acquired a crucial resource from the WLS to help her continue to respond creatively in an unrelenting context.

In addition to gaining insight into how she may have contributed to her difficulties with gaining visibility, Eva's reflection on the feedback also altered her view of the context. While she continued to feel that her center's culture was challenging for women who chose to pursue roles that were inconsistent with gender-role ascriptions, she also recognized that there were individuals within her environment that recognized and valued her capabilities. The feedback from co-workers suggested that others wanted to see her share her ideas more willingly.

Building on Transformative Insights and Cultivating a New Habit Pattern

Although WLS alumnae described having moments of insight and radical perspective change during the course, I also explored the crucial issue of whether these changes impacted their behavior in a sustained way after the course. To address this, I also analyzed the data with two interrelated questions in mind: Did the WLS alumnae build upon the insights gained from the WLS to cultivate a new pattern of thinking? And what, if any, behavioral changes ensued from this?

My analysis suggests that the WLS put into motion a slow but steady process of transformation from hidden leadership to visible leadership. In stories of visible leadership, WLS alumnae described themselves engaging in *self-affirming* and *context-mitigating* thought processes. These thought processes are characterized by acknowledging one's strengths and realistically assessing the situation relative to obstacles and opportunities for taking action. Reversing habitual thought processes, however, required effort. Visible leaders described, "catching themselves" having self-diminishing and context-amplifying thoughts and consciously "interrupting" these and cultivating a new pattern of thinking and acting.

Hidden leaders described employing several means to build upon the transformative insights from the WLS after returning to work. One of these was the recall and application of problem-relevant knowledge from the WLS. Angela described her internal conflict with suppressing aspects of herself that were devalued in her center. As described next, theoretical ideas regarding the role of leaders in building high-performing teams gave her a way to incorporate her personal values related to modesty and collaboration into her thinking about what effective leadership entailed. Here she describes the impact of this insight on her subsequent behavior when returning to work:

> In one sense, theory kept me from totally modeling the behaviors I was seeing. It helped me see that, for what I'm trying to do, some of my own ways of working are valuable. One of the big things out of the training course was the idea of teamwork and looking for complementarity. I realized from this that I'm quite strong on finding complementarity. I'm good at the big ideas and initiating things, and I need somebody who's detail-oriented to complement me, and to make sure things get done. So, that was probably the big thing I got out of the course in terms of my own work. To look for those complements.

Another crucial means for continuous learning and change were the relationships created in the WLS. In Chapter 3, I described how learning in a women-only environment fostered safety and transformational change. The depth of learning that took place in these interactions helped to build long-lasting bonds that continued to foster learning and change long after the WLS was over. As Angela and Eva describe next, relationships were critical to their capacity to change their habitual pattern of hiding. Angela emphasized the importance of just catching up with women in the WLS and the continuous exchange of experiences: "I see many of the WLS alumnae at CGIAR meetings, I often take the time to talk with other women about their experiences, about what are the challenges we're having, what strategies other centers are using. We do a lot of networking just by e-mail as well."

In addition to swapping stories and experiences, continuous learning also takes place by actively seeking on-going advice about specific issues and problems encountered at work. Angela again explained:

> Somebody I worked with on the (XYZ) program had a problem with one of the team members just basically walking away from the project and not delivering. She and I were at a meeting together in France a couple weeks ago, and we had several rounds of conversation about what to do about that problem and who she should be talking to and strategies for dealing with it. Certainly I would feel comfortable talking with her about a similar problem. Sometimes it helps when it's not at your own center.

Relationships were also a source of continuous encouragement and inspiration. Consider Eva's comment about her on-going contact with her WLS feedback-buddy as well as her staying connected with other WLS alumnae from her cohort:

> I kept in contact with my buddy person in another center, and we were sharing every success. I have just come from Indonesia where we had a meeting on gender and diversity, and I met one of those ladies who was with me in the 1999 course, and she has grown up so much both as a person and in the position that she has. When you talk to somebody and in a meeting after six years, you notice the difference between what the person was at that time—that shyness—and the person they are now. During one week, I saw two people who had grown from being the shy person, very hidden person, to people who had developed those abilities they had previously hidden, all through those exercises of leadership in the WLS course.

In addition to relationships and theory, mindful attention and critical reflection were important means of building on transformative insights.[3] Hidden leaders described the role of recalling transformative insights from the WLS in situations when they caught themselves engaging in old habitual patterns. In these accounts, hidden leaders described conjuring up the "Aha" moments from the training. They recalled the shift in perspective, the insights, how they felt, and the possibilities they had seen for themselves in the WLS. When they recalled these moments, they were able to self-regulate: pause and reflect on their current circumstances. Sometimes, an actual object from the training activated mindful reflection. In Chapter 3 I described how one of the functions of physical objects was anchoring meaning (e.g., bracelets used to signify women's strengths). These objects were one means of recalling critical lessons from the WLS and applying those lessons to circumstances arising in the workplace. In Chapter 2, for example, I described how Claudia repeatedly returned to a feedback letter from a senior woman on her WLS team who had encouraged her not to discount her ideas. Re-reading this letter, she told herself: "She told me not to look at my being young as a constraint. I should have more confidence—that is so true." Similarly Rosaria recalled a story of feedback from WLS team members. Previously I had described how she had given her colleagues extensive written feedback on her observations of their behaviors throughout the program but none could think of anything to say about her because she had been very quiet. Surprised by the quality and depth of her feedback, her feedback-buddies affirmed that her quietness was a strength because it allowed her be observant and thoughtful. But, they added, her keen observations and ideas were hidden because she did not share them with others. Rosaria understood why her work colleagues had misunderstood her and she embraced the encouragement that her WLS feedback-buddies had given her to share her thoughts. Rosaria said that this singular feedback of affirmation was, "the most memorable moment from the leadership training."

Self-diminishing and context-amplifying thoughts create a belief in the lack of personal agency and exaggerate the influence of context. Critical insights from the WLS brought hidden leaders' attention to their habitual patterns. Theoretical insights, relationships, and recall of transformative insights were valuable means of sustaining change. Each of these means enabled hidden leaders to repeatedly encounter, "catch," pause, examine, and reevaluate their habitual patterns as these were automatically activated and repeated in specific circumstances at work. The repetition of this reflective process sensitized hidden leaders' perception of, and heightened their capacity to recognize when old patterns emerged. Their ability to pause and redirect themselves more deliberately, weakening their habitual pattern of self-diminishing and context-amplifying thinking, while strengthening their capacity to more quickly and easily engage in self-affirming and context-mitigating thoughts. We next turn to the visible leader behaviors that this new thought process fostered.

Behaviors of Visible Leadership

Being visible is the opposite of hiding in that it involves trying to make something evident, clear, or detectable to others. Visible leadership behaviors occur when hidden leaders express and publicly take ownership of their ideas, insights, knowledge, and skills. Earlier, I described three behavioral strategies of hidden leaders: self-censorship, rare and controlled speech, and obstructed visibility. This section will describe how, by cultivating self-affirming and context-mitigating thought patterns, hidden leaders reversed these earlier behavioral tendencies. Stories of visible leadership reveal that those who self-censored described speaking up, those who engaged in rare and controlled speech described speaking spontaneously, and those who struggled with obstructed visibility developed increased capacity for strategic action.

The reader may recall that the critical learning event in the WLS for Rosaria resulted from feedback provided by her WLS teammates. Her teammates had noted that while Rosaria had very good observational skills that allowed her to recognize things others missed, she did not share her insight. They encouraged her to have confidence in her ideas and share them for others' benefit. Rosaria took this to heart, repeatedly telling herself: "I just needed the confidence that what I'm thinking is right. It may not be always right, but expressing what I thought came very easy and naturally." When she returned to work, she decided to: "Open up myself, expressing what I think and what I feel. At the same time, I feel I'm open now to more ideas, including opposing ideas."

This new perspective gave Rosaria the courage to use her observational skills to tackle the thorny interpersonal issues to which she had responded with hurt and withdrawal. After the WLS, she was able to engage colleagues, offering her observations with empathy, compassion, and understanding. In the dialogue that follows, Rosaria shared a story of how she had given difficult feedback to a colleague who was perceived as a problem by the team:

ROSARIA: She was really difficult to deal with.

INTERVIEWER: How was she being problematic?

ROSARIA: She was very aggressive, and very impulsive. She's also very much output-oriented so she wants to do things, everything, and all at the same time. I also found her having difficulty focusing on one thing. And I felt that this was creating stress to her subordinates, creating stress to herself, as well, and creating stress to others with whom she's working, including myself. So, I took the opportunity to share my observations. I had to carefully plan. I really wanted to help her, and I wanted to make the effort to help her, because I know I can do something, and I want to try it. Then I wanted to give her feedback and to express it in a way that says: "I am concerned." I was trying to be careful and conscious so that she won't misinterpret my feedback.

INTERVIEWER: What did you say to her?

ROSARIA: What I told her is: "Don't misinterpret others, that they do not like you. Maybe you want to consider changing the tone of your voice when you want to talk to them. Or maybe be careful with the choice of words. You may not be aware, but your tone and your choice of words are hurting them." Then, I also observed how she responded to everything I told her.

INTERVIEWER: So you saw a change as you were talking to her?

ROSARIA: I think I was the only one who could really talk to her well and really advise her that, "Okay, maybe you have to dress more appropriately. This place is a corporate environment." Her dressing is not good. So I have to carefully tell her that we are going to this meeting and it would be good if you would be in proper corporate attire. She's really chubby, and then she will wear these sleeveless tops that are very thin, and you can see her undergarments through the thin fabric. What I find inappropriate is that she would be dealing with senior staff, and it's really not appropriate.

INTERVIEWER: And she responded well to that?

ROSARIA: Yeah, she responded to that. They would ask, other people would ask me, "Did you tell her to dress appropriately this time?" What's interesting is whenever other colleagues would want to tell her something, they would tell me first. I've become the messenger.

INTERVIEWER: Do you think that her relationship with others has improved, too?

ROSARIA: Yes. But, of course, it took time.

INTERVIEWER: What difference do you see in how you dealt with situations such as this before and after the course?

ROSARIA: It's basically the confidence. Before the course, I thought it was just a matter of luck or something like that. Another thing—my comments and my feedback were very candid, very frank, but they didn't sound intimidating. And I think that really gives me the comfort. It's just a matter of articulating.

A second pre-WLS behavior was rare and controlled speech. This is where the hidden leader would speak only after having done extensive research in a topic area and after having very firmly set the agenda for what will be discussed. Because it takes time and effort to be fully prepared to speak on a topic, hidden leaders that engaged in this behavior were rarely heard from. Exercising visible leadership for this group entailed not only speaking up more but also learning to speak spontaneously, without extensive forethought and planning.

Ayana's pre-WLS story related to being dismayed when her well-thought-out communications strategy did not even register when she described it in a team meeting. Her tendency to be quiet had resulted in a situation where she could not establish presence when she was finally ready to speak. For this reason, Ayana worked on developing a presence in her team. One area where she practiced this was in meetings:

The Advanced Leadership course just made me stronger in meetings. For example, I can speak my mind. And I don't prepare, even though I don't have any idea what's going on, if I have something in my mind, I'll just speak it out. What I decided after the WLS course was to participate in meetings and have three points in mind before the meeting. I have no clue about a subject matter, then I wouldn't go to a meeting, but if I have a clue of what's going on, and even if people don't raise the three points I have in mind, I'll get out of this meeting with my two or three points said. And the more meetings for me, the better, because I can practice. Sometimes it could be a boring topic, but still I have something to say about it, and I can participate and that's wonderful.

Ayana also made sure she was seen and accounted for rather than accept merely being an unacknowledged presence in a group. She described one meeting that she attended where:

The main speaker addressed the audience as "the wise gentlemen in front of us." And then he went around, and I raised my hand like, "Hello!" And he went, "Oh, I'm sorry. You're there." I was like, "Oh, of course!" And so they went around this table—it was a round table, actually—asking for concrete opinions, or questions, or whatever. If it were before the course, maybe I wouldn't have said anything.

Ayana also gave her colleagues direct feedback when she felt discounted. She described a situation in which there was conflict with a peer who treated her in a dismissive manner. After the course, she decided that she needed to do something about how she felt about her colleague's treatment of her. She stated:

So, when I came back, I was like, "Okay, I've had enough of this and I'd just rather stop this right now." So, I just waited for a good time to talk with her, and one day, I was very clear, and I had the guts to go to her office and tell her, "I don't like this and this from you. Could you please stop it and just treat me as your equal" kind of thing. And that really stopped her from doing that. And I thought, "My God. I've just spent one year taking on this rubbish." It just cost me, one day to talk with her. And it wasn't even ten minutes conversation. It wasn't so hard. That was it. And now she's very careful.

Eva's leadership had been limited by obstructed visibility, the final pre-WLS leadership behavior. Despite her desire to have her work noticed and acknowledged, her center's norms and organizational hierarchy obstructed the visibility of her contributions and capabilities. Fortunately for her, a situation had arisen where these structural constraints were to come into question. This led to a reevaluation of reporting relationships and eventually more visibility of her skills. At the time of the interview Eva had been promoted to a researcher position and her recruitment category had been upgraded from national to international staff. This was a huge leap involving an upward trajectory in status along two important dimensions. However, she found that these markers of status were constantly challenged, and she had to find ways of defending her achievements.

Eva enjoyed her work greatly, but to remain respected and be taken seriously, she had to be vigilant. Eva said that there were several ways in which she felt vulnerable: being the only female on her team, her previous designation as national staff, and her lacking a Ph.D. These dimensions added nuanced identity markers that made Eva an outsider among the ranks of her team. Yet Eva was determined to preserve her visibility and develop strategies to circumnavigate the marginalization traps she encountered. She credited the WLS for her increased astuteness and capacity to respond to these situations.

Eva explained that what set her apart from her international research colleagues were not the objective and material markers of difference such as salary and position. What she had to contend with were perceptions:

EVA: The perception that people have about a person that has been national staff and is now international is a constant challenge to credibility. For example, when I came to the research area, the first thing we did was a very thoughtful and rigorous study of the center's culture around diversity. We paid a great deal of attention to detail and every step was done with rigor. It was well-done. It was a one-year study with feedback from high caliber people. When we presented it to the management team for the first time, it was kind of disqualified by one of the directors who pointed out several minor details. So I was seen at the time as "not a researcher" or the project having "not having much rigor" because of me. So we were thinking at the time, well, if it were a foreigner who recently arrived to the institution that had presented the data, the response would have been: "Oh, that is a very important study."

INTERVIEWER: How did you come to the conclusion that if you had foreign staff doing it, it would have received a different kind of response?

EVA: It is a perception.

INTERVIEWER: Your perception?

EVA: No, no, even in that study we could prove that it is kind of our culture that if a foreigner does it, then it has respect and is well received. The difference between internationally recruited and nationally recruited staff is high. So, that is the perception that we have.

INTERVIEWER: Did you describe your methodology in light of the concerns about the rigor of the study?

EVA: Of course, I had to. Finally, we could prove that we had a rigorously designed study. But if another person had presented it, maybe it would have been received from the very beginning. That person wouldn't have had to make the effort we had to make to demonstrate and argue to prove that the methodology was okay.

INTERVIEWER: I was wondering if what you gained from the WLS course was useful to you in terms of making your voice heard in this particular situation.

EVA: I definitely had, in myself, some tools acquired from the WLS. One was the persuasiveness that I have gained by knowing that I am valuable, that I have to preserve my self-confidence. I have gained self-confidence that otherwise I wouldn't have been able to respond. During that research presentation, where somebody was just trying to throw my work out, I wouldn't have responded the way I did if I didn't have the tools as a woman and a leader to have self-confidence. I didn't just let it go. I just sent him a message after the meeting saying, "Maybe there was a misunderstanding here about the methodology we used; let me explain a bit about it." Yeah, I learned to be persuasive, to be more self-confident. Before the course, I may have abandoned the idea. So I gained self-confidence, I gained the tools to handle many situations, and that is unconscious. I couldn't think of exactly which of the tools helped me to deal more with self-confidence now, but I'm sure that course was critical.

As the discussion about the WLS continued, Eva pointed out that her confidence came from new knowledge and skills but most critically from relationships, "having allies," as she described it. She explained that, when she encountered difficulties (such as the one described in the case of the research project), she would tap into her network of WLS alums for substantive and strategic feedback: "I would ask: 'What do you think of this? I'm sure this is a good methodology and a serious study. What do you think?'" By doing this, she fundamentally reversed an old habit of thinking she just had to keep her head down and expect her contributions to be taken seriously and recognized. This habit had come from not just the lack of tools, but also, from isolation from other women. With an extended network available, she continued to build her skills to respond to the dynamic circumstances that repeatedly hid her capabilities. As she stated: "Unconsciously, I used tools from the WLS to persuade or to push an idea through and be self-confident of what we have done and how to be assertive." What follows is an extended story of one hidden leader, Angela, whose leadership dilemma was introduced in the opening story of this chapter. The extended story below is condensed but by sharing it here, some of the complexity and nuance behind each of the leadership stories that were told to me can be illustrated.

Angela's Story of Hiding and Transformative Insight From the WLS

Angela's pre-WLS experience had to do with how she coped with an organizational culture that she experienced as intolerant, even hostile, to cultural diversity. Angela was an American that had been raised in India, where she had been socialized to embrace the values of modesty, humility, and group harmony. Early in her career, she encountered a clash between these values and the individualistic and competitive culture that was dominant within her research center. Suppressing the former values and embracing the latter, she had emerged as a respected leader but felt conflicted. The WLS course helped Angela affirm and reintegrate suppressed aspects of her personal style. Three themes from Angela's story will be described here: experiencing a clash between her values and those of her center; conforming to organizational expectations; and transformative insight in the WLS.

Experiencing a Culture Clash

Many stories of cultural adaptation start with the clash between an individual's expectations and those of the organization.[4] These clashes, often painful, confusing, and difficult to overcome, are significant experiences that are often vividly recalled. When asked to characterize her leadership effectiveness after the WLS course, Angela responded, "very effective," and, chuckling, added that this very response demonstrated the significant changes she has made in order to survive in her center.

> When I first started working at my center, I would underplay what I was good at. I had been raised with this idea that women shouldn't speak too much and that tooting your own horn was not a good thing. Our culture is very much that you should be modest and other people should praise.

Her modesty, however, was a disadvantage in her center.

> It used to be that the nastier the question you asked at seminars, the more points you got for being intelligent. They would ask questions in a way that implied, "You idiot. Why on earth would you run your regression that way?" Now, there's a little bit nicer tone in the way questions are being asked.

Being a woman also contributed to her outsider status. Women's accomplishments were reined in by attributing success to something other than professionalism and competence. "When I told my boss that the World Bank was interested in funding me to do some work, he said, 'What'd you do, bat your pretty eyes at them?' It was a joke, but I took great offense."

Being rendered invisible also minimized women:

> At a donor meeting, a senior official at my Center was asked to introduce his staff to the donors. He went around the room introducing people but cut things off just before he got to me. I was standing in the back, but I was wearing a red suit. He just didn't see me at all. It wasn't purposeful. He was quite embarrassed when it was pointed out that one person had not been introduced.

A final factor that contributed to her outsider status was her profession. She said: "Sometimes I felt like it was a hostile environment. I was undervalued. In fact, when I first came, the only people who were valued were economists who could do quantitative analysis." She concluded that, to be taken seriously in her center, one had to be an economist, male, and exhibit assertive behaviors. She observed that other colleagues—including men who did not exhibit prototypical masculine characteristics—were struggling with similar issues as her. One of these was an Asian man who was a world-renowned expert in his discipline. She felt that the new division director, a European man, did not respect the Asian man despite the fact that he was a very highly respected scholar. For example, her Asian colleague, so not to appear immodest would couch his assertions:

> My (Asian colleague) wasn't playing the game. He just stayed true to his sensibilities. When he would couch his recommendations with modesty when speaking with our (European colleague). He would say, "well, from the little I know of Indian agriculture." This is one of the very, very highly respected experts on Indian agriculture. That's a code for saying, "Well I know more about this than you." But, my new boss would just take him at face value and sort of say, "Well, see, he doesn't know much about Indian agriculture." Because modesty wasn't an excessive flaw of my new boss.

The immediate outcome of this cross-cultural misunderstanding was the European boss' lack of respect and recognition of the expertise that Angela's Asian colleague brought to the research project of the center. In the long run, the Asian colleague's contract was not renewed. Angela said there were several others whose careers similarly suffered because of their modesty.

Initially, Angela voiced her concerns, hoping that her colleague's expertise would be valued and respected. She also recognized that, in many ways, he and she were in the same boat. Her collaborative and relational values were at odds with those of self-differentiation and individualism that were normative in her center. Similarly, her modesty was at odds with the assertiveness and self-promotion that was appreciated and recognized. So, when her initial efforts to advocate for others ("ranting" as she described it), failed to make a difference, she concluded that her only choice was to conform. She was modest, female, and not an economist. She decided, of these, gender was immutable, her profession was only partially negotiable, but the third, modesty, was malleable. This was an area in which she made the greatest modification. She stated:

> I decided that if I was going out, I was going out on my own terms, not because I had been fired or let go. I couldn't just wait for my boss to discover that I was brilliant. I had to periodically tell him that I was a respected authority in my area. I needed to speak up in

meetings and things like that. Now I enjoy it when I get a good question. I feel more confident, so it doesn't threaten me as much.

Survival by Conforming to the Organization's Culture

Angela learned a great deal about what was expected from listening and watching. She learned how to manage interpersonal relationships in a manner that was expected. In seminars, she started to ask questions and learned that asking questions in a nasty tone was not to be taken personally; it was a challenge, part of the normal give and take in her center:

> Now I enjoy it when I get a good question. I feel more confident, so it doesn't threaten me as much. Of course, since I might get annoyed if it's asked really nastily, I'll usually picture the person asking the question as an idiot.

As for her discipline, she found she had to demonstrate that she could do the complicated statistical analyses that the economists were known for. She demonstrated her competence and skill as a quantitative researcher and learned to make sure that other people understood the value of her contributions. She made it a point to let her boss know that, within her discipline, she was "one of the top-ten in the world."

Transformative Insights in WLS

Angela's efforts to conform had a very positive effect on her professional credibility: she was taken seriously and she moved up the organizational hierarchy. Yet she expressed uneasiness about suppressing a valued aspect of herself that had been a source of ambivalence and inner conflict when she came to the WLS. She dealt with this by trying to coach others and also to advocate on their behalf. In particular, she told one story in which she coached a young Asian female scientist to become assertive, and another story where she advocated on behalf of a modest senior Asian researcher. Not only were these actions unsuccessful by her own account, they also reflected her ambivalence and internal conflict regarding what needed to change: the individual (first story) or the organization (second story). Angela's uneasiness reflected the fact that, when valued aspects of the self are hidden, individuals experience discomfort, confusion, and dissonance.

For Angela, the most significant impact of the WLS course was the realization that she did not have to fully conform, that she could and should retain aspects of herself that she valued. She stated:

> The training course gave me understanding that some of my instinctive ways of doing things were right or had value, that I didn't need

to absorb every aspect of the organization's culture, that there was value in the way I was. So in one sense, the course kept me from losing myself totally to the behaviors and working culture I was observing.

Expression of Previously Suppressed Behaviors

Angela previously hid a valued attribute of modesty, but during the WLS, colleagues affirmed the value of this quality. As she reflected on this, she came to realize that her boss had recognized her modesty and her ability to relate to a wide variety of people and had identified this as a skill that was needed to lead a team. Angela described how this affirmation influenced how she was able to reframe self-aspects she had previously regarded as a liability, as strengths:

> Fairness and some of these other traits where I may be a little different from the other researchers actually worked in my favor and were real assets in this program. So the women's leadership training course helped me to realize that some of these other traits I had might be assets too. A lot of programs had fallen down over the issue that the lead center took most of the money. But instead of giving out a couple of big research grants, we focused on providing public goods that everybody could get. Once we built up a track record and brought in more money, we developed clear processes and governance for allocation in which all centers have a say in the way the program was operated. It was the willingness to listen and play fair. These were the overriding values.

Summary

In the case of the transformation from hidden to visible leadership, the WLS training did indeed contribute to change in participants' habitual patterns of thinking, feeling, and acting. Further, these changes enabled participants to exercise leadership more effectively. Prior to the WLS, hidden leaders engaged in self-diminishing and context-amplifying patterns of thinking and feeling which produced hiding behaviors manifested in self-censorship, rare and controlled speech, and obstructed visibility. Shifts in habitual patterns, effected by critical learning in the WLS gave way to a new pattern of self-affirming and context-mitigating thinking. This new pattern fostered visible leadership behaviors. Stories of visible leadership reveal that those who self-censored described speaking up, those who engaged in rare and controlled speech described speaking spontaneously, and those who struggled with obstructed effort developed increased capacity for strategic action. As described by the participants, the WLS training enabled them to emerge from hidden leadership to a more effective visible leadership.

Notes

1. See Fletcher (1999) for a detailed analysis of how women's competence is "disappeared" by structural barriers and cultural practices.
2. See Steele and Aronson (1995).
3. See Kuechler and Stedham (2017) for a discussion on cultivating mindfulness in a management classroom setting.
4. In a different context, for example, see Debebe (2008).

References

Debebe, G. (2008). Cross-cultural competence and power-based rules: A Native American case study. *International Journal of Intercultural Relations, 32*(5), 399–414.

Fletcher, J. K. (1999). *Disappearing acts: Gender, power, and relational competence at work.* Boston, MA: MIT Press.

Kuechler, W., & Stedham, Y. (2017). Management education and transformational learning: The integration of mindfulness in an MBA course. *Journal of Management Education, 42*(1), 8–33.

Steele, C. M., & Aronson, J. S. (1995). Stereotype threat and the intellectual test performance of African Americans. *Journal of Personality and Social Psychology, 69*(5), 797–811.

5 Transformation From Inflexible to Receptive Leadership

> I knew that I needed to change A for B. Before the course I knew that A wasn't the right thing, but I didn't know an alternative.
>
> *Ana, Inflexible Leader*

This chapter explores the second leadership transformation produced by the WLS, from *inflexible* to *receptive* leadership. The analysis will show that the WLS fostered greater leadership effectiveness through this transformation by fostering a shift in a habitual, *self-amplifying* and *context-dismissing* thinking that was at the root of inflexible leadership behavior. This pattern of thinking was enacted in situations that were ambiguous and complex. By self-amplifying, I refer to a tendency to grasp at one's beliefs and assumptions when faced with uncertainty, and by context-dismissing, I refer to the tendency to make untested, often negative assumptions about others' motivations, intent, or values. Inflexible leaders engaged in both of these thought processes simultaneously, defending their perspective and rejecting external cues. Although this behavior may have enabled them to feel some sense of control, it blocked insight into the demands of context, resulted in lack of effectiveness, and further entrenched the habitual thought pattern.

The transformation to receptive leadership, evidenced in the development of *self-tempering* and *context-regarding* thought processes was based on a newfound realization of the value and importance of information from the environment as providing critical clues to what is necessary for goal achievement. Receptive leaders asserted the validity of and need to account for both their own views as well as those of others. As stories of receptive leaders suggest, post-WLS involved embracing receptive leaders embraced "not knowing," were willing to be curious about their environment, and were eager to find new, creative possibilities from weaving their own knowledge with those of others.

Fifty-two percent of WLS interviewees told stories pertaining to the transformation from inflexible to receptive leadership. While inflexible leadership stories pertained to leadership behaviors prior to the WLS, receptive leadership stories pertained to leadership behaviors after the WLS. Inflexible/receptive leaders were also represented in all recruitment categories with 46 percent recruited internationally, nine percent recruited regionally, 36 percent recruited nationally, and nine percent having a special designation of being employees of a national government. They held a variety of positions at different levels of the hierarchy. Specifically, the position classification distributions among inflexible/receptive leaders were: 25 percent program leaders, 41 percent scientists/researchers, 17 percent managers, and 17 percent theme leader. None of those classified as inflexible/receptive leaders held the "technician/administrator" position.

Let's begin our consideration of this leader category with the story of Ibsituu, a theme leader responsible in part for the coordination of a system-wide project. Ibsituu described her leadership effectiveness prior to the WLS as "somewhat effective." Although she often received verbal support for her ideas people would often leave her with the task of implementing the vision. She didn't have the understanding or guidance needed "for getting people excited and working together, with everybody pulling their own weight and being part of a big idea."

One of the most important lessons Ibsituu learned from the WLS Negotiation Course was that she did not have to do everything herself:

> One of the major things I still remember from that course—which was many years ago—is a better understanding of the fact that not everybody's like me and, if I want people to appreciate the fact that we are doing something together, I have to recognize what I can bring to it, what I can't bring to it, and what other people can bring to it. For a period of time, I felt I needed to do everything myself.

One of the most important insights articulated in the preceding statement was that, in order to engage others, she would have to take into account their differing concerns and desires. This required skillful negotiation and modification of her tendency to engage in "strong-willed" negotiation—insisting that things be done her way:

> There was one particularly memorable moment in the Negotiation Course. We were role-playing about a development project in a port area that would create shopping malls and commercial activity. I was representing the government, while other people were representing NGOs and trade unions and various others. One of my colleagues had been instructed not to compromise under any circumstances. In fact, the instructor said: "I'll give you a bottle of wine if you do not compromise." And she didn't. Everybody else was willing to compromise, and she just refused. She was brilliant. And because I was

the government, I started out with a heavy hand and everybody was telling me to shut up.

Although Ibsituu's team was unsuccessful in this particular negotiation, but she learned several lessons that have served her well. One lesson came from the bottle of wine that had been promised to their negotiating partner without the group's knowledge: "I realized there could be a wildcard that you don't anticipate, and that's the bottle of wine." To negotiate effectively required an understanding of the desires and motivations of others:

> You think you're absolutely right, but everyone else is going to think they're absolutely right as well. I've got very strong opinions. Before I did this training, my tendency was to argue until people capitulated. But training made me recognize that, if I win out of sheer force of will, it's not going to be a happy alliance because other people will feel like they've given in or lost. It's much, much better to come to a common agreement where everybody feels they've won something.

Ibsituu's story reveals a key theme that runs through the varied accounts of inflexible leadership: inflexible leaders had come to rely on a set of ideas, assumptions, and strategies that had enabled them to lead effectively in the past or in some other context. Their leadership dilemma came into clear focus when they encountered the limits of these practiced approaches. When their efforts proved ineffective, inflexible leaders vigorously leaned into what had worked for them in the past, attempting to impose their will on their environment. When this approach inevitably failed, there was confusion and a tendency to grasp more tightly at their assumptions and to see the environment as flawed.

This chapter will illustrate that inflexible leaders' self-affirming and context-dismissing thought patterns produced a distortion that was the exact opposite of hidden leadership. Whereas hidden leaders dismissed self-aspects, inflexible leaders clung to what they knew. Whereas hidden leaders perceived the context as all powerful, inflexible leaders dismissed the cues from the context and attempted to impose their will on it. Both habitual patterns were responses to discomfort with engaging the inherent ambiguity and flux of the environment. The following sections draw upon the stories of inflexible leaders to illuminate their habitual patterns of thinking, feeling, and acting, how these patterns shifted from critical learning experiences in the WLS, and how these changes were manifested in new patterns of receptive leadership that I refer to as self-tempering and context-regarding.

Behaviors of Inflexible Leadership

Inflexible leadership stories were not about dramatic and short-lived situations but of chronic on-going difficulties in which individuals persisted with well-practiced patterns of thought and behavior despite disappointing results. Inflexible leaders described three types of behaviors: inaction, isolation, and mishandling emotions. *Inaction* refers to a state of paralysis or being stopped in one's tracks as a result of not understanding another's actions and the appropriate way to respond to it. Kanya's story of a salary negotiation illustrates inaction. Kanya was baffled about what had gone wrong upon learning that she had been undercut in a salary negotiation that she had assumed had been fair. This negotiation occurred when her position changed from a part-time consultant to a full-time employee. As she explained:

> My supervisor liked what I had to offer and said, "We can draw up a contract for you." He left the salary negotiation to someone else. I was totally unprepared for a tough negotiation. The Director of Finance and Administration (DFA) just casually asked me a few questions about what I was getting where, and based on that, he made an offer.

Initially, Kanya did not realize there was a problem. But later, she and a colleague had a conversation in which she learned that she had been undercut in the salary offer:

> After this negotiation, I went to talk to the other statistician who nearly knocked my head off. He said, "You spoiled it for everybody. You could have asked for three times as much as this, and the Director General (DG) would have approved it." The problem was that I got negotiated down when I went from my consultant rate to a full-time rate because they fixed the rate at the same level that I was working part-time. I was putting in three times what I was normally doing as a consultant, but the rates were the same. But I wasn't capable of negotiating out of that.

Kanya's negotiation experience left her with a bad taste in her mouth and a lot of confusion. She had learned that she should have been offered a higher salary but had no idea what went wrong or what she might have been able to do about it.

Isolation refers to the situation in which a person avoids, or is avoided by, individuals or groups with whom one is interdependent. In Harriet's case, isolation was self-imposed. Right out of graduate school, Harriett had accepted a new job to lead a multidisciplinary, cross-cultural, and geographically dispersed research team. Although Harriet described herself as a somewhat reclusive person, her story of self-isolation suggests that there was much more at work than a personality predisposition. Harriet was faced with a chaotic, fluid, and stressful work setting without any support. It was in this environment that she reacted to isolate herself.

As already stated, Harriet was hired right out of graduate school. Her center was brand new with an entrepreneurial and egalitarian spirit, but there was very little formalization. This mix was simultaneously exciting, demanding, and frustrating for Harriett:

> I had been accustomed to working in a very hierarchical organization. My new center was a brand-new organization, and there were no models to follow. Every week we were discussing everything from what kind of microwave to order to what the staff vacation policy should be and what color the carpet should be. You just can't imagine the amount of extra issues we dealt with while we were supposed to design a totally new program and get our work done and hire staff. So, it was wonderful and exciting, but I think that just created a lot of stress.

Not only was she new to the country and the workplace, but Harriet was also faced with a very stressful work environment. While her colleagues relied on one another for support, the perceived differences between herself and her colleagues created social distance that Harriet felt she could not overcome:

> I think I was also the only woman in the organization in the beginning, and I was a young woman. They were all men. They all sat in the meeting room and had lunch together. They had children in the schools and I didn't so I didn't get to know people that way. With colleagues I felt very self-conscious and didn't like to join them for lunch.

Harriet had a contentious relationship with her boss, and this amplified the stress of the workplace. Although she recognized that he was under a lot of pressure, she disliked how he dealt with people:

> My boss at the time—we were all under so much stress—would get into temper tantrums, and we would get into fierce fights. I had no respect for him at the time because I didn't think he was doing his work properly, and he didn't think I was doing my work properly. We were all struggling to get what this model of the center should be.

Harriet was technically proficient but did not have a lot of management expertise, yet she was expected to create and manage a research team. For Harriet to be effective in her work, she had to devote time to developing managerial skills. But in the fluid and contentious environment where roles were not clearly defined, she was not afforded the space to focus on her job.

Harriet described the managerial difficulties she faced with a geographically dispersed, multidisciplinary team whose expertise did not cohere:

> I was given people to lead, but their research had no real coherence, and they were based all over the world, and I didn't even know where to begin. I had no skills. I had never done this before and was thrown in the pot. Communication was a problem, building a team was a problem. I knew what my vision was, but having a shared vision was a problem.

In the midst of all this, Harriet withdrew into a zone of comfort: "I pulled into my own little shell and just tried to do my work, because I thought that was the way I was going to get things done." This resulted in a negative performance evaluation and warning that her contract may not be renewed. Eventually, Harriet's situation improved. Her boss left, reducing stress, she had a few years under her belt, and she had more responsibilities. But Harriet said: "I still felt ineffective even though I was less angry and calmer and less stressed. I wasn't effective in bringing people together because I didn't have these skills yet."

In contrast to Harriett, Cosima's isolation was a result of others' hostility and silence. Her small program "was charged with working with everybody" to implement a system-wide change. A few constituents, senior management of the CGIAR Centers, were immediately supportive of her efforts and expressed interest in working with her. However, as she described, her perception was that most constituents did not see her initiative as "useful or relevant, not worth putting the time into." While a few expressed this sentiment openly and in a hostile manner, most were silent. It was this silent group of constituents, whom she could not read, that frustrated her most:

> You're sitting in an office, communicating with people all over the world, but certain pockets just never respond. You're getting a flurry of correspondence and feedback, positive and negative and everything in between from others, which is great, because they care. But when you're getting dead silence, that's what failure feels like.

Cosima faced the daunting task of engaging senior management in her center's initiative without understanding why most of them failed to respond to her communications. She said: "I had fifteen fiercely independent organizations to work with, all at different starting points." Cosima began working with the enthusiastic center and decided to entice the silent group by continually communicating about her activities. Numerous specific initiatives and policies resulted from the first collaboration. However, despite widely sharing these activities within the CGIAR, senior management in most centers remained unresponsive. Cosima felt very discouraged: "No matter how many announcements we sent out, no matter how many times we made our services available, we never got an answer."

Mismanagement of negative emotions involves expressing emotions in such a way that entrenches and/or exacerbates a problematic situation. As we know from the large literature on emotional intelligence, an ability to manage emotions, particularly negative ones, is an essential leadership competency.[1] Yet, most people struggle with managing emotions well and find themselves triggered into habitual routines by strong emotions. Unregulated emotions can be so powerful that they sweep a person into an automatic involuntary "fight" or "flight" response, rendering them unable to think through the situation and make informed choices about how to act.[2] Inflexible leaders that mismanaged negative emotions found themselves reacting too quickly and in a defensive and often hostile way when they encountered situations that they perceived as threatening in some way.

As explained previously, Harriett described instances when her anger at her boss over her perception of his incompetence turned into "fierce fights." In contrast, Josephine did not "fight." Instead, her response was to "flee" confrontation. Her inability to manage the anger and pain she felt as a result of her boss's hostility and negative attitude towards women resulted in her decision to leave her previous job:

> I was one of the program leaders. I found myself writing a lot of project proposals for the program and winning some funds and keeping contacts with colleagues in other countries. This did not impress my boss very much. He said, "This woman is now turning to be a director more than myself. Whoever comes to this station has to see her first, has to ask about her." He would say, "Ah, but this is just a lady. This is just a woman." So instead of reflecting positively on me, somehow, it ended up being a conflict. And at a certain stage, I actually had to move elsewhere so I wouldn't continue experiencing this kind of treatment.

Ana, a national staff, also mismanaged her emotions by suppressing her frustration and anger at her team, isolating herself from them and eliciting a reciprocal response. Before the WLS she rated herself as "somewhat effective" when asked how she would characterize her leadership effectiveness. She explained that she was good at getting things done and achieving results, but not effective in managing relationships. Ana's focus on tasks over relationships meant that she not only pushed herself intensely but expected others to do so as well. Most critically, she did not give others the opportunity to provide input. Rather, she wanted the work moving at her pace and a standard *she* found to be acceptable. She described her intensity, stating:

> I worked on developing training materials with my team. I was under a lot of pressure. Members on the team would not get their parts

done on time, and I would get frustrated and do it myself. For me it was: "Let's get it done, on time, with the highest quality." I could move on quickly and then wait until they would digest what they had to do. And sometimes people would feel too much pressure or that I was not sensitive to what they were feeling. People on my team felt they could not express themselves without risking that I would be upset. I would not wait, or I would just take standards for granted, so I would leave them behind. I was aware that something was wrong, but I didn't know the right way to deal with it.

In each of the descriptions of inflexible leadership described here, the individuals had a particular strategy that had worked for them in the past, one they trusted and relied on. Problems arose when these well-honed behaviors proved ineffective. In these cases, instead of taking a step back and examining why their efforts failed, inflexible leaders did more of what they were used to doing with the same unsuccessful outcomes. The result was frustration, disappointment, and confusion about why their efforts did not bear the desired fruit.

Discovery and Transformation of Habitual Patterns of Thinking

A habitual pattern of self-amplifying and context-dismissing thinking shaped inflexible behaviors. In this pattern of thinking, the person engages in a self-referential circular thought process in which they draw on their assumptions, beliefs, and past experiences to justify their view of a situation that is ambiguous and confusing. This process inhibits curiosity and a search for explanations from the environment, especially explanations that are outside the individual's frame of reference. I will return to the examples of inflexible leadership cited in the previous section to illustrate this dynamic. I will also show how the WLS fostered critical learning experiences that enabled inflexible leaders to recognize their blind spots, and to provide them with fresh perspectives on how they could expand their inquiry about their environments.

Self-amplifying and context-dismissing thought processes were enacted in at least three ways: out-of-context thinking, rationalization, and negative judgment. To understand out-of-context thinking, we need to recall a key point discussed in Chapter 2, namely that habitual patterns of thinking and acting are products of socialization. Society cultivates and normalizes a particular pattern of thinking, feeling, and acting to generate a shared basis for members to anticipate one another's actions and achieve mutual intelligibility. Once internalized, shared habits become taken for granted. They come into view when something occurs that disrupts expectations, a phenomenon that has been well documented in the cross-cultural communication literature.[3]

Out-of-context thinking is common in cross-cultural situations. Kanya's inaction in the salary negotiation story was a result of her out-of-context thinking. In the WLS Negotiation course, Kanya realized that her failed salary negotiation was a result of culturally conditioned and untested assumptions about the nature of the salary setting process. During the process, Kanya assumed that an impersonal, formal, and highly bureaucratic process set salaries, obviating the need for negotiation. The salary setting process in use at her center stood in sharp contrast to this, however. Kanya was surprised by the lack of formality, stating: "there were no formal salary scales, a pay structure, or basic grades and scales." Consequently, Kanya did not have a reference point to judge whether her salary was appropriate or not. What she discovered later, in discussions with co-workers, was that the salary she received was indeed not appropriate.

Kanya's assumption about a formal salary negotiation process had something to do with her sense of dignity. Specifically, she went into the negotiation with a decidedly negative view of salary negotiation: "Just asking for something is like polite begging. If I'm entitled to something, then I should be getting it." Kanya also explained that having a formal process prevents conflict and bad feelings. By creating a formal process that precluded the need for having a back-and-forth, positive relationships between the employee and administrator could be ensured. Finally, Kanya observed that although negotiations were viewed as "polite begging" in her cultural context, this did not mean that negotiations never occurred. Rather, negotiating was seen as a civic virtue when it was done on behalf of *others*: "Before the WLS I had no problems negotiating something for somebody else, but for myself, it's very difficult." Therefore, negotiations are used in ways that promote cohesion and builds relationships.

The negotiations course in the WLS allowed Kanya to reflect on and became aware of the assumptions she had about the negotiations process. She also learned about the norms that governed the negotiation process in her center. Finally, the WLS course helped Kanya to reframe how she thought about negotiation in the context of the WLS. She described how she learned to view negotiation differently to reflect the norms of the center:

> I think the biggest takeaway was that negotiation doesn't need to be a conflict. I mean, asking something—that was a big hurdle for me, but after the negotiation course, I was like, "Yeah, it's okay to ask." And then I always had this concept/idea of negotiation as a confrontation. I also didn't have the language to say, "Look, I'm not getting what I'm worth."

As suggested in the last sentence in the preceding quote, Kanya had never considered negotiation as a process in which the employee has a say in establishing the value or "worth" they brought to the organization. In the negotiations course, Kanya learned essentials of effective negotiation:

objectively assessing one's skills, establishing a collaborative conversation to reach a shared understanding of one's skills, and reaching agreement on fair compensation. To objectively assess her skills, she learned that she needed to not underestimate or over-estimate her contributions but to concretely and objectively document her accomplishments:

> I learned that one needs to collect enough documented evidence to allow for a conversation about the weight of what I was contributing. I needed to show that I have something to put on the table. I needed to do a self-analysis—and this means making an objective assessment of my own inputs and my own abilities.

Having documented evidence of one's contributions was important but not sufficient. The documentation did not speak for itself. Rather, it was a place to begin, an objectively rendered description about a person's track record that could be shared with another person as a basis for a conversation about salary. Her reframing of what negotiation is—a collaborative conversation—and what it is not—begging or a confrontation—helped Kanya see herself being able to use this document in a way that preserved her dignity and concern for the relationship: "the document was a way for me to express my feelings and thoughts in a non-confrontational way, in a very objective way. That is so powerful. It gave me a template for having that difficult conversation."

The negotiations course provided Kanya with a new perspective, one that was aligned with how her center operated. All of this was new to her, something that she would have to practice in order to become an adept negotiator. But the WLS course helped her recognize that the learning curve was not all uphill. She had some of the skills critical to negotiation already. In the following quote she describes how she gained this insight through positive feedback, provided by WLS alumnae:

> Let me give you an example of positive feedback, which played a huge role for me. In the WLS, we did a role play where I was supposed to be the supervisor and I was supposed to be having a discussion with a subordinate who wanted to go off and work on another project while she's having a full-load here. After the role-play, one of the participants said, "My god, you're so analytical." People make comments like that about your positive attributes, which you have never realized that you have. This is just one example. Or, you might hear "You communicate so well, you're so empathic." Lots of things about you that you don't know because you've never done a self-assessment. I mean, these are senior people watching this, and if they think that of you, you go back to your institute carrying all these things. That gives you huge confidence.

In this manner, Kanya resolved her out-of-context thinking in a positive manner.

Rationalization was another way in which inflexible leaders enacted self-amplifying and context-dismissing thinking. Rationalization involves formulating a justification for a preferred course of action by validating some dimensions of a situation and not paying attention to or down-playing other dimensions. In the previous section, I described how Harriet had self-isolated. Recall that Harriet faced a challenging situation: new to the country and center, little management experience, a boss who shouted at people, the only female, and lacking social support. During the WLS, Harriet had the opportunity to reflect upon this experience and uncover how she rationalized her choice to isolate and not seek social support:

> I didn't make myself liked, and I didn't care about people not liking me. I didn't realize it was important for people to at least think that I was nice, you know, whatever I might truly be. And that people's positive attitude toward you would then lead to other positive behavior in the organization. Basically, after two years, I got a letter telling me that I was out of the organization in three months unless I finished these three publications, but that was just a foil because other people also didn't have publications. They were ready to get rid of me, and then things really turned around after that.

Harriett described the WLS as "absolutely transformational." One of the inputs that catalyzed the transformation was 360-degree feedback obtained from her co-workers. She said that the feedback "shocked" her:

> I didn't recognize what problems I had. Where I thought I was strong, other people saw me as weak. I remember particularly an item that I didn't really think mattered that much, "She handles her emotions well." I got rated really poorly on that one, as you can imagine from all the shouting matches with my boss. Generally, I rated poorly on management. I was shocked, but it was very constructive. I'm one of those people who like getting feedback, even though it may hurt. I thought it was one of the most amazing ways to motivate me, to learn. I thought it was a great tool. A wonderful way to start the course off.

Coincidentally, she was presented with an opportunity to reflect concretely about how she related to people during the course. Harriet was exposed to theories of personality, and a personality inventory was also administered. One of her work colleagues, someone whose work she had dismissed as "superficial and not well done" and whom she had characterized as a person who "did not take criticism well," happened to be in the course with her. During the discussion of their personality types, Harriet could understand her colleague's behavior from the colleague's point of view. She realized that she had misunderstood her colleague and reflected on how hurtful her behaviors towards this person must have been:

> It opened up a channel between us. Where I had seen an antagonistic relationship before, suddenly I could empathize, and it allowed me to communicate with her in a completely different way. Basically, I listened to her and respected what she said more. I wanted to spend more time with her and trust her opinion more, but it took a long time to build up the trust again. I had definitely hurt her along the way. I was definitely too arrogant about being smart. And, you know, I'm not that smart, but I thought I was smart. And she was fifteen years older than me and a lot wiser. I should have been more respectful.

Like Harriet, Cosima had also been isolated, but in her case, key stakeholders whose cooperation was needed to implement her system-wide program imposed her isolation. Prior to the WLS, she expended energy to engage both those stakeholders who were enthusiastic to work with her *and* those who ignored her communications. When she came to the WLS, she was demoralized by the continued silence of the latter group. Theoretical input shifted this view. Whereas she had previously assumed that she had to expend energy to engage with everyone, she discovered that she could be more strategic in her approach. Here she describes her "Aha" moment when new possibilities flooded her mind as she was presented with theory:

> I remember during the course when this model of allies, opponents, and fence-sitters was presented, that I just had this light bulb go off in my head. And I was like, "Right, that's what I'm facing." I immediately pictured all of those constituents in those three categories. I could immediately place them in my head. And once I had that, I thought, okay, here are my allies. Here's who I can turn to for support and where I can deliver, right away, and start having results. For the others, I concretely thought about their information needs, and then I started thinking about how I could move fence-sitters and opponents into allies, but that was going to be a longer-term effort. I was first going to start with my allies.

She also describes how she benefited from the coaching provided by WLS participants as she considered how to apply the insights from the framework in the context of the CGIAR culture:

> By being with a lot of other women from the CGIAR and hearing their stories and hearing their own strategies, it was educating me

about what works and what doesn't work. You know, there's a lot of learning among us, not just from the trainers, but among the women. It kind of grounds you in a reality of the organization. I might have this great idea, but after having listened to all these women I realize that would never work. And it gave me an opportunity to test ideas with them. "Do you think this would work? Do you think that would work?" And they would tell me what they thought: "Oh, do that. Please come to us first." I think that's one of the things that happen in the course. You get these powerful mental models like your allies, fence-sitters, and opponents. Then, you discuss how to work with each of those ideas. And then you're also creating a network and allies among the course participants, so a nice combination of models and application.

Cosima assumed that focusing on relationships was necessary to engage stakeholders. In contrast to her, Ana, whose story was described earlier, elevated task performance over relationships. Although their assumptions were different, both Ana and Cosima engaged in rationalization, emphasizing one aspect of the leader's role and ignoring the other. Both expressed indignation about others' behavior but did not see their blind spots. Cosima thought that building relationships was important, while Ana thought that getting the task done was important. As described previously, theoretical insights and coaching gave Cosima a more balanced view.

The third means of enacting self-amplifying and context-dismissing thinking was *negative judgment*. Josephine's story illustrates how she made negative judgments in response to her boss's attitude towards her. She reflected on how she would respond to perceived affronts: "I could be emotional and feel the person didn't respect me. In the past, whenever I faced something like that, I would respond immediately with very strong sentiment, which sometimes would not help."

Ana also engaged in negative thinking, and like Josephine, this resulted in emotional mismanagement. As described in the previous section, Ana had been impatient with the slow pace at which her team worked, and she had the habit of just doing everything herself. A personality inventory administered in the WLS gave her insight into her intense behavior. She stated that she viewed herself as a "high achiever" and expected of others what she expected of herself. But this posture also elicited negative judgments when others chose not to comply, which stood in the way of her building a high-performing team. Theoretical input enabled Ana to understand that good leaders not only attend to the task but also to relationships:

In the first course, we studied how to come up with an effective team. And we had a diagram with like 12 different things that make a team effective. I saw myself as an achiever, more of the kind that takes pride, getting things done and creating and coming up with solutions. But if you're a leader, you have to nurture. I saw that I was paying too much attention and giving too much weight to something and just ignoring other things. But the weaknesses were in relating to my team, so I also learned to be an effective team member, to be an effective leader, because I'm part of the team. So it's a matter of playing the right role at the right time. And you need to focus on the task and the relationships simultaneously.

There was a particularly poignant experiential exercise that brought this message home to Ana in a very embodied way:

ANA: We did some exercises in which we were blindfolded. And we had some strengths, and we had some weaknesses. In one of those exercises, I had to be the leader, and the other I had to be just a team member. So, for me, those exercises were very illustrative of what you should do and what you shouldn't do in a team as a leader and as a team member. If you deal with people effectively, they collaborate. People are not as difficult as we think they are. What is difficult is to relate. Once you learn to deal with people effectively, you can lead.

INTERVIEWER: So, tell me what happened in that exercise.

ANA: In one exercise where I had to be the leader, we had to cross a bridge and if we were not together, we would fall and die. So, I was aware that I had to take care of it. I was blindfolded. I was in the middle, listening to the ones who were in the front, the ones in the back, and the ones on the sides, and asking people to pay attention so we could be safe. And we actually crossed the bridge, and nobody died. If you are the leader, you have to listen to everybody. You have to decide when to move and the whole team has to move together. That was a good lesson.

In another exercise, I was a team member. I could see, but I was mute. And my leader was blind, and she could ask from other people. I could see, and I could just move my hands to tell her yes or no. I had to be creative. And it was tough. It was a strain. But I could see it was an opportunity for all the people to perform their duties well, so it was learning not to interfere in somebody else's role. If you interfere, then you remove the opportunity from them to do their best.

INTERVIEWER: That's very powerful. What were the most important things that you gained from this exercise?

ANA: One was to be aware of what is necessary in a team. Things that created the condition for the team to perform well or for the team to fail, and a lot of that has to do with the leader and with members playing the right role right. The other thing I learned was the importance of persuading, influencing, networking. Things get done because people do them. Teams are effective because of the mix of personalities and performance, but the technical aspects are too valued in organizations at the expense of the personal things. By learning to be an effective team member, I started to become an effective leader. That was something I learned from the first course.

Building on Transformative Insights and Cultivating a New Habit Pattern

My analysis suggests that the transformative insights catalyzed in the WLS put into motion a slow but steady process of transformation from inflexible to receptive leadership. In stories of receptive leadership, WLS alumnae described themselves engaging in *self-tempering* and *context-regarding* thought processes. This new thought process was characterized by acknowledging the need to account for both one's own views as well as those of others. Each receptive leader experienced an "Aha" moment in the WLS. It was as if someone had removed a blind spot, illuminating a missing piece that rendered a vexing situation sensible. Inflexible leaders left the WLS with intention and determination to do things differently. Ana's comment below reflects a spirit and tone that came through clearly in my interviews with receptive leaders: taking responsibility for the earlier leadership challenges, understanding what was missing, and embracing the needed changes:

> This course gave me the answers, or it helped me find the answers. It showed that I was responsible for the situation with my team and gave me hints of the desired behaviors. So that I could just go ahead and change my behavior. I knew that I needed to change A for B. Before the course I knew that A wasn't the right thing, but I didn't know an alternative.

Changing habitual patterns, however, does not occur overnight. It is gradual, with new patterns emerging in time and through deliberate effort. When the WLS participants returned to their workplaces and personal lives, it was reasonable to expect that the demands of these contexts would soon take over. Further, these immediate demands would elicit the well-worn neural pathways of habitual thought and action. Almost all the inflexible leaders described facing this pivotal period when they were faced with the challenge of building on transformative insights in real-time. However, the "Aha" moment and the insights from the WLS generally took hold. These insights had a subtle but powerful influence on future perception, thinking, and acting. One person described it as:

> The best effect was felt immediately, a month or two months after the course. You remember a lot of things that were said. I suppose the

ideas that had become applicable, are those that have the potential of bringing about a positive change in you. For example, I had forgotten a lot of what I learned, but the empathy part sticks with me, because I kind of felt that this is something that I need to observe and analyze in my management style because I kind of felt that that was one thing I had not given much thought to. Things that I'm already practicing or things that are not so applicable to me, I had actually really forgotten, you know?

Like in the case of hidden leaders, discussed in the previous chapter, inflexible leaders described three means through which the insights from the WLS informed their thoughts and actions after the WLS: recall, relationships, and mindful attention and critical reflection. I illustrate each briefly in this section.

With regard to *recall*, Kanya described how recall of "episodes" from the workshop would foster small changes that influenced behavior in a snowball effect:

> You go to the course, you remember these episodes from the course, then you're much more confident to take the negotiation. So you do a little one first, and then it grows exponentially. The more confidence you get, the bigger things you can go for.

Ana similarly described how she used a physical object from the training, a toy ladder, to recall a critical insight, reflect on it in situations where the insight was relevant, and take mindful action. I have already described the use of objects (Chapter 2, Claudia's use of a letter) or memorable episodes (Chapter 4, Rosaria remembering feedback). In the following quote, Ana describes how she used the toy ladder to recall the lessons about reasoning from the WLS:

> They gave us toys, for the segment on difficult conversations, one of the exercises was working up and down the ladder of inference. And they gave us some plastic ladders, and I brought it back with me and I have it here on my bulletin board, just to remind me that I should not take things for granted and should not withhold information that the other person might need to understand. The ladder is a symbol and has meaning. You decide what you want the symbol to mean, because it doesn't have a meaning by itself. When I see the ladder, that was my way of remembering my commitment—I went to this course and I learned, but I have to bring that learning back and put it to work. Otherwise, it will be a waste of time.

Recalling a salient training episode is not a passive activity if the recollection awakens commitment and brings the person back to the excitement they felt when they had a moment of clarity. Ana described how the ladder of inference was a tool she used to slow down and listen:

> I started to slow down, to be very aware of my behavior, of the intensity of my behavior, watching every word I would say, the tone of my voice, and reading peoples' reactions, and asking more questions rather than giving instructions. Paying attention to what I would say or the other person would say, the things that were different. I started praising people for what they were doing, and making people feel comfortable and good about what they were doing and about working for me.

As underscored by nearly all the WLS alumnae, *relationships* were also critical to continual learning in the WLS. As discussed in Chapters 2 and 3, relationships amongst WLS alumnae were sources of continual inspiration, encouragement, coaching, and strategizing. Sometimes, WLS alumnae, including inflexible leaders, obtained intensive feedback from one another as they attempted to navigate specific difficult situations. Thus, relationships contributed not only to the strengthening of insights gained from the training but also to the continual growth and development of inflexible leaders.

Self-amplifying and context-dismissing thoughts narrowed the perceptions of inflexible leaders and locked them into a pattern of trying to impose their will on their environment. Theoretical insights, feedback, coaching, and other exercises of the WLS expanded their perception of situations, showing them their unconscious assumptions and revealing the potential that exists in opening themselves up to understanding their environments. These insights were pivotal turning points for inflexible leaders. What did not make sense in the past could now be rendered meaningful, and they could also see the changes that were needed on their part. These changes were sustained after the WLS by means of recall, relationships, and mindful attention and critical reflection in specific workplace challenges. As they caught themselves, paused, reflected, and tried out new behaviors, these alternative responses cultivated a new pattern of thinking. We next turn to the receptive leader behaviors that followed from self-tempering and context-regarding thought processes.

Behaviors of Receptive Leadership

Receptivity is the opposite of inflexibility. When faced with situations they could not understand, inflexible leaders exhibited tunnel vision tendencies and clung to their perspective with a sense of indignation. While inflexible leaders recognized that they could not explain others' behaviors in these problematic situations, they were unable to understand their environment on its own terms. As described previously, critical learning in the WLS not only fostered self-awareness into these habitual thought processes but also began to generate a shift. After the WLS, inflexible leaders began to cultivate a different way of thinking—self-tempering and context-affirming—that facilitated a transformation to receptive leadership. While receptive leaders had a point of view, they held these tentatively, with openness to others' perspectives and with a recognition that their prior assumptions and understandings would evolve from engaging with others.

Changes in perception elicited changes in thought, feeling, and behavior. Stories of receptive leaders revealed that those who previously engaged in inaction exercised agency, those who were isolated built relationships, and those who mismanaged their emotions were better at regulating their emotions. Kanya's story illustrates a movement from inaction to agency. The insights she gained in the negotiations course changed not only the meaning Kanya attached to negotiation but also provided Kanya with the knowledge and skills needed to negotiate effectively. These new ideas and tools were instrumental in her expanded agency as a negotiator. I return to the salary issue, which was problematic prior to the WLS.

The process of renegotiating her salary was circuitous and required patience, risk-taking, and diligence to document her accomplishments. When she returned to her center, Kanya discussed her concerns about her salary with her supervisor. However, he told her that, had she accepted the inclusion of a six-month probationary period in her contract, her salary could have been re-negotiated when the probationary period was over. But since she had insisted on a fixed contract, revising her salary would be very difficult. She interpreted his refusal to mean that her boss lacked influence with the DG and/or was unwilling to advocate for her. Although this disappointed Kanya, she took the long view, and began to build relationships within her center. This turned out to be very important and helpful in the salary re-negotiation process:

> I was becoming a bit more assertive, expressing my opinions, and asking more questions at the seminars. I had basically talked to a lot of people. I was listening more. I was putting my face to everybody, trying to see what advice they would give me on how to engineer myself into a decent salary.

Eventually Kanya decided that, to receive a salary increase, she would have to pursue a Ph.D. degree, and her project leader was willing to support her application. While this process was underway, the DG approached her with a job offer in Nairobi, Kenya. Kanya believed that the DG had become aware of her desire to increase her salary through the network she had built for herself. The DG encouraged her to take the job instead of pursuing the Ph.D. She said, "the DG convinced me that this is a good idea to go to Nairobi and at a system-wide level, you can get a publication. I was smart enough to realize, that if I refuse this offer, the others might not get approved." She decided to give the job in Nairobi a try.

The move to Nairobi was a crucial step. Her boss turned out to be a WLS alumnus, providing Kanya with much needed encouragement, support, and advice:

> I got personal coaching from my supervisor and a lot of personal feedback. Positive feedback. Anything that you're really good at or which she appreciates, she tells you. And about six months of having that hammered into you, it changes your psychology, really. Everybody needs at least six months with a supervisor like that, someone who constantly focuses on your strong points, and you realize, my god, how many strong points I have! It's useful telling you what you do wrong and how can you correct it, but it's much more powerful to tell you what you're good at.

Kanya's confidence grew immensely. At some point, her center also published salary classifications, grades, and scales. Armed with greater confidence in her abilities, knowledge of the rules of negotiation in her center, a well-documented track record, a network of colleagues and peers who supported her, and formal pay scales to refer to, Kanya decided to re-negotiate her salary:

> The pay scales were made transparent. They were published as proper scales and grades. There was a classification system, and there were competencies. We also had a manual that had very clear competencies as to what you need to do to get to the next grade. So, given the classification guidelines and what competencies you need to have, I could compare that to the competencies I did have and say, "Hey, look, there's a match here." By the end of the year, I had a very clear justification of why I thought I should be promoted to the next level. I also received extensive feedback from WLS peers and peers within the center before submitting the proposal. It's a whole process of writing and redrafting. The performance appraisal system had also improved a lot. Then I got my performance appraisal written in a way that I thought, "Okay, I think this might be convincing." I put in a lot of effort in that. And of course, my boss read my first draft. I got feedback from her, then I redrafted it. And my promotion was approved, and that was quite a surprise for me, a very pleasant surprise. When I got the letter, I nearly fell off my chair.

Harriet and Cosima were isolated from others. Their post-WLS stories involved efforts to *build relationships*. During the WLS, Harriet had been administered a personality test. This had given her insight into how differences based in personality could cause conflict. She had been struck by how this insight changed her perspective about a co-worker who happened to also be a participant during the WLS. She commented how, knowing about personality differences and in particular the differences between her and her co-worker, had led her to listen, release negative judgment, and in the process learn both to appreciate her co-worker and understand how her previous actions towards her co-worker had been hurtful.

This experience was important to how she approached others at work. Although by the time she came to the WLS things had settled down at work, she was still seen as someone who could not manage others. Harriet's newfound recognition of personality differences, as well has her keen observation of the team building techniques from the WLS, provided her with not only knowledge and skills that she previously lacked but insights that addressed her difficulties:

> I decided to focus on one team in particular. It was a field-based team in (South American country). I put that team together, and I built it with complimentary skills, with people having clear goals. We worked so hard, for the first time in two years, on building the skills of that team. I took a lot of the skills that I had seen in that leadership course, a lot of the training types of things, and I repeated them with our team. Everything from the energizers to trying to describe what your strengths and weaknesses were, I repeated with our team. And I built this very, very tight group that's worked together now for six years, very successfully, even though some members of the team have moved on. The group has used reflection, and the feedback techniques in a routine way, and we've built that into an adaptive management framework that we've written about. And we've learned along the way that things ebb and flow depending on how much effort you put into them. So, I put in a lot of effort those first two years, and then once things were rolling, I let it drift, or glide, I should say, for another two years. And then I realized, "Uh oh, you have to keep working at it." It builds on its own momentum. The last eighteen months or so we've put more elbow grease into making it work. But that's something I'm actually very proud of.

Although Harriett and Cosima were isolated, there was a striking difference. Harriett had self-isolated, while Cosima was isolated by the refusal of key stakeholders to respond to her communications about the system-wide effort she headed up. Initially, Cosima worked very hard to engage stakeholders who ignored her, but during the WLS she was presented with a theoretical framework that completely changed this approach. This framework, which classified stakeholders into the three categories of allies, opponents, and stakeholders, not only gave her a way to think about her own stakeholders but also how to invest her time and energy in engaging them. A key insight during a coaching session had to do with how to apply the insights of the framework to a scientific, data-driven organization like the CGIAR. Cosima went straight to work after the WLS:

> I think it was in the leadership course that I was able to think things through and come out feeling more confident that focusing on those where the door was open was the right thing to do. I wasn't taking the easy way out. And yet, to make sure I gave concerted effort, giving information to the others and trying to understand what kinds of information would make them happy. And that's when I became very data driven, recognizing the culture of the organization and doing lots of survey work and hitting them with data, more data. The fact that there was a problem we needed to address couldn't be denied because there it was in the numbers. Facts, facts, facts—I moved us immediately away from jargon and theory. I present our own facts and figures and trends and challenges. So, I think the leadership course helped me understand that I needed to run a fact-driven program.

Cosima's efforts paid off: "Now we only have two centers that we don't work with: one silent and one hostile. I mean, compared to where we started, I consider this a wonderful condition to be in."

Ana and Josephine mismanaged their emotions prior to the WLS, by avoiding conflict. After the WLS, they learned to better regulate their emotions and cultivate empathy and appreciation of others. This empathetic response enabled them to find constructive ways to deal with sensitive situations. Ana had been judgmental about the quality and pace of her team's work. She had decided to do all the work herself, conveying to others that they weren't needed, damaging her relationships with colleagues in the process. Ana described how she managed her intensity in order to repair a damaged relationship:

ANA: After the course, I turned an enemy into a friend. We used to be friends a long time ago, but when we came to work in this office, there was some misunderstanding about things and some rivalry. I thought he felt jealous, and he felt uncomfortable, and he developed a negative attitude toward me. So I had to withdraw, keep at a distance because he wasn't feeling comfortable with me. We couldn't do anything together. To repair our relationship, first I focused on not doing anything that he would interpret negatively.
INTERVIEWER: Like what?
ANA: Reinforcing that, if we could not be friends, we would not be enemies.

INTERVIEWER: So you knew some of the things that he tended to misinterpret.

ANA: Yes. I knew that whatever I would do was going to be taken as a threat.

INTERVIEWER: Whatever you would do?

ANA: For example, I was given a project that he had expected to get. And I did well on that project, and he resented it. So I guess that was sort of the ignition, the thing that set it off. So, I focused on not doing things that he would interpret badly.

INTERVIEWER: So, if you were assigned a project and he would have perhaps wanted for himself, would you have turned that down?

ANA: No. I was better qualified. I think that's why I was given it. It was a very good project, an interesting project, a good opportunity for me.

INTERVIEWER: I'm trying to understand, you know, your statement about not doing anything that would make him resentful.

ANA: Not just adding to his negative feelings. I mean he had to live with the fact that I had a project. So I was not being pretentious, for example, or giving opinions on things that he would do—I kept distance and respect. And I never attacked him. There was another person here who wanted to take advantage of that situation and put me against him. And I told him, like two or three times, "Listen, you go first and talk to this guy. When you two agree, you come and talk to me, because I'm not going to do anything behind his back. I'm not going to play that game." So at the end, one day, he was doing a publication, and he needed some help with that. And that has been part of my job for many years. So he came and asked me to do that for him while he was on a trip. I was surprised that he would do that, and I said, "Yes, I will help you with that. Tell me what you expect and tell me where the publication is in the process and I will take care of it. No problem." And from there, he started to come and share things with me. His concerns, his fears, his negative feelings. We were friends again, as we had been in the past.

INTERVIEWER: Did you ever talk about your relationship?

ANA: No, I left it open, because if he wants to do it, fine. If not, it's okay. I appreciate him. I thought of it as, okay, this was the direction of our friendship and now we can move on. We're friends again. No problem. Sometimes he asks for opinion or advice and I give it to him in a respectful way, and it's up to him to decide. I give him an opinion and if he wants to take it into account, okay. If he doesn't want to take it into account, it's okay.

I have thus far described the nature of inflexible and receptive leadership and have also described the critical learning experiences that fostered this transformation. I would now like to return to Ibsituu, the inflexible leader whose leadership dilemma had been introduced at the opening of this chapter. In the extended account of her story, as follows, I will provide a detailed description of how the insights from the WLS course informed changes in her leadership behavior upon returning to work. This extended account will hopefully provide a holistic sense of the complexity of the leadership challenges that were described as well as how the learning from the WLS informed subsequent behavior. Ibsituu's story is particularly interesting because it provides an example of when an individual reverted back to old habits and realizing this, changed course.

Ibsituu: Making a Problematic Restructuring Work Effectively

In the opening to this chapter I described Ibsituu's pre-WLS leadership story, as well as the transformative insight she gained from the WLS. Recall that one of the most important lessons from the WLS Negotiation Course was that she did not have to do everything herself, that she needed to learn how to negotiate with others to create collaborative partnerships. Prior to the course, Ibsituu was accustomed to imposing her will through sheer stubbornness. However, during the negotiations course, she was engaged in a role play that changed her understanding of negotiating for collaborative outcomes. In the WLS role play, not only was she confronted with a very strong negotiator, but also with an individual whose motivations she did not understand. During the processing of the role play, she learned that understanding others' motivations was critical to finding a solution that all would accept.

Problematic Restructuring

Indeed, the lessons from the WLS proved significant in how Ibsituu participated in a sensitive negotiation aimed at making a problematic organizational restructuring work for all involved. Ibsituu had been charged with leading a discipline area that had staff in several regions. Some regional directors committed a full-time staff person, some a part-time staff person and, because these individuals reported to the regional director and not Ibsituu, her efforts to engage them were not always successful.

Subsequent restructuring (moving from a regional to a thematic structure) brought significant upheaval to this less-than-perfect arrangement. Scientific activities previously carried out by the regional offices were brought together into program areas and administered by a program director. Non-program functions that required center-wide coordination were grouped into research and support units. Ibsituu was named director of one of these units, but she did not have authority over the individuals who worked in her discipline area across the regions. The regional staff members were part of her unit in theory but, in practice, they continued to report to the regional directors.

This lack of authority plus a lack of funding had implications for Ibsituu's effectiveness, as well as the effectiveness of the other unit heads. She had no way to define or evaluate activities in her area, and she lacked resources that could provide an incentive. Without authority or resources, Ibsituu and her colleagues felt their hands were tied. As she stated:

> There were huge expectations, but how were we going to operate? Everyone said to us, "Well, senior management has said it'll work out, so it'll work out." And we always said, "How?" They never acknowledged that it was a problem. It was very frustrating and very irritating. Finally, we got people to engage and say, "Okay, yeah, we're going to take this seriously, we've got to take this seriously."

Framing the Problem Effectively

One of the things that she and the unit leaders did was to frame their task within the context of the center's strategic goals. One of those objectives directly related to her discipline area. Framing the argument in the context of the center's strategy proved to be an extremely powerful negotiation move, putting her, as well as her colleagues responsible for the support units, in a strong negotiating position. More importantly, it gave them a means of communicating with each of the key stakeholders within the organization to figure out how to make the new structure work.

Armed with this framing, Ibsituu first approached staff within the programmatic areas that worked on functions related to her unit. She and her colleagues then approached the program directors, regional directors and, finally, the director general to discuss common ground and how each could contribute to the task of focusing on the importance of an integrated center-wide initiative with joint planning and staff accountability. The inclusion of key stakeholders proved very effective in getting buy-in for their ideas from each group.

> I've never had the funds to bring together all the people in the regions who have responsibility for my discipline area. Trying to forge a team without ever having them together in one place is impossible. Bringing them together would mean that I would work with people in the regions (who report to other people), and we collectively would come up with a work plan, and they would commit a certain percentage of their time to this collective work plan, and they would then be accountable for that time within the terms of their performance agreement. Then I would be involved in assessing their performance based on the time that they have given to this.
>
> And that's big. Then for management to say, "Okay, we're going to go to our donors and say that our stakeholders have said this is vitally important and so this is significant," that's a huge step. And it happened through individual conversations and interactions between

the support units, all of which had similar issues in terms of how we get the regional people engaged with us.

Making and Recovering From a Blunder

While she had made a great deal of progress getting the buy-in and commitment of key stakeholders in this restructuring, there was one critical meeting, involving the DG, four program directors, and the heads of the support units, in which she made a blunder. This mistake threatened to undo all the good work she and her colleagues had done to create common ground:

> I had a really bad moment. We (the heads of the support units) went in on the offensive and said, "Half of the six objectives that have been identified in the strategy represent our work. We've got no resources and no staff, and we're expected to cover 50 percent. So, the question is not how do we serve you but how do you serve us?" And they hated that. It was too aggressive. I was speaking on behalf of the three research and support units, and they felt I was being too aggressive.

When she left the meeting, she and her colleagues revised their strategy:

> We said, okay, we'll just put the same argument in a less aggressive form. As opposed to saying, it's your responsibility to help us, we said, you know, it's in both our interests, this is how we can help each other. They obviously know that three of the six objectives address our areas, so let's put it in a way that's going to be palatable to them and is not going to feel threatening in terms of their responsibility and authority.

The next day they met with the program directors again. Their goal was to try out their new approach:

> It was one day later, and it was extraordinary. We basically said, "Let's work out our common problems and come to some way of working together." And it worked out fine. In fact, it was funny, because after that session, on the last day, people were saying things like: this is fabulous, go for it, everything is great, everything you said is wonderful, we're definitely supportive. I was thrilled and stunned. We kind of got a standing ovation.

Importantly, Ibsituu's insights from the negotiation course informed her practice in this situation:

> I don't think I consciously thought, "Oh, I need to remember what I learned in the training." I definitely went out of that first meeting

and thought, "Oh, that was stupid. What I really need to be thinking about is making everybody comfortable. That their needs are going to be met and we're all going to be pulling towards the greater good, and it's not just about what Ibsituu wants and what the other research and support units want, but they also see that it's going to benefit them." I certainly think I internalized lessons from the course that led me to that way of thinking.

What was not stated, but was apparent in her story, was that she internalized much more than the crucial lesson concerning her own strong-willed negotiating style. She also learned to be clear about her desire and to take others' desires into consideration. Although one of the program directors had asked her why she was so surprised that the group had fully supported her and the other support units' heads after the difficult conversation, it is clear from this story that, given the initial resistance and the year-long effort that was involved, getting everyone on board and to the point of agreement was not a *fait accompli*—it was accomplished through skillful negotiation.

Summary

The WLS facilitated a transformation from inflexible to receptive leadership through effecting a shift in a habitual self-affirming and context-dismissing pattern of thought and action. When met with situations they did not understand and in which their well-honed and practiced methods did not result in desired outcomes, inflexible leaders exhibited tunnel vision tendencies. They responded by digging in, clinging to their view of a situation as well as their methods, disregarding the cues from the environment, and attempting to impose their will on the environment. Pre-WLS inflexible behaviors included: inaction, isolation, and mismanagement of emotions. These behaviors created a rift between themselves and others and diminished the capacity of inflexible leaders to influence others. The WLS fostered transformational learning which was manifested in a shift to self-tempering and context-regarding thought processes, based on a newfound realization of the value and importance of information from the environment as critical to goal achievement. Beyond goal achievement, inflexible leaders recognized that their controlling response to uncertainty robbed others of choice, excluded others' ideas, and suppressed others' needs. They felt that releasing control and letting others influence the course of events was the right thing to do. Stories of receptive leadership revealed that those who previously engaged in inaction exercised agency, those who were isolated built relationships, and those who mismanaged emotions were better at regulating their emotions. These shifts contributed to greater leadership effectiveness by increasing inflexible leaders' capacity to take in information from the external environment and by enabling them to enlist others support in what they were trying to achieve.

Notes

1. See Goleman et al. (2001), Cote et al. (2010), and Gardner and Stough (2002).
2. The internal thought process underlying the practice of mismanaging negative emotions has been discussed at length in the literature on emotional intelligence (Goleman, 1998) and conversational skills (Ellinor & Gerard, 1998). These discussions indicate that, when faced with stressful situations that give rise to emotions such as fear or anger, we tend to adopt a fight/flight mode, leading to defensive or offensive and inappropriate actions based on negative judgments and unexplored assumptions.
3. See Hall (1981), Triandis (2006), Hofstede (2005), and Debebe (2012).

References

Cote, S., Lopes, P. N., Salovey, P., & Miners, C. T. (2010). Emotional intelligence and leadership emergence in small groups. *The Leadership Quarterly, 21*(3), 496–508.

Debebe, G. (2012). *Navigating power: Cross-cultural competence and coordination Navajoland*. Lanham, MD: Lexington Books.

Goleman, D. (1998). *Working with emotional intelligence*. New York: Bantam Boo.

Ellinor, L., & Gerard, G. (1998). *Dialogue: Rediscover the transforming power of conversation*. New York, NY: John Wiley & Son.

Gardner, L., & Stough, C. (2002). Examining the relationship between leadership and emotional intelligence in senior level managers. *Leadership & Organization Development Journal, 23*(2), 68–78.

Goleman, D., Boyatzis, R., & McKee, A. (2001). Primal leadership: The hidden driver of great performance. *Harvard Business Review, 79*(11), 42–51.

Hall, E. T. (1981). *The silent language*. New York, NY: Doubleday.

Hofstede, G., & Hofstede, G. J. (2005). *Cultures and organizations: software of the mind*. New York, NY: McGraw-Hill.

Triandis, H. C. (2006). Cultural intelligence in organizations. *Group and Organization Management, 31*(1), 20–26.

6 Transformation From Intuitive to Deliberate Leadership

> Defining what all the concepts are, what all the components are, and which components need building on, I now see the ones that need improving, and when they have a name, I now know how I can improve them.
>
> *Miora, Intuitive Leader*

Intuitive leaders based their actions on their sense of what the group and organization needed, as well as their own personal values and sense of what their role should be in the group. They listened deeply to gain insights assessing situations, and they responded in purposeful ways by accounting for both the demands of the situation and their roles and values. Intuitive leaders often met with success in their leadership efforts, and they were relatively confident in their capacity to lead. But because their leadership behaviors were informed by tacit knowledge, they were unable to articulate the grounds for their actions.[1] For example, in the following quote, Afeen conveys this idea when asked to explain why she rated herself as a "somewhat effective" leader instead of a "very effective" one:

> I suppose I didn't say "very effective" because I feel that, at that time, I didn't have much of a basis for the way I did things. And that would lead into saying that the course actually helped me put names and labels to what I was doing.

As these reflections show, Afeen's self-assessment had to do with the lack of explicit and formal knowledge that could guide and validate her intuitive choices.

Although intuitive leaders were generally effective, some also described situations in which they encountered persistent difficulties. In these cases, intuitive leaders applied their sharp observational skills to uncover the source of resistance and possible levers of influence. Such situations are emblematic of the leadership dilemma of intuitive leaders. Because they did not fully understand why they were effective leaders, they could not conceptualize what they could do differently when their efforts met with opposition.

Seventeen percent of the WLS interviewees told stories that pertained to the transformation from intuitive to deliberate leadership. While intuitive leadership stories related to leadership behaviors prior to the WLS, deliberate leadership stories were about leadership behaviors after the WLS. The position classification distributions among intuitive/deliberate leaders were as follows: 25 percent theme leaders, 25 percent director/scientists/researchers, 50 percent manager/administrator. None of those classified as intuitive/deliberate leaders held the "technician" position. Twenty five percent of intuitive/deliberate leaders were recruited nationally, while 75 percent were recruited internationally.

I will begin with a brief story of an intuitive leader that I refer to as Miora. At the time of the interview, Miora was a researcher who had moved from Australia to a Southeast Asian country where she was tasked with managing a research lab. Miora had been very effective in a similar job in Australia, and she had been particularly skilled at developing others and building a highly motivated team. In her new lab, she met with success doing the same thing, but she also encountered a few individuals whom she could not motivate. Despite the surface similarity of her new job to her previous one, Miora discovered a key difference—while she had known how to motivate people in her home country, she was at a loss for how to do so in her new milieu. She noticed that there were a lot of tensions between some of her internationally recruited colleagues and their nationally recruited counterparts. Indeed, some of the international staff told her that the national staff were "stupid, lazy, and useless," and Miora was uncomfortable with these negative and stereotypical interpretations. Nevertheless, she was puzzled by what she felt was a lack of commitment and professionalism on the part of one of the national technicians in her lab. Wanting to avoid replicating the tension and conflict that she saw around her, Miora went about asking questions:

> I don't think I've got any tension in my group, even with the guy that I can't reach. But I look at other groups—I don't know if it's because I'm still quite new or because I'm asking question, but I look at other groups and really wonder what joy, if any, the international staff get in their jobs.

Miora's story illustrates a key theme that runs through the varied accounts of intuitive leadership. In the preceding example, Miora's inquiry is focused externally in that she tries to understand her environment. But part of the problem in motivating her staff lay in her own approach—she also needed to turn her inquiry inward. Based on their experiences of leading others, intuitive leaders felt they were effective as leaders, but their inability to consciously articulate and reflect upon the knowledge that guided their actions proved to be a stumbling block when they encountered resistance. It was precisely at this juncture that they needed to be able to reflect on the knowledge that informed their interpretation of situations and assess whether it was appropriate in the circumstances where they met with resistance. The shift to deliberate leadership entailed the acquisition and use of theoretical knowledge that explained the basis of their tacit knowledge as well as its limits. It also involved acquisition of knowledge that addressed their challenges and expanded their capacity for leading.

The stories of intuitive leaders are characterized by a habitual thought pattern that I describe as *self-unaware* and *context-constrained*. The self-unaware thought process is characterized by a sense of confidence in an ability to lead but an inability to explain one's successes and/or leadership difficulties. A context-constrained thought process is evident in situations where intuitive leaders struggle to discern some aspects of their environment and thereby express both confusion and inquisitiveness about it. The remainder of this chapter draws on stories from interviews to illustrate these habitual patterns of thought and action, and how shifts facilitated by critical learning in the WLS fostered the *self-aware* and *context-discerning* thought processes of deliberate leadership. In particular, I will demonstrate how deliberate leaders' greater awareness of their intuitive processes sensitized them to the fact that they needed to draw on these processes with greater intentionality, recognizing that their intuitive processes were not suitable for all circumstances. The chapter will close by returning to an extended account of Miora's story. We now proceed to a description of the behaviors of intuitive leaders.

Intuitive Leadership Behavior

Intuitive leaders described two types of leadership behaviors: unreflective attuned responsiveness and shutting others down. *Unreflective attuned responsiveness* refers to sensing the needs of others, based on what is implicitly or explicitly conveyed, and responding to these needs in a manner that one deems is appropriate for one's role in the group. The idea of "unreflective" suggests that the knowledge used to understand a situation and act on it is preconscious and therefore unexamined. Prior to attending the WLS, Afeen served as coordinator of a cross-national multidisciplinary research team. In her role, she facilitated communication among the geographically dispersed members. Although her activities were subtle and behind-the-scenes, Afeen said that her boss recognized and rewarded her for it, promoting her to other positions where her skills were needed.

Afeen's research team was composed of scientists from multiple disciplines and countries, as well as farmers from several countries. The idea for the team arose from conversations among a small group of scientists who felt that the practical value of their work could be enhanced by collaborative research in which all stakeholders—scientists and farmers—worked together from project inception to project implementation. As Afeen explained, this idea gave the group a "common agenda," and one of the paradigms used by the group was "making the whole greater than the sum of the individual parts." Afeen felt that the multidisciplinary and multinational team that came into existence from this shared vision had developed a good working relationship and that the team had many successes that were replicated in the CGIAR. Referring to the camaraderie and cohesion of the team, Afeen said: "There is a real sense of people being committed to that general area of research and a readiness to work together."

The group's success did not occur overnight or without challenges. The most notable challenges stemmed from disciplinary and linguistic differences.

> I had a project that was in five different countries, and we had a number of national partners as well as partners from three international centers. So one of the challenges was to keep people communicating, interested, and part of the process.

Afeen worried that, if these challenges were not managed, they could potentially lead to disengagement of some group members, threatening participation and collaborative decision-making. From her perspective, it was essential to manage these differences in a way that promoted the goals that motivated the formation of the group in the first place.

As already stated, one communication challenge stemmed from disciplinary differences. In the following quote, Afeen described the layers of differences arising from the way that the scientists on the team were trained to think and work and how she helped manage them:

> We were trying to have an integrated approach, and our team consisted of the specialties within the crop livestock system—crop raters, livestock scientists, soil scientists, and social scientists including economists. We found that you can deal with the disciplinary differences by giving people a shared format. For example, if you say to everybody, "Okay you should write a protocol before you do this piece of research," rather than just saying "write your part for the research protocol," you actually give a format and say, "This is the format, and these are the sections you need to fill in." Or, "Here is an example." Or something like that. If you try and get similar sets of information from everybody, even though some might be in English and some might be in French, it is manageable. We also were trying to work very closely with farmers. Sometimes you would find some reluctance in the scientists who had been used to doing research at

a station by themselves, for much of their lives, and when you now challenge them and say, "Okay, we need you to work with farmers and just let them do whatever they want to do." The reaction would be, "Well, okay, but I want to plant it and look after it in the farmer's field." Because people feel that their research is being put on the line or something like this, it was quite challenging for some people in the group.

Another communication challenge stemmed from language differences. In this next quote, Afeen differentiated between the dynamics of face-to-face and email communication and specifically described the subtle ways that language use patterns in face-to-face communication can include some while excluding others. Her description illustrates her attunement to these dynamics and the various experiments that she and others in the team developed to ensure inclusion and participation of all members:

> Since the research we were doing was a little bit new and different, it was important to get everybody on the same wavelength. The team was composed of both Anglophone and Francophone people. To get people on the same wavelength, you need to communicate clearly, whether you're using English or French and whether you're doing e-mail or all sitting around the table. If you're working as I was in West Africa, mostly the language that's used is English and French at the international level. Very often if you are in a meeting, not by e-mail or something like that, it's very easy to slip into talking in English and feeling comfortable with that and you leave out Francophone people who don't have enough English language skills to be part of it. At times we would have translators. Other times we would manage as a group—we almost always had two or three people in the group who were bilingual and then try to use them as much as possible. You might realize later that the conversation has gone on without translation and try to get Francophone members caught up a bit.

Afeen was aware that addressing the communication challenges in a multinational and multidisciplinary team was not merely about addressing differences based in culture and discipline. It was also about being aware that people are sensitive to the power dynamics of a group and that this can influence inclusion, engagement, and cooperation. As she described, one area where this concern was manifested was in the choice of which language to speak in face-to-face meetings. Translation was a helpful way to deal with this on a practical level, but the fact that the Francophone members were in the position of being translated to also created a dominance of English over French. By holding meetings in different geographic locales—sometimes French-speaking countries and sometimes English-speaking ones—the group simultaneously addressed the linguistic problem and most importantly established mutuality and equality among its members. Although it is unclear whether this was initiated by Afeen or someone else in the group, the following quote showed Afeen's sensitivity to this dynamic and its impact on communication within the group:

> One of the other things that we did was that we were working in three countries initially and then five, and we made sure that we never met in the same country one year after the other. We always went to a different place and tried to make sure that everybody was aware of different situations in different countries and things like that.

Like Afeen, Eleanor also engaged in attuned responsiveness. In her case, she was advocating for spousal health insurance coverage for the national staff in her center. Her efforts began when she discovered that her fellow internationally recruited colleagues had spousal health care coverage but that she and the other national staff did not. She saw this as a "big injustice" not only because of how this policy impacted her personally but also on principle. She decided to do something about it: "I revealed it, I talked about it, and I managed to have it changed in the staff policy. I had to be very diplomatic and do a lot of groundwork to be effective." As she described in the following quote, this groundwork included talking with her colleagues to understand their needs and wants, as well as talking with Human Resources to request hard data and facts. She reflected that, because she was able to maintain good relations with both the HR staff and her colleagues, "no one felt I was meddling where I shouldn't be meddling." After doing this groundwork, she approached her supervisor and told him what her investigation had revealed. In addition to sharing the facts, she also argued for fairness and equity between national and international staff. Although she had a personal stake in the outcome, she focused on the equity concerns, particularly as it related to gender equity, because, as it turned out, most of the international staff were men, while most of the national staff were female. She told her boss:

> Things have changed in the workplace, and perhaps this has been overlooked. I was perhaps the only one in the institution at this time who could see it, because it affected me directly. But it would be in the interest of all of the institution to correct. It's time that there's more equal treatment of females and males in the working environment, and it would be nice if this would be changed.

When she presented her arguments, Eleanor noticed that her supervisor "was a little bit surprised," but he listened and was convinced. After a few months, the changes she had advocated were incorporated into HR policy.

Eleanor used her capacity for attuned responsiveness to guide her in advocating for many other changes. For example, she observed that, while female national staff had maternity leave provisions, the female internationally recruited staff did not. Although she recognized that this was likely due to the fact that there was a dearth of women recruited internationally, she nonetheless decided to take action because the situation was unfair. As in the case of her advocacy for health insurance for national staff, she relied upon careful research, data collection, and listening to others to successfully seek and secure maternity leave for internationally recruited women.

Intuitive leaders' efforts succeeded due to their capacity to observe and interpret the environment and drawing on tacit knowledge they were quite skillful at assessing the needs and wants of stakeholders as well as any obstacles there might be in achieving their goals. But there were some instances where they met with resistance, their efforts to influence others' behavior failed, and they could not understand why. Nevertheless, they were clear in their goals and purposes. In these circumstances, they engaged in the second behavior, namely, *shutting others down*. Shutting others down involves a posture of asserting one's perspective with an attitude of indignation and unreceptiveness to others' when others failed to cooperate or do what the leader expects. At first blush, the rigidity entailed in their posture might seem similar to that of inflexible leaders. But there is a crucial difference—while inflexible leaders dismissed the environment in an effort to reduce anxiety arising from ambiguity, intuitive leaders actively sought clues from their environment in an effort to understand it. Although intuitive leaders were able to prevail, their actions caused some tension, and they wished they understood how they could have more skillfully gotten others' participation.

Chipo saw herself as a flexible and effective leader, someone who could get things done without having formal authority. She described herself as such: "Sometimes I apply authority and other times my social power. I have built rapport with managers and contemporaries. When I want to get things done, I can get them to give me what I want." But not all her relationships were as smooth. In some cases, people were coercive and unwilling to abide by the rules and procedures she was expected to enforce. In these cases, she had to resort to shutting others down. For example, when a scientist asked her to circumvent normal purchasing channels and order items, she refused:

> He wanted me to give the money in cash to people to go and buy things. And I said, "No, I will not do that. We still have to go by the rules." I didn't want to jeopardize our funds and our name just because he wanted some people to buy things for him. But I told him: "Why don't you go through the normal channels to get these tools, through the processing unit?" He didn't like it, but I stood my

ground. I was not going to shift. He didn't like it, and apparently because he was furious with me, he actually wanted me to be sacked. I didn't say anything to his abusive behavior. I just made sure I did my job to the best of my ability.

Fortunately, her boss supported her actions. Eventually, management knew of the scientist's potentially unethical behavior, along with Chipo's effective resistance to his efforts, and he was let go. Chipo was satisfied that she had managed to protect the interests of her center and maintained her own ethical standards. However, she would have liked to have been able to manage such situations more smoothly. At first, she thought that the reason why she had to resort to shutting down the researcher was because she did not have the title of "manager." She thought that the solution to her problem would have been to ensure that her position was graded at the appropriate level where she could expect people to accept her authority. After the WLS, however, she would learn that she could handle these types of situations with more skill at whatever hierarchical level she found herself.

Eleanor describes another situation of shutting people down, but she too was not comfortable with the reaction she engendered. Eleanor said that she often communicated in a very direct, task-focused manner and that sometimes this ruffled feathers and made some people "insecure." Others' reactions clearly irritated her:

> Sometimes I am a very frank and open person, and I think sometimes this is threatening to insecure people. And there were two or three instances where I simply said, "Look, this is what I believe in and that's why I'm acting this way." It's simply my personality, but I think I have become a little bit more diplomatic because I don't want to put insecure people into a situation where they feel, "Oh, she wants to get her way." There are other ways one can handle difficult situations.

Discovery and Transformation of Habitual Patterns of Thinking

As explained earlier, intuitive leaders' successes came from their ability to draw on tacit knowledge, but they did not have a way of understanding the ideas and principles that informed their perception and behavior. The internalized and unconscious nature of tacit knowledge contributed to intuitive leaders' habitual self-unaware and context-constrained pattern of thinking. Self-unaware thought processes were not problematic when intuitive leaders' efforts were successful. However, when resistance was encountered, the tacit knowledge that informed their practice was a barrier to their learning. Unable to conceptualize and articulate the grounds upon which they formulated their strategies, they could not get a handle on why they failed and what they might do differently. The result of this was context-constrained thinking that involved confusion and irritation at the circumstances that they could not understand.

Self-unaware and context-constrained thought processes were enacted through heedlessness and the absence of empathy. The notion of heedlessness brings to mind negative notions such as being reckless or careless. Here, however, the term merely refers to not being watchful, thoughtful, and attentive. It means that one looks through a prism but is unreflective and therefore unaware of the prism. The difficulty of being heedful is enhanced by the ephemeral nature of the thinking process and the taken-for-granted nature of assumptions. From this definition, it is easy to see that heedlessness is actually quite widespread and common.

As described in the previous section, Afeen was attentive and responsive to the communicative challenges of her team. At one level, Afeen and her team were cognizant that their linguistic and disciplinary differences could create communication difficulties. Translating this intellectual knowledge into face-to-face discernment and response was the basis of her cross-cultural competence. Afeen's discernment came from observing a variety of verbal and non-verbal cues, and her assessment of the team's needs evolved in real-time. What Afeen could not articulate, however, was the knowledge that she drew upon to discern and interpret these needs consistently. During the WLS, Afeen gained some insights into this matter when she was introduced to the Myers Briggs personality framework and took the associated personality test. Reflecting on her personality type, particularly the dimension of "Introversion," Afeen began to reflect on the processes that informed her intuition. In the following quote, she described this recognition, as well as the feeling of being affirmed and confident with the usefulness of her introverted nature:[2]

> When you're in a group, the people that seem to be leaders are the noisy ones. The quiet people you think are not so much leaders, but in fact it's not necessarily the case. The Myers Briggs was helpful because it helped me to understand that I could have potential as a leader although I am not an extrovert. This was reinforced later in the course when we had one of these team exercises where I was the leader. Many of the people in the group were very surprised, and that included me, at the way I was able to lead the group without having an extroverted style but through quiet encouragement from the back.

When heedlessness produces positive outcomes, the basis of one's success is rarely considered. The WLS helped Afeen become more aware and heedful of her natural posture towards gathering and appraising information. Greater self-awareness is the basis for understanding how one functions and why one's actions have the effect they do (positive or negative). As Afeen explains in the next quote, naming herself as an introvert and understanding how this influenced her behavior in a group helped her see how she influenced others and contributed:

> What I learned helped me put names to things. I think it was that growing self-awareness and confidence that many of the things that I did instinctively were reinforced and encouraged that this was a good way to go about things. And there actually was a rationale behind what I did that could be described.

When difficulties arose, as they are bound to do, intuitive leaders paused and reflected upon the context but not the tacit knowledge upon which they based their actions. For example, when Miora accepted a job managing a research lab in a Southeast Asian country, the first thing she did was to modernize the facilities and update the skills of the lab technicians. She assumed that this would lift morale. In the following quote, she expresses her confusion about one of the technicians in her lab who remained uninterested despite the many changes she made to improve the work environment and the technician's skills.

> The first thing I did was to send all the technicians off for computer training. I had one researcher and three technicians, and the two of the technicians really enjoyed going off for computer training and enjoyed learning and really loved seeing how we could make things so much faster and really loved it. We did a lot of laughing and a lot of development of ideas and a lot of bringing the program together. One guy just didn't enjoy the computer program, didn't enjoy going to learn how to use computers, hasn't enjoyed anything. I just can't reach him.

Self-unaware and context-constrained thinking was also enacted by means of lack of empathy. Empathy refers to the capacity to step into another person's shoes, to see a situation from the point of view of another person. Sympathy relies on emotional identification with another. Sympathy can come into play as a complement to empathy when a person can use their imagination and experiences to literally sense and feel how another person might feel in a given situation. Because we all appreciate being the recipients of empathy, we tend to think of the capacity for empathy in another person as a virtue and its absence as a vice. Although understandable, this normative perspective does little to help us understand how empathy is achieved. I would argue that the presence of empathy is not a marker of integrity, although the two can co-exist (e.g., empathy can also be employed to manipulate). Empathy a skill. Specifically, relational psychologists suggest that empathy is generated in interactions and it helps those involved create a connection of mutual cognitive and affective attunement. [3]

Exercising empathy is difficult when we are faced with time pressure, uncertainty, cultural differences, and many other stressful situations common in workplaces. Miora's difficulty in expressing empathy was complicated by all these factors. For Miora, one of the most important insights resulting her from the WLS was recognizing that her difficulties with motivating colleagues stemmed from a lack of empathy. In the next quote, Miora reflects on how this insight enabled her to make sense of a situation with a colleague in her previous job in her home country. Miora identified her leadership style as pace-setting, which was characterized by a hard-driving and competitive posture. This posture proved to be a stumbling block when she and her colleagues were preparing for conference presentations:

> One of the important lessons from the course was when we were defining leadership styles. I identified as a pace-setting leader, which made me think of something that happened that I didn't understand at the time, but after we learned about leadership styles, it was clear, I understood what had happened. I thought about somebody who was on my team in (country). We were all getting ready to go to a conference, and you've got to put in a hard week before it, getting the talks ready and practicing the talks. I was on maternity leave, so I was coming in specially for these practice talks. Three out of our four talks went beautifully, and one didn't. And the person who was responsible for the one talk just hadn't been putting the hours in to make it beautiful, and she kind of expected me to do it. And the day before we were supposed to go, she said she was not going to go to the conference and was talking of leaving. We convinced her to go to the conference. But what I learned at the course was that I had subjected her to too much pace-setting without enough coaching. And she was quite new. I couldn't understand at the time, why she suddenly pulled out and why she expected me to do it all. Now I think I do. I pushed her too hard and expected too much, and she wasn't ready to give it.

Miora realized that her hard-driving, pace-setting style was also at the root of her difficulties in her work setting in Southeast Asia. In this context, however, the complexity of being empathetic was exacerbated by cultural differences. The reader may recall the discussion of out-of-context thinking, a process which was discussed in Chapter 5. Out-of-context thinking results from unconsciously using culturally conditioned and untested assumptions to formulate expectations of appropriate behaviors. While Miora's communication with her colleagues in her home country had been facilitated by shared cultural expectations, here she struggled to understand the behaviors of some technicians in her team. On the one hand, she rejected the stereotypes bandied about by some of the international staff that the host country nationals were "lazy." But she struggled to understand why some of the technicians lacked the work ethic she expected. Although the WLS course did not directly address her questions, she did discern the implications of her pace-setting style of leadership on her capacity to step back and be self-aware. It also taught her something about the complexity of exercising empathy when differences are encountered. In the dialogue below, she describes an exercise in which differences are manifested when two people with varying tendencies of physical movement are asked to synchronize so as not to drop an object:

MIORA: I had my finger on one end of the stick and my partner had her finger on the other end, and we can just use one finger. And we had to move the sticks and not drop them. That was the day that I really realized that the amount of energy in people is genetically different. My partner wanted to be very slow and I wanted to dance the sticks all over the place and try not to drop them, but I couldn't. I really had to restrain myself. I noticed that, other energetically compatible pairs were walking around with the sticks and not dropping them. And then that's when I first realized that if, genetically you have a lot of physical energy, it's worth preserving your energy to make mental energy as well.

INTERVIEWER: I see. And what was the practical implication for you in that?

MIORA: Well, the lower-energy people just didn't have the excitement that the higher-energy people could have. It was just two very different ways of operating. Having a lot of energy makes you want to do a lot of things.

INTERVIEWER: One thing that strikes me is that how we move our bodies is cultural as well. If you have two people from two different cultures trying to dance together, their differences in body movement may reflect the cultural norms with which they grew up. I'm just throwing this out for you to comment on.

MIORA: I'm sure. I'm sure that that's one of the factors that frustrates me. I move fast and (host country nationals) move slow. What it means practically is that I've slightly changed my lifestyle.

Chipo also struggled with being empathetic, especially when she was defensive and angry. Recall from earlier that, prior to the WLS, she had shut down a scientist who had asked her to procure lab equipment and skirt formal purchasing protocol. She had refused to do this and had "held her ground." During the WLS, she gained greater self-awareness and realized that while her leadership strengths lay in her flexibility (using social influence or authority depending on the situation), she struggled with establishing cooperative exchanges when she strongly disagreed with someone or when others approached her in an aggressive way. She said:

CHIPO: The areas where I need to learn more is my ability to be more cooperative, because I tend to be someone that when I see things going wrong, I just cannot take it. I won't take it. But at the course that I attended in May, I saw the need to be more cooperative.

INTERVIEWER: What kinds of situations would this apply to? What are you thinking about?

CHIPO: Okay, for example, if somebody came up with an opinion and I disagree with that opinion, I would tell the person I am not in support of this, saying "It is not going to work, and I cannot see it working." And that is it. Now I think I would want to listen more to that person's side of the story. Understand the person better. How does this person feel about the situation? And see where we compromise. Come to a midpoint maybe where our opinions might meet. And then we can find ways of doing things in such a way that we would end up doing things properly without going against organizational policy and achieve the same end. In the case of the scientist, I would still not allow him to defraud the organization. But I might just want to make him realize where he is going wrong.

For Chipo, "being cooperative" was a broad idea. With respect to the scientist, for instance, being cooperative did not mean giving him what he wanted when she knew this to be inappropriate. Rather, it meant engaging him in a spirit of cooperation with the aim of helping him understand why his request was not acceptable. It also meant trying to understand his needs to see if these could be met by acceptable means. Thus, cooperation had more to do with *how* she engaged others, with greater empathy, rather than abdicating to avoid conflict. Chipo and other intuitive leaders built on the powerful insights they had after the WLS and by doing so, were able to refine their leadership behaviors.

Building on Transformative Insights and Cultivating a New Habit Pattern

The WLS put into motion a slow but steady process of transformation from intuitive to deliberate leadership. Transformation to deliberate leadership did not happen immediately. As described in Chapter 2, transformative insights are "Aha" moments in which a person's inquiry results in clarity, shifting habitual patterns in deep and meaningful ways that alter future perception. This does not mean that the old pattern goes away; it reasserts itself repeatedly until a new pattern is developed through conscious and deliberate effort and repetition. In Chapter 4, for example, I described how hidden leaders continually "caught themselves" engaging in habitual thought processes and altered these intentionally. Intuitive leaders said that the lessons of the WLS were "at the back of the mind." In the extended story of Ibsituu's inflexible leadership at the end of Chapter 5 we saw how she learned to catch herself after she reverted back to old habits. But we saw that the sensitivity to her habits and the conviction to change generated by the transformative insight of the WLS helped her bounce back and do something different such that the desired habit eventually took hold.

When WLS alumnae returned to work, they built on the transformative insights from the WLS. Being able to name their intuitive processes was a very important part of the process of cultivating self-aware and context-discerning thought processes. Learning about her leadership style as well as the exercise with the sticks gave Miora some powerful insights. One of these insights had to do with toning down her pace-setting leadership style and exercising relationally oriented styles like coaching or affiliative. Theoretical discussions concerning empathy and emotional self-regulation gave her the language to conceptualize what she was trying to accomplish, and this in turn helped her practice:

> Critical ideas were empathy, self-awareness, self-regulation, and leadership style. I think I practiced all of the things in some sort of jumbled way. But defining what all the concepts are, what all the components are, and which components need building on, I now see the ones that need improving, and when they have a name, I now know how I can improve them. For example, let's take self-regulation, "I need to regulate." That's a much nicer way of saying it than to say, "I need to take a deep breath and count to ten." Maybe it's the scientist in me, but thinking I need to regulate has much more meaning for me than I must count to ten and take a deep breath. And it's just the process, as well. Instead of taking a deep breath and counting to ten, it almost sounds like it's a force within you. Self-regulation sounds like a process that your body's going through that you're now dealing with.

Miora recognized that practicing self-regulation and empathy were not only necessary in order to tone down her pace-setting style but also to conserve energy and improve her overall well-being. Recall that her insight regarding how she used her energy had come from the exercise with the dancing sticks, described earlier.[4] This insight as well as the one related to her pace-setting leadership style seemed to converge on the idea that she tended to have a hard-driving high-energy predisposition. In her efforts to slow down, step back, and create space and time that was not consumed by work, she had to undertake significant changes in her lifestyle. Specifically, Miora decided to practice conserving her energy. In the dialogue below she discusses these efforts:

MIORA: I decided to work on self-regulation and preserving my physical energy.

INTERVIEWER: So are you saying if you conserve your physical energy, you have more energy for the mental work that you have to do.

MIORA: Not conserve, but if you look out to observe it, if you nurture your physical energy and care for it, then everything else will be better. You don't struggle through the day. And the interaction between physical and mental energy is much better. For me to see, that there are genetic differences between people's physical energy, and that having a high level of physical energy naturally is a gift to be looked after. So that's what gave me the motivation to look after it a bit better.

INTERVIEWER: So what did you do?

MIORA: Before the course I'd work and play hard. But now I try and play a little less hard. I try to eat better, drink less, go to bed earlier, try to look after myself better. I'm seeing a really big difference in my physical and mental well-being. I'm very busy. I have three small children. Here (in Southeast Asia) you have someone to help you take care of them. We have two fantastic people working for us during the day, not weekends. Learning to conserve my energy helped me with my family. Instead of putting the kids to sleep, opening a bottle of wine and sharing it, now we put them to sleep and I end up falling asleep with one of them. I've just been having more time with them. I've now got a completely different way of looking after myself, I used to compromise the energy I use.

Like Miora, Eleanor was also struck by the concept of managing energy and her insights had implications that went well beyond work. Eleanor explained:

> I've worked on being calm. I think to be calm and contained and see things clearly, it's very important to recognize that when your body and your mind are continuously under stress and you don't manage the stress, you simply can't respond the same way to a very stressful environment.

The learning of the WLS was also kept alive and cultivated through relationships. Not only did intuitive leaders stay connected with WLS alumnae, but they also built relationships with female colleagues in their centers. They found that being connected with other women in the WLS network provided access to senior women whom they did not personally know. For example, Eleanor said that she made a habit of joining female colleagues in her center for lunch or coffee, and this allowed her to build an immediate network on which she relied for social support, advice, and information sharing. She said: "One gets energy from this type of social contact."

Colleagues and relationships established through the WLS were also regular sources of advice and counsel, and this helped Eleanor think more deliberately about how she responded to tricky work situations. Eleanor described the calming effect of having someone to empathize with you: "In difficult times, if you can share your story, the transition is better and easier, your self-confidence is strengthened, and you can go into the next phase with confidence and a positive attitude."

Behaviors of Deliberate Leadership

The cultivation of transformative insights strengthened intuitive leaders' awareness of their intuitive processes and allowed them to better reflect on their practice as leaders. This cultivation involved using theoretical concepts that had helped them name their intuitive processes to observe themselves in action and to guide their actions. Through these efforts, intuitive leaders refined their practice, nurturing a self-aware and context-discerning thought process that characterized deliberate leadership. The transformation to deliberate leadership was evidenced in greater capacity for awareness and regulation of the intuitive processes that guide behavior, and the capacity to choose new approaches attuned to the situation and self.

Deliberate leaders demonstrated self-aware and context-discerning thought processes after the WLS in situations where their intuitive processes had previously been successful, as well as in those situations where they encountered resistance. After the WLS, for example, Afeen had been promoted from coordinator of a research team to theme leader. In her new role, she was responsible for several multidisciplinary and cross-national research themes around the world. Reflecting on the impact of the WLS on how she led this team, Afeen referenced one of the transformative insights she had gained during the negotiations course. Prior to the WLS, Afeen had been a good negotiator but she had the self-concept of someone who avoided negotiations in an effort to avoid conflict. During the WLS, Afeen learned that the real skill of effective negotiators was the capacity to integrate the different perspectives and desires of the individuals involved in a negotiation. She also realized that she was already adept at this. Here she tells a story of how she drew on this insight to navigate a delicate situation in which a prominent researcher needed to align his research with the new direction of the center.

AFEEN: One challenge is that the whole institute is trying to move to a somewhat different agenda. You have some people who tend to want to operate in the way they've always operated. But the challenge is how to move people forward and to do that in a way that people feel respected and empowered and know that their skills are still very valuable even though you're trying to get them to change a bit in how they use those skills. I have one operating project leader who's a very good scientist, well-recognized in the field, and has been working on a particular agenda for a number of years. Now we as management want him to move away from the fairly fixed and focused agenda that he's been working on for a very long time. That means that we have to get him to think a bit differently. We need to get him to disengage from a number of activities and people he's been work-ing with, or maybe relate somewhat differently to them, to use the experiences they've gained through that agenda to address something that's somewhat of a different scale. And the way I've gone about thinking how to work with him it is to take a positive and encourag-ing approach, looking at what he's good at and thinking about what he feels positive about and coming with suggestions along those lines so that he can feel good about moving forward.

INTERVIEWER: How did that work out?

AFEEN: To some extent, we're still in it, but one of the first steps was for me to recognize that I tend to be a logical person and wanting to understand what the situation is. So one of the first steps was to say, "How do you see things? Where do you see your work program over the next year? Can you articulate how you're going to spend your time and so on and so forth? What are your priorities?"

INTERVIEWER: And how did he react to that?

AFEEN: Very positively. In this particular case, this was somebody who really liked to feel in control of things. And then, the next step was to have a discussion that involves not just me, but my boss as well to discuss much more broadly: Where might be the agenda? Where is the institute going? And to ask him, "Okay, now think about this and come back to us and let's discuss some more." And then the next step is to bring suggestions, to hear his suggestions and also bring a new suggestion as well from my side, then I discuss with my boss, and hopefully he says that's okay and go back to the person. That would enable them to really wind up the agenda they've been pursuing, and they can move to something new rather than trying to juggle the two things at once.

INTERVIEWER: So, did it work?

AFEEN: Well, I think so. It was received very positively and now we have to figure out the details of how to implement it. We had to think of a way to move forward in a way that makes him feel comfort-able about finishing up things that he's working on currently and thinking about positive ways of moving forward and not just saying, "You've got to stop that and change." Trying to give options. I guess the lesson from the course that I mentioned, in terms of putting quite a lot of thought into other peoples' perspectives and so on is probably what helped with this process. I don't think I found it easy but having thought about things and gotten some ideas and discussed them, it went much better than I would have thought it would.

A few things are notable about the preceding exchange. First, Afeen had a very deliberate, step-by-step method for reaching agreement. Second, she began with a recognition of her strengths and how she tended to approach things: "I tend to be a very logical person, wanting to understand the situation." Third, she exhibited empathy towards the scientist. Specifically, she understood that he valued having control, autonomy, and power over things, and she formulated a process where he could retain this. Finally, Afeen's step-by-step process ensured that each stakeholder's interests and needs were incorporated in the transition of her colleague to the global agenda to which the Institute was headed. This included not only creating a substantive agreement that aligned all stakeholder interests but also creating a plan for implementation that would attend to the researcher's needs as he made the shift. Thus, in the preceding exchange Afeen described how she applied the principles of the negotiation course with deliberation in a self-aware and context-discerning manner.

The insights from the WLS were also very helpful to intuitive leaders who had previously encountered resistance. Eleanor was one of these individuals. In her case, insights about her Myers Briggs personality profile helped her understand how her logical and task-focused approach could ruffle feathers. Her response to others' reactions had previously been to shut them down and judge them harshly. After the WLS, she thought about these encounters differently. She recognized that others' reactions might not be about being insecure, as she had previously assumed, but to her irritability and seeming disinterest to their needs. Next, Eleanor describes how she tempered her irritation and thoughtfully sought to understand where others were coming from. She used her understanding of others to appeal to them:

> If you have people who are insecure, and my previous supervisor was very insecure, and I realized his weakness, I consciously tried to find another strategy to get what I need. I think one thing I learned in the course, it's very important to give feedback, and when you are in meetings, to summarize, to paraphrase, so that people really feel that you have listened to them and you have understood them. I used to come in with my idea and that's what we have to do, and I used to just come out with it and say "support me." But now I try to do everything that will make my boss feel something was his idea, and at the end I wanted support for a specific activity, and it doesn't make

me unhappy if he then promotes it as his own idea. You know, the important thing is that things get done.

As described earlier, Chipo learned the importance of being more cooperative, even when she felt that others' behaviors or goals were inappropriate. For her, being cooperative did not mean going along but rather not shutting others down, showing empathy but also trying to be heard. After the WLS, she had a situation in which lab technicians that she managed began to slack off, to come in late, or not come in at all. She said that she had spoken to several of the technicians about this problem in an effort to get them to change but to no avail. So, instead of confronting them and making it a battle, she decided to introduce the idea of "clocking-in."

> I met with the staff one day and I told them, "Okay I want to know who are our latecomers. When you come in in the morning, you need to clock-in. 7:30 is your resumption time so anyone who comes after 7:30 will be graded as a late comer." That's where we have a record of those who come late. To my surprise, people have improved. People who would not get to work until 8, 8:30, or even 9 in the morning have improved greatly. You see them come in before 7:30, you see them coming in maybe a little after 7:30, which to me is an improvement.

In this situation, Chipo created a formal structure and process for regulating the work hours of the staff. This impersonal tool was a means of establishing shared understandings and norms. It produced objective information that could be used to hold people accountable and served as a tool to structure the workday. Chipo said that the staff simply abided with this de-personalized tool and there had been no problems since it was introduced.

I now turn to an extended story of the transformation from intuitive to deliberate leadership. This story, introduced at the beginning of this chapter, concerns Miora's efforts to understand how to motivate her staff. The problem revolves around her trying to understand why she had been effective at doing this in her country but only somewhat successful in the new country in which she now leads a lab. Miora had to unpack at least two sources of tacit knowledge that informed her use of intuition to lead—cultural and leadership style.

Miora's Story of Finding What Makes "Them" Tick

It had only been a few years since Miora, a researcher, moved to a new country to manage a research laboratory. Prior to taking on her new post, she had been in a similar role in her home country. But despite the surface similarities, there was one important difference. While she had known how to motivate people in her home country, she was at a loss for how to do this in her new milieu.

The WLS Leadership course helped her to understand some of her tendencies in terms of leadership styles. When applied to her staff, this enabled her to understand her successes (with two staff members), failures (with two staff members), and to reach out to a staff member whose potential she recognized. This leadership story is a good example of how a WLS alumnus deliberately used knowledge acquired in the course to gain insight into her intuitive processes and fine-tune her leadership behavior in the area of developing others:[5]

> I had worked in exactly the same position at an organization in my home country where I would have considered myself a very effective leader. I had a team, a little smaller but with the same sorts of goals, but everyone was basically from the same country and had the same focus. Culturally I understood what made them tick and how to get the best out of them. Here, I struggle with some people, with the culture. I find myself getting very frustrated by the lack of commitment to a deadline, the lack of willingness to take ownership of a project, and I get frustrated by my inability (with two people in particular) to make them excited about their work. And so, I struggle.

Although frustrated, she also had some clear successes. The course was crucial in helping her understand her leadership style and diagnosing why she had been effective with two people while she had not been very effective with two others. It also helped her appreciate the importance of self-regulation and how her impatience was getting in her way of using a more effective leadership style. More specifically, she realized that, while she had employed an "affiliative" style with the former two team members, she had used her more-preferred "pace-setting" style with the latter. Despite the recognition that her two successes were linked to her use of an affiliative style, she decided that investing in the two problematic individuals was not a priority. Instead, she resolved to invest time and effort in another staff member whom she recognized as smart and motivated and deserving of more "affiliative" attention. While the affiliative style was time-consuming, it produced the kinds of results she wanted for the team.

Two Coaching Successes

Miora had had success in motivating two of her staff. One was a woman who had been with the center for a long time but had been "shunted from lab to lab." Miora recognized that this woman was bright and spent time in helping her develop:

> I sat down with her for a couple of hours, gave her the list of the research projects that I wanted to have in the lab, asked her what portion of her time she would like to put into either service or research or a split, and which projects she'd like to have. She decided she would be fully research but, when we began, she decided she would be a little bit of service as well.

This arrangement worked very well. This staff person was very resourceful and excited about the project. Miora taught her how to use some new equipment, and the staff person soon fully assumed the responsibility of managing it. Miora said this woman went further and "wrote up the research she had been doing into a poster presentation, and I got her into an international conference."

Miora also had success in working with another staff member who came to the center with a year of research experience:

> She's one of the brightest people I've ever worked with. I explained the project to her and she took it, and she has been generating so many nice results. But she wants to move up in her career. I knew I was going to lose her, so I searched far and wide and found her a really good Ph.D. program. So she won't only get the Ph.D., she'll get it from a good institute.

Miora was aware that her two successes had to do with the fact that she made an effort to find out what her team members were interested in and supported their developmental goals through resources and encouragement. With the first woman, there was also an interpersonal connection that facilitated the coaching and mentoring that resulted in the subordinate's professional growth. With the second woman, the coaching and mentoring was initiated differently. Miora was very impressed with her intelligence and skills and decided to coach and mentor her after she learned from another source that this staff member wanted to pursue a Ph.D. program and would leave if she were accepted into one.

Two Coaching Failures

The two staff members that Miora was not able to engage were a man, a full-time permanent member of her staff, and a woman employed in another unit who had come on board for a specific project:

> He is a research technician, does a lot of research, but he works in the service program. I couldn't reach him at all, and I still don't know

how to, not even after the course. He pretends his English is terrible, but it's actually not bad. He's just not interested and does not make a good contribution to the lab.

She tried, unsuccessfully, to engage him, moving him out of the service area and asking him what he really wanted to do. Thinking that it might be fieldwork, she designed some field experiments, but he was not interested. She put him back in the lab because that is where he said he wanted to be, but he did not show any real interest there either. Finally, out of desperation, she gave him a low score on his annual evaluation hoping that this would alert him to his developmental needs and propel him into action. However, that alienated him even further:

> He avoids me like the plague, and I can't get beyond the "Yes ma'am, yes ma'am." And that is definitely a cultural thing. Everyone else I've managed to convince to call me by my first name. I try when I sit down to talk with him to get a dialogue going about what he wants to do, but everything I suggest is "Yes, ma'am." And that is the biggest obstacle: I haven't found a way to communicate with him yet. I thought I could manage all people. . . . He's my first failure.

The second problematic coaching story is a woman who arrived already having a fairly senior position. She came highly recommended from a quality lab and was interested in the work she was doing. The problem, however, was that she could not work independently and appeared to be less qualified than expected:

> She's on a really nice project that I think is quite a simple one, but she just doesn't get it, doesn't get excited about it, doesn't use initiative at all. I haven't been able to push the button to get the fire in her belly on a project.

Because the situations surrounding these two individuals were different, Miora felt that her strategy with them also had to be different.

The Staff With Potential

While Miora had her successes and failures in developing staff, there was a man who fell in a more ambiguous category. She described him as "a very smart fellow" with aspirations to make things better for himself and wanting to pursue a Ph.D. He was a hard worker and had managed to get to the center on his own merits. But he faced significant obstacles. He supported a family on his meager salary, making it difficult to push forward with his professional development goals. Although she saw his potential, Miora said: "I didn't get behind him before I took the course because I knew it would take a lot of work." One insight from the course was that, to build up the capacity of the center, she needed to invest in coaching this man.

The Impact of the WLS Leadership Course

The WLS course introduced Miora to concepts and definitions of leadership styles and emotional intelligence. These concepts and definitions were very helpful to her because, by giving names to leadership styles, she became aware of her tacit practices, was introduced to alternative practices she had not considered, and could see the ones that needed improving. Learning the various types of leadership styles helped her define her preferred leadership style—pace-setting—and recognize the conditions under which another style might be more effective:

> So, pace-setting is my default, but now I know that I should try harder with other styles, such as "coaching" and "affiliated" styles, and the "authoritative" one, the "visionary" one. I think I'm not too bad at it, but I've got to be conscious of applying it, and recognize that I've got to "coach" a bit more.

Similarly, learning about her emotional intelligence and particularly the concept of "self-regulation" facilitated a diagnosis of how she managed her emotions and how she could do a better job in stressful situations. In general, even though she previously did not have definitions for all the leadership styles, she still had an intuitive understanding of the processes.[6]

> I think I practiced all of the things in some sort of jumbled way. But by defining all the components, I recognize which components need building on. I now know that my self-regulation needs a bit of building up or that I need to do a bit of coaching here, or I need to do a bit of the authoritative, the visionary, the affiliative, the democratic, the pace-setting, and this one, the autocratic.

Miora found these insights to be particularly helpful in understanding her successes and failures in motivating her staff. Although her preferred mode was pace-setting, she had used the affiliative style with both individuals she had been able to motivate. She recognized that she can be affiliative initially, to help launch someone, but then wants to switch to a pace-setting style and watch them "run with it." When the mentee's response fits with her preferences, as it did with the two individuals with whom she had been successful, then she is effective. However, as she found in the cases where she had been unsuccessful in coaching subordinates, neither individual complemented her style. She learned that, when faced with this type of situation, she becomes impatient and the relationship does not produce expected outcomes.

Recommitting Self to Developing an Underutilized Resource

These insights helped Miora make important decisions and changes in her leadership behaviors after the course. For example, her new insights made a difference with the staff member with potential in whom she had not previously invested time. She said that, after the course, she decided to coach and develop this man. He had a lot of potential and she recognized that her leadership style would work with him:

> I knew that he was just coasting but was a really bright fellow. I knew that I didn't need to lead him very much scientifically, he's really good. I hadn't put as much into getting to know him. So I've started doing that now.

In light of this, she decided to use a more affiliative style with this person. "I'm trying to give him a stipend and get him enrolled in a university. Things like that. I'm trying to be far more affiliative and do far more coaching and a little less pace-setting. And a bit more visionary too." She had some discussions with him to find out what his career and life goals were, and she began to help him move forward with these goals. Specifically, she helped him with the university application process. She said this effort made a difference in his morale. "I'm sensing a much more positive energy from him and more of a commitment to his job. It's not that he was slacking off or anything, but now he's giving more. I feel that he's much happier to be here."

Summary

In the case of the transformation from intuitive to deliberate leadership, the WLS produced a subtle change in the habitual self-unaware and context-constrained patterns of thinking and feeling. Intuitive leaders had been effective in many areas but they seemed to have some areas of chronic difficulties. The WLS gave them theories and conceptual language for understanding the chronic leadership difficulties; equally important, theories helped them understand their successes as well. In particular, theories gave them insight into the tacit knowledge they drew upon to develop an intuitive sense of what was needed in a particular situation. By understanding this, intuitive leaders were able to access insights about processes they had previously utilized but not been consciously aware of. This was helpful because when they encountered difficulties in their leadership efforts they were able to be self-reflective and willing to learn new ways that required more conscious thinking. The transformation to deliberate leadership was characterized by a self-aware and context-discerning pattern of thinking, feeling, and acting. This involved being more intentional in how they made use of their intuitive processes and applying them to situations in which these were an asset and learning new styles where these were limitations.

Notes

1. Michael Polanyi (1966) is credited with coining the term tacit knowledge and making the assertion "we can know more than we can tell" to characterize the essence of tacit knowledge or tacit knowing.
2. This is similar to the point made in the popular book by Cain (2013).
3. See Miller (1976), Miller and Stiver (1997), Kaplan (1990), and Jordan (1990).
4. In the next chapter I will discuss the transformation from depleted to inspired leadership. The question of leadership and well-being and energy use will be a topic that will be discussed in more depth. The reader may readily recognize how widespread and relevant the problem of managing energy in work and life has become to modern life, deeply intertwined as it has become with technology.
5. Readers who are interested in obtaining more information on the theoretical ideas described in this story can consult Goleman et al. (2004).
6. An excellent introduction and discussion of emotional intelligence can be found in Goleman (2000).

References

Cain, S. (2013). *Quite: The power of introverts in a world that can't stop talking.* New York, NY: Broadway Paperbacks.

Goleman, D. (2000). *Working with emotional intelligence.* New York, NY: Bantam.

Goleman, D., Boyatzis, R. E., & McKee, A. (2004). *Primal leadership: Learning to lead with emotional intelligence.* Boston, MA: Harvard Business School Press.

Jordan, J. V. (1990). Relational development through empathy: Therapeutic applications. *Work in Progress, 40,* 11–14. Wellesely, MA: Stone Center for Developmental Services and Studies.

Kaplan, A. G. (1990). Empathy and its vicissitudes. *Work in Progress, 40,* 6–10. Wellesely, MA: Stone Center for Developmental Services and Studies.

Miller, J. B. (1976). *Toward a new psychology of women.* Boston, MA: Beacon Press.

Miller, J. B., & Stiver, I. P. (1997). *The healing connection: How women form relationships in therapy and in life.* Boston, MA: Beacon Press.

Polanyi, M. (1966). *The tacit dimension.* London, UK: Routledge.

7 Transformation From Depleted to Inspired Leadership

> The idea of having power has no draw for me at all. I want to have autonomy, I want to be able to do the things I want to do.
>
> *May, an Inspired Leader*

This chapter explores the final leadership transformation produced by the WLS, from *depleted* to *inspired* leadership. The analysis will show that the WLS fostered greater leadership effectiveness through this transformation by fostering a shift in a habitual, self-affirming, context-obliged pattern of thinking and feeling that shaped depleted leadership behaviors. In general, self-affirming thoughts have to do with an individual's positive appraisal of, and attachment to, self-aspects such as values, beliefs, skills, and the like. Recall from Chapter 5 that inflexible leaders also engaged in self-affirming thoughts but the nature of self-affirming thinking that they described differed in an important way from that of depleted leaders. Namely, while inflexible leaders clung to what they knew and what worked for them in the past, the depleted leaders were deeply motivated by their principles and values. The first had a grasping quality, the second an anchoring one.

A context-obliged thought process produces behavior that is depleting. In understanding this, it is important to note the distinction between responsibility and obligation. One is expected to do one's job, but this is a matter of discharging one's responsibilities. Obligation, however, does not come from the formal dictates of a position but rather from discretion compelled by a personal feeling of being bound by duty or values. Depleted leaders recognized the pervasive and entrenched nature of organizational processes, including culture, hierarchical norms, and group and interpersonal conflict. Given their values, they felt an obligation to use their skills and insights to influence these processes. Relaxing into the flow of how things were done was not viable given their values and sense of duty. To discharge their sense of obligation, often going counter to entrenched organizational currents, meant they had to exercise patience, persistence, discipline, and self-regulation. They also had to be alert and vigilant. This state of arousal was cognitively and emotionally demanding work and while it produced results, it was also depleting.

The post-WLS leadership stories of depleted leaders reflected a transformation to inspired leadership in which self-affirming and context-aligned thought processes replaced the earlier self-affirming and context-obliged processes. While the context had not changed, inspired leaders had. The shift to context-aligned thinking came from the recognition of the personal cost of acting out of obligation to address problems others would not. Context-obliged thinking led to behaviors in which an individual did more than their share, shouldering the responsibility of manifesting an ideal that was not aligned with their context. While many of the goals of depleted leaders, such as promoting collaboration or harmonious relationships, were helpful to their teams and organizations, their willingness to bear the inordinate burden of effort to achieve these outcomes removed the accountability of other participants while placing a constraining burden on themselves. The shift to context-aligned thinking arose from the recognition that acting out of obligation alone was costly to depleted leaders, creating disequilibrium and diminishing their capacity to adequately attend to their own and their families' well-being. This recognition compelled depleted leaders to begin to take their own feelings, well-being, and priorities into consideration as they selected roles and activities that energized them by allowing them to simultaneously meet the needs of their organizations, their families, and themselves.

Nine percent of the WLS interviewees told stories that pertained to the transformation from depleted to inspired leadership. The position classification distributions among depleted/inspired leaders were as follows: 50 percent were scientist/researcher and 50 percent were in an administrative/coordinator capacity. None held the position of theme leader or manager. In terms of recruitment categories, 50 percent of depleted/inspired leaders were internationally recruited, while the other 50 percent were nationally recruited.

This leadership transformation category is notable for its small size, with only two out of the 24 interviewees providing stories of the transformation from depleted to inspired leadership. Although modest in number, these two individuals provided accounts that were unique and pertained to an important issue facing both women and men, namely, how to reconcile their desire to be of service to others with the need to attend to the well-being of themselves and their families. The stories of depleted leaders suggest that the work-life balance perspective does *not* accurately frame the problem or provide answers to how they might deal with the tensions they experienced in their daily lives. A key problem is the posited duality between work on the one hand and life on the other. The stories contained in this chapter concretely show what most people know from experience: the individual worker is a whole being, and work and life are not independent. Rather, the energy a person expends in one domain affects the energy available for the other. The demands of work can be so excessive such that a person may not have the mental and emotional energy to respond to the demands of personal care and family life.

My analysis of depleted/inspired leader stories suggests that it is not possible to adequately address the problem of the management of energy allocation through the idea of balance.[1] Instead of balance, a more apt idea might be *fulfillment*. This does not refer to fulfillment in work or in life because work and family are parts of a life that is experienced holistically. Rather, fulfillment is about managing the boundaries of work and home by deciding what is important to the person and seeking to optimize the expenditure of time and energy in a way that is congruent with one's deepest values. This optimization will ensure that the individual is inspired and energized by their life, even if some of the things they do with their time are challenging and difficult. It is also important to underscore that such choices cannot be made with a "plan" and a "goal." Rather, the choices emerge from reflection on values what is important and what matters at a particular point in time and by seeking opportunities in one's environment to more closely live a life that reflects one's current understanding of what's important.[2]

This chapter describes stories of the transformation from depleted to inspired leadership undertaken by two individuals that I refer to as Asdis and May. Their stories will support the idea that depletion results from managing the demands of work and life through the prism of obligation, and inspiration emerges from managing life with the intent to find fulfillment in life *as a whole*. Both women built their capacity for inspired leadership by gaining clarity on how their activities, while congruent with their values, were depleting—not aligned with their desire to be energized by their activities. Seeking to optimize their time in such a way that they could experience more fulfillment, they learned to exercise greater agency in choosing how to use their time at work and at home.

Unlike the other three leadership transformations discussed in the preceding chapters, the transformation from depletion to inspiration was not neatly marked by the transition point of the WLS, with a depleted pattern "before" and an inspired one "after." In the case of one depleted leader, Asdis, the transformation to context-aligned thinking had already taken place prior to the WLS, whereas in the case of the other depleted leader, May, the shift from context-obliged to context-aligned thinking did not occur for some time after the course. Nevertheless, the WLS course had an important role for both—affirming the choice of the former and catalyzing a new thought process for the latter—and produced and reinforced a shift that I call inspired leadership. This impact will be described more fully in the remainder of this chapter. Because there are only two individuals whose stories were categorized as depleted/inspired, this chapter will tell their stories in-depth and will not contain an extended story at the end.

Behaviors of Depleted Leadership

The notion of depletion is closely related to the concept of "organizational burnout."[3] According to Maslach (2015), "burnout is a syndrome of emotional exhaustion, depersonalization, and reduced personal accomplishment that can occur among people who do 'people work' of some kind" (p. 2). Burnout is the result of chronic depletion of a person's intellectual, emotional, and spiritual energy over a long period of time. The idea of depletion suggests that the expenditure of effort draws on and reduces energy rather than produces greater capacity and vitality. Depletion results when an individual is simply reactive to external demands—others' wants and needs—without sufficient reflection upon one's own needs and priorities. It is not that caring for and responding to others is inconsistent with the wants and needs of depleted leaders; indeed it may often be compelling to them for precisely this reason. Their stories suggest that depletion can result when one fails to reflect on the impact of caring work on one's well-being. As their stories suggest, addressing depletion requires taking a step back, taking stock, prioritizing self-care along with care of others, and developing inner-directed set of intentions that guides decisions about what kinds of activities are fulfilling and allow for both care of self and care of others. Caught in a reactive-response pattern, depleted leaders were unable to create internal space and downtime to formulate the intentions that could guide how they would respond to external demands to preserve mental and emotional energy and sustain spirit and inspiration.

Depleted leaders were very confident in their skills and abilities, and were confident in their capacity to contribute to their organizations. Beyond confidence in their technical competence, they were also clear about their values. This meant they not only had a deep desire to contribute to the organization, but they were guided by their sense of what ought to be. A matter that was critical to their capacity to reverse the process of depletion was that the values that motivated depleted leaders were not limited to the narrow sphere of work but also to home life. They felt an obligation to do their best to be of service in both domains.

Depleted leaders described two types of behavior: endurance and carrying others' problems. *Endurance* contains an aspect having to do with how a person feels as well as an aspect having to do with how she carries these feelings in her environment. Endurance involves the emotional capacity to allow the co-existence of contradictory emotions, both negative (e.g., suffering, hurt, and anger) and positive (e.g., self-confidence, values, ideals, and imagined positive possibilities). The positive emotions make it possible to tolerate the negative ones, making sustained, even inspired, action in difficult situations possible by eliciting patience, tolerance, and discipline. These qualities enable the individual to stay the course and see something difficult through to closure and hopefully, to satisfaction.

The capacity for endurance allowed depleted leaders to cope with neglect and scrutiny. Neglect has to do with indifference, coolness, and inattention toward another. Neglect elicits feelings of being unimportant to others, unconnected, excluded, and unneeded. Being the target of neglect is painful, but individuals do have a choice in how they respond to it. Sometimes people react by making negative attributions to others, directing their pain and anger outward, and adopting an antagonistic posture. This is where neglect can elicit aggressive responses that redirect a person's action to getting back at others rather than a goal they might have. Other times, people could direct negative attributions to themselves and end up feeling worthless. This too can lead to reduced self-efficacy, hope, and optimism, and withdrawal of effort towards goal achievement (Luthans et al., 2015; Debebe, 2017). Endurance is a resilient response to neglect. Enduring neglect involves feeling the negative feelings rather than denying the pain that comes from neglect. Enduring also involves feeling the positive feelings along with one's commitments to one's goals, rather than minimizing or discounting these in the face of the negative feelings. These positive feelings make the painful experiences resulting from neglect tolerable and allow the individual to persist in a course of action that is meaningful and worthwhile to the person. I begin with Asdis' story of endurance and follow with, May's story of endurance and carrying others' problems.

Asdis' Story of Depletion

Asdis' story had to do with enduring neglect. Asdis was a European woman who had been living in a Southern African country before she was hired in her center. Because she was recruited from the local setting, her job was classified a national recruit. In her new job in the communications unit of her center, Asdis was tasked with creating a website to showcase the center's research programs and activities. She decided that undertaking this project would be made easier if there were a community of webmasters from other centers to whom she could turn for information and mutual support. So without telling her boss, she contacted people in other centers who were in similar roles. Next, she describes her boss' reluctant response when he learned she had done this:

> I wrote a lot of emails to people in research centers all over the world, saying: "Hi. We are trying to do a new website and I'm sure we have a lot of things to share. I would like to learn from you. Perhaps we can build a kind of mailing list and keep in touch and enrich ourselves in shared knowledge." I got answers from about half of these people. We were very excited. And then I told my boss about it. He wasn't excited about the idea. I think it was because our website wasn't launched at that time and he would have liked to have something to show to

them. And, he didn't know me—perhaps he didn't trust what I was planning to do. And I stopped and never continued with the network.

Although she was disappointed by her boss' lack of support, she decided to move forward with building the website. Asdis worked with the project leaders responsible for her center's research programs. In addition, her boss approached the information technology (IT) unit with the goal of securing their help in setting up the website. In both sets of relationships, Asdis sought to contribute to the organization, and she was deeply motivated by a strong desire to work with others in a way that fostered cohesion and collaboration. She repeatedly expressed the desire to build positive relationships and to learn from others to produce the best outcome. These desires shaped what she hoped would transpire in her interactions with IT and the research teams.

Asdis approached the research teams carefully, gauging their needs and trying to determine how best to work with each unique team. Her vision was to establish a partnership. She said, "In this project I could motivate people from all over the institute. It's not, 'okay, we from the communications unit will now lead this project and do everything ourselves and you will give us your information.'" Rather, as she describes here, Asdis sought to find a counterpart in each team, offer her expertise to the level desired by each team, and take the lead from each team when it came to content and details of web presentation:

I went to see each project manager, and said, "Just to let you know, the center has 15 projects, and each project is doing a different kind of research. And so our idea was to have a website where each of these 15 projects can have their own project website. We know that you would like to have a website. We are working on this, and we want to help you. I know that you as project leader are very busy and will not have the time to sit down with me for hours. So what I want to suggest to you is to look in your team, who would be the most suitable person to do this with me." So I generally started to work with the secretaries or the project assistant or the researcher whoever was IT-enthusiastic or interested in web stuff. The project leaders were happy not to be obliged to do it themselves. Some of them were a little bit surprised, thinking "my secretary will not be able to do it," and I told him "well I think she will." This way, I motivated people who wanted to learn something new. From more or less nothing, no web knowledge in the center, we built a network of thirty people who have some kind of expertise in it. We always knew that they would not do it all alone, but we gave them the freedom to choose if they want to do it alone, if they want a lot of support, or a little support. So, I think this kind of leadership-building has worked quite well.

Not only was Asdis pleased with the outcome of her work with the research teams, but she was also pleased with the process of working with the projects and the relationships she built. The process of working with IT, as well as the nature of the relationship with IT, however, was more complicated because the parties involved had different, unacknowledged expectations of how they would work. Asdis said that, from her viewpoint, IT was less motivated to work with others when they could not claim sole responsibility and credit. She relayed the following story to describe one episode where this was manifested and created tension:

> I was informed by the head of the unit that the IT people were doing a website on their own and they were going to use the design that we had developed for the website, but they wouldn't do it with us, and they wouldn't check the content with us. They would publish it because they have access to the server and the machines, and they wouldn't even inform us. So what I did was, very stupidly, I sent an e-mail saying that I just saw the new website. I think they did a great job, I wondered why they did it alone and without respective of the design guidelines, the content wasn't edited, and I was regretting that they weren't working with us in a team as we agreed to do it. So this was a big problem. They didn't respond, but other people told me that they talked to my boss. My boss was in conflict with them, too, but they let him know that they think I'm kind of crazy to be so arrogant to think that they need to work with me.

In the quote above Asdis suggests that the IT people saw her as overstepping her role and authority. However, the problem that surfaced went beyond this. In the following quote Asdis alludes to an underlying philosophical difference. From her view, for IT, achieving a positive outcome and getting credit was important, while for Asdis, her boss, and indeed others in communications, producing a positive outcome through relationship-building and collaboration was important. She stated:

> The main conflict was that, from our point of view, the IT people collaborate when they are project leaders. When they are sure to get all the credit for everything. When they have to work in a team and people from several units are involved, and if they are not the leader, they are not so motivated because they can't say, "We did it." They completely have this perception of "You are my client and I solve your problem," which is the logical IT point of view, because in most projects you are completely lost and you need the IT people to repair your computer.

Although she recognized how the specialized technical knowledge of IT might have contributed to IT's client-expert model of service delivery,

Asdis clearly saw that in some situations, IT could adopt a more partnership model. To Asdis, the fact that IT chose not to do this when it was possible to do suggested that conflict in the IT posture and that of communications reflected the individual preferences of the heads of the respective units. Asdis said, "My boss is very collaborative and transparent. He's not interested in politics, problems, and tensions. The IT guy is the complete contrary. He wants to be the 'boss.'"

Although the differing approaches of the heads of IT and communications may have reflected differing values and priorities, one cannot ignore the organizational influences that might also have been at play. Too frequently, organizations overtly encourage teamwork, but in practice, they rarely recognize and reward it. While the IT boss claimed credit and accrued rewards for IT's work, the communication team's efforts were neither recognized or rewarded. Asdis recounts with chagrin:

> We won't get credit here. The IT people have very high credit with the Director General. We have never found a way to prove that our work, without talking so much about it, is of high quality, so there's always this kind of frustration that we are working so hard and we're doing something very effective and that it never gets the credit it deserves because the IT people are doing so much more public relations than we do. Our DG loves this guy, because he is so ambitious. He would come to you at 3:00 in the morning and repair your computer. The DG just thinks "This guy is solving all my problems. He never criticizes; he always says that I am wonderful."

The preceding account suggests that another factor that likely contributed to the IT unit head's preference for an individualistic approach was the tendency of the organization to recognize and reward individual contributors over outcomes produced through team effort. Given this, why did the communications unit as a whole, including Asdis and her boss, persist in trying to establish cooperative relationships? It is clear they understood the organizational incentive structure well. Why would Asdis and her boss choose to work with others collaboratively when it was not encouraged or rewarded? One plausible answer is that they personally embraced collaboration as a more rewarding mode of working. Their efforts suggest that they may have believed they could turn things around either through motivating collaboration, as they did with the project teams, or through persuasion with IT. After all, who would argue against a collaborative ideal?

As it became apparent that IT was not interested, Asdis said that she and her boss initially fought back by choosing to "confront IT, and not avoid the conflict. We had a time where we weren't talking much to each other." However, when a confrontational strategy worsened the conflict, Asdis and her boss stepped back to reflect, and clarify their intentions:

We saw that there's no way to win the battle because we are not the fighters, that they are. We're not able to sell our souls for being the little stars at the center. We want to do a good job, and it's much more fun than to spend our daily work struggling with the IT people.

This proved to be a crucial turning point not only for the communications unit but also for the individuals within it, leading to the decision to expend their energy in a direction aligned with their aspirations. Asdis said that both she and her boss had endured difficult personal circumstances and they agreed on the importance of giving work its proper place in life, ensuring that work demands do not bleed into life and deprive them of the energy they needed for themselves and for their families. For her part, Asdis had young children with chronic health issues. Using her energy wisely at work was not a luxury, but a necessity. She was very clear in her own mind that seeking visibility and recognition, which were externally driven activities, did not have a place in her priorities. She wanted to be of service to others, work collaboratively, and enjoy both her work and colleagues. But she also did not want to put all her energy into work. She wanted to have some mental and emotional energy when she went home—to meet her kids' needs and enjoy her family life:

> What I really trust from my experience is that being modest takes more time, but I have the feeling that I'm getting where I want to get without so much stress. I'm starting to do more difficult and demanding things when I feel ready. I always tell myself, "Well, I can't be very aggressive because I have three kids and I have a family and I have to have a balance between my work and my family." When you are aggressive, you put all your energy into work, and I can't do it.

Clarifying what was important to them was only the first step; what followed was figuring out what that meant for their future direction. Although Asdis' used the terminology of work-life balance, the substance of what she had to say was richer and far less mechanistic in its imagery. She was seeking to optimize the expenditure of time and energy using her desire for holistic fulfillment in the totality of her life as a guide. Next she described the initial period of uncertainty and then the discovery of a new direction aligned with her values and with the needs of researchers in her center:

> So for a while we just did nothing. We didn't make plans for new web projects, and then we kind of discovered the world of knowledge management in the sense of knowledge sharing. Not IT, but tools and techniques that help people to share their knowledge. This is something that is very useful for our researchers because sometimes they

need ideas on how to share their knowledge better. So we are really excited to develop our expertise in this knowledge area, and we don't need so much IT stuff. This knowledge-sharing field is pretty much related to my way of thinking about my job. I found a field, or an activity, which resolved my dilemma. I am more at peace with myself. I need to have energy when I come home, or in general for my heart, my soul. I think it's better this way, and I'm quite happy with it.

May's Story of Depletion

As can be seen from the preceding story, Asdis had made the transformation from depleted to inspired leadership prior to the WLS. May, the second depleted leader, was the opposite. She engaged in depleted leader behaviors before the WLS and continued to do so for some time afterwards. May engaged in two behaviors of depleted leadership: carrying the organizations' problems and enduring scrutiny. *Carrying the organization's problems* refers to the situation where a person fills a void in an organization or group by assuming an unpleasant or difficult role. In doing so, they become the covert carrier of that role, relieving others of their responsibility to do their fair share of unpleasant and difficult work. While May was an accomplished and organized researcher and leader, one issue in her story had to do with her center's over-reliance on her to manage difficult people and difficult situations.[4]

While Asdis encountered indifference to her contributions, May was sought out to pacify difficult people, smooth over differences, help people find common ground, build bridges, and mentor and develop difficult but talented scientists. May saw a need for her particular skill set. Referring to her colleagues, she said, "They're all thinkers. I'm a feeler, so I make a big contribution in realizing that people are offended or realizing that there is a 'feeling' problem going on. I'm also very goal-oriented, and productive." As May described below, she was the one they turned to so as to keep things on track:

> I dealt pretty well with difficult situations. We had some people who were difficult, and people would give them to me to take care of because I was able to manage them better. If you're in a meeting and you need someone to smooth things over and bring people together when they're not agreeing, that sort of thing, I thought I was really good at that. I think that I'm sensitive to what other people are feeling.

Despite being compelled to respond to the void in interpersonal skills in her center and despite being skilled at doing so, May, like most people, disliked dealing with difficult people and situations. She particularly disliked seeing hurt in others and having to quell her irritation at the petty and political behavior that would sometimes emerge. Although her instinct was to avoid these situations, she would nonetheless persuade and goad herself to act if she were needed:

> It's difficult for me to do. I usually manage to do it, but I don't like to hurt the person's feelings, and I worry about it for a long time before I get around to doing it. They say, "If you're worried about it, just do it." Well, of course I should just do it, but I don't always because I just can't bring myself to.

May also engaged in the behavior of *enduring scrutiny*. Scrutiny can be carried out in a benign and routinized manner. In this case, terms such as analysis, inspection, or review are fitting—there is not necessarily an agenda but rather a routine evaluation process that organizations frequently undertake. But there are also times when scrutiny can take on a negative and aggressive connotation such as in nit-picking and fault-finding, aimed to either intimidate or shame a target. Enduring scrutiny involves feeling and holding and not denying the anger, fear, and sense of injustice that can arise from being overly scrutinized, while at the same time focusing on the values and goals toward which one is working. These latter positive feelings make the perceived and felt aggression tolerable and allow the individual to persist in a course of action that is inherently satisfying.

May's story of enduring scrutiny occurred in the context of her efforts to lead a team that was developing and implementing an innovative research method. Given her boss' skepticism, May's efforts to implement the new methodology required that she defend it from her boss' many efforts to derail the effort in its vulnerable and nascent stages. The source of her boss' skepticism was hard to pin down. On the one hand, the aim of the research method, to harness the contributions of both scientists and farmers in a collaborative research partnership, was aligned with the egalitarian aspirations and values of her center. Despite these espoused values, which her boss also embraced in principle, his behavior suggested an aversion to its practical implications, at least in the context of the research method she and others were in the process of developing. The result, as she described, was a chaotic response to her efforts in the context of the research she was leading:

> It was a very schizophrenic sort of environment. The DG, compared to the other centers, was absolutely not top-down. He had an explicit philosophy to have a flat organization. But he was also very autocratic. It was not a particularly hierarchical situation, but they were trying to figure out how not to be hierarchical, and so we came up with this model of not being hierarchical, but it was all new and strange and they had to think if they really wanted to do that or not,

or if they wanted us to do it. Our approach involved some risks. You don't have perceived control, which you have in a very top-down approach. We didn't have a controlled experiment, and we had a lot of discussions around that. They didn't complain about the idea of being bottom-up, it's like motherhood and apple pie: you can't say that you shouldn't be bottom-up.

In an effort to ensure rigor and especially quell her boss' nervousness about the new methodology, May formed an advisory committee of international experts to provide critique and feedback. But May speculated that her supervisor must have viewed the advisory board as a body ostensibly set up to rubber-stamp her project and say, "Oh yes, that's wonderful." To monitor the group's proceedings, the DG "asked a friend of his to keep an eye on us, pressure us, and keep asking difficult questions. He put this guy in a difficult situation because, his friend, who was supposed to be a sort of spy, actually agreed with what we were doing."

Her boss also used the board of trustees as another tool in his scrutiny of her team's proceedings and work:

> He was worried about our rigor. Because he had the power, he asked me to defend this approach over and over again. And I did. I had to justify it repeatedly with our leaders and with the board of trustees. It was crazy how many times I had to make presentations, particularly to the board. And it was completely instigated by him.

In addition, May also had to buffer the teams working in the various research sites from these political dynamics so they could implement each project with minimal distraction. These research teams each participated in the development of the method, aligning their approaches and working to develop a single, unified methodology. May had to maintain the morale of these teams by working effectively with the project leaders from the various research sites. Cohesion and task focus were critical because the collective effort was involved in the development of the method, and the collective effort was under scrutiny with May as the defender. Whenever May saw potential for threat to the cohesion of the teams in their joint effort, she made sure to deal with it. She did this with enormous skill, displaying her ability to understand the motivations and needs of people who were difficult and to show them how their needs could be met within the team. By doing this, she averted breakdown among the teams, ammunition that her boss might have found useful. In the following quote she described one situation where a researcher who headed a project at one of the sites threatened the fragile dynamic that May was trying to manage:

> I needed to get one the leader from one of our sites to come around. And that involved a lot of patience with her because she was irritating.

I would do something that I thought was completely fair and, somehow, she would figure out a way that it was not fair. So then I would have to patiently take a deep breath and explain, "Oh, no, no, that wasn't what I meant." Or I'd have to somehow add a phrase to a document to satisfy the particular perspective of her team. She took the fact that I was using phraseology developed by another team a little bit as "They're favoring that other team over me." So we changed the title of the program to be consistent with the title of the overall program title she used for her old program. So, we did it because we thought it doesn't really make any difference what the title is, and it will keep her happy.

Asdis and May had shared experiences of enduring. Endurance suggests persistence and prevailing in the face of forces that discourage the pursuit of endeavors or aspirations that are misaligned with the norms and structure of the organization. Endurance can be draining but it has a hidden positive aspect—the capacity to stay focused on forward momentum despite pressures. May and Anna endured by the force of their commitments and values but at a cost to themselves. What they needed was to redirect their capacity for focus on desired goals in environments that are supportive and enlivening while veering away, as much as possible, from those environments that are draining.

Discovery and Transformation of Habitual Patterns of Thinking

For both Asdis and May, the WLS experience played an important role in the transformation of the self-affirming, context-obliged thinking that shaped depleted behavior. Recall that, prior to the WLS, Asdis had already made the shift to a self-affirming and context-aligned pattern of thinking. May, on the other hand, had not. In the case of Asdis, the WLS affirmed the changes she had made and strengthened her commitment to her own choices, strengthening and reinforcing inspired leadership. In the case of May, the WLS placed her in the company of other women with whom she could identify. This identification was powerful even if May did not appear to explore the implications for her during or immediately after the WLS. May's insights were latent and dormant, only to resurface and inform her thinking in transformative ways years later, after she left her demanding and depleting role as project leader.

Context-aligned thinking is where the individual makes a conscious choice about how they will expend their time and mental and emotional energy to achieve fulfillment in the totality of her life, both work and personal. For both Asdis and May, a significant insight from the WLS came from the recognition of the personal costs of unchecked and uncritical expenditure of energy on context-obliged thinking. Recall from earlier the decisive and powerful language Asdis used to describe how she saw the costs: "We're not able to sell our souls for being the little stars at the center," and "I need to have energy when I come home, or in general for my heart, my soul. I think it's better this way, and I'm quite happy with it." For her, "selling our souls" was not just about the choice to behave a certain way—competitive or collaborative. Rather, it was fundamentally about deciding to be motivated by the desire to be fulfilled rather than strive for or be incentivized by external recognition. Based on these convictions, Asdis began to actively take steps to design her job with the goal of maximizing the potential for working collaboratively with others.[5]

In Asdis' case, given that the shift to context-aligned thinking and practice occurred prior to the WLS, a question that is relevant to this study is what, if any, impact resulted from participating in the leadership development activities. It is fair to say that the transformative effect of the WLS was not in catalyzing a shift in Asdis' thought process. Rather, the WLS affirmed the changes Asdis had made from working through the challenging workplace experiences described earlier. Affirmation is a subtle, but very important dimension of reinforcing and sustaining positive change. For many of the WLS alumnae, feedback from other participants, women they admired and respected, relieved self-doubt and fostered confidence and commitment in their choices. This was particularly important for depleted leaders because their desire to pursue fulfillment over external recognition and accolades put them in a position where their chosen course was out of sync with the motivations and behaviors deemed "normal" or desirable in their environments. Asdis recounts the impact of affirmation from the course:

ASDIS: The feedback we got from our teams after some role-playing exercises that we did was memorable. That was very useful.

INTERVIEWER: How was that useful?

ASDIS: Well, it more or less confirmed what I knew about myself, but you see it differently when others tell you about it.

INTERVIEWER: What were those things?

ASDIS: Well, I remember clearly that what came out of it is that I'm potentially a very good leader, but I'm to some extent impatient, and I show my emotions very clearly. So, one moment I can be the one who motivates the whole team. Another moment, when I'm thinking we're not doing fine, I would just show it, and this can offend people in the team because I would say, "Okay, this is not what I want to do." So it's helpful to know yourself better in order to be able, a bit more, to anticipate.

INTERVIEWER: Anticipate what?

ASDIS: Different situations in work, and kind of plan your behavior or try to adapt your behavior in advance. Actually, something that is coming into my mind right now is that when I left (European country), I was really in a leader position. I got a lot of credit, and I was in a very good moment of my young career. I left, and when I arrived in (Southern African country) I didn't speak the language. I learned the language, and then I had another child. I started to work in the American school, I was overqualified for the job, but it was okay because I was happy to do something and to communicate in the local language and get to know people. But then when I realized that my first son had a serious health issue—I really personally lost my self-confidence at that time. So when I started to work in my center, I wasn't at all in this self-confident position I was when I left (European country). When I was in (European country), I was quite sure I was able to lead, have responsibilities in project coordination or in my field of expertise. Then I lost this feeling, and the course helped me to give me again this idea or this ambition or this feeling that I'm able to do this again.

INTERVIEWER: That's a powerful story.

ASDIS: How I lead, it's not really changed, but I've had confirmation from the course that what I did very intuitively before the course—there were a lot of good things in there. This was very much confirmed now with the things I learned on knowledge-sharing. So I tried to continue, for example, to trust my intuition. So, now I trust myself more. I am happy with my own choices. I don't see it as something that could be a weakness.

For May, the impact of the WLS was more complicated. Either at the time of the WLS or afterwards, May was in the position of leading several research teams experimenting with participatory research methods. I have already explained how she endured scrutiny from her boss in leading these teams. Given the vigilance that May had to maintain to defend the activities of these teams, she did not have the luxury to relax and explore the full implications of what she had learned in the WLS. Thus, the impact of the WLS on her can be divided into two periods: acquisition of knowledge and skills during and immediately after the WLS, and the surfacing of insights from the WLS years later, after her term as project leader was successfully completed, effecting a shift to context-aligned thinking.

In the first period, May was keyed into what she could learn from the WLS that had direct relevance for the research teams she was leading. May recalled an exercise during the WLS that demonstrated the value of leveraging diversity in a team. The exercise showed, in a very concrete and verifiable way, the benefit of assembling people with different skills and perspectives and drawing out and using these skills and perspectives to achieve a goal. This matter was at the heart of participatory action research, and May took note of that. She envisioned how she could modify and use this exercise in her discussions at work in order to shift the understandings and perspectives of her boss and others who were skeptical about what she and her teams felt was a valuable research approach. She also felt that the verifiable nature of the exercise would be palatable to the scientific audience she wanted to address. Here she describes this "Aha" moment:

> The course reinforced the value of diversity. For years I've felt that there was a huge value in diversity, but in that course, they did some team things that showed the value of actually incorporating input from a variety of points of view. I do remember there was one exercise where there was some real evidence of the added value from incorporating diversity. And so, I think that reinforced my existing feelings about that and also maybe gave me some concrete evidence that I could present to other people when I was arguing for our very inclusive approach.

As helpful as the WLS exercise was in her persuasion efforts, the preceding example shows that the WLS contributed to May's knowledge acquisition, but not to her transformative learning. It was not until after she had successfully served out her term as project leader that May appears to have reflected on the full implications of what she had learned in the WLS. This turned out to be transformative. Freed from the onerous responsibility of leading the research teams under scrutiny, the dormant insights from the WLS emerged as she contemplated what she should do next. She recalled one of the things that struck her the most during the WLS, namely that being with other women she was able to recognize their shared concerns:

> I think the opportunity to get together with other women and to share some of the difficulties they're having is really, really valuable. A lot of the women were saying that, in the group I was with, they had felt that they were all alone in their center and nobody else had these problems and here they came and ran across a whole bunch of women having very similar problems. The course gives you some ways for addressing these things.

These shared concerns were relevant as May began to contemplate her next move. As she explains below, after her four-year term leading the difficult project, several colleagues encouraged her to consider applying for a Director General position. Although this was a testament to their confidence in her leadership, she was acutely aware of the cost of assuming a formal leadership role. May was proud of what she had done for her center, but she was drained by the politics and the scrutiny she had endured. It was at this point that she could recall the transformative insights from the WLS. This appears to have been the catalyst for May's shifting from a habitual context-obliged to a new context-aligned pattern of thinking. She attributes to insights from the WLS:

MAY: After being a team leader of this project for four years—I was very happy to stop being a formal leader. I still do a lot of leadership things informally. I didn't apply for a program director position. I'm not applying for a DG position, although people keep saying, "You should apply for that," because I don't want to spend all my time in meetings and with the level of stress that you have and with the demands from above and the demands from below so that you have no life except work. I think what really needs to be done is that the context needs to change if you want to get women to be more involved in formal leadership. I talked to a lot of people who are my age, a lot of senior women who are very capable. The idea of being a DG and sitting in those formal meetings, all dressed up in formal clothes, talking about non-substance, being political, just sounds so objectionable to me.

INTERVIEWER: Do you think that that kind of professional life is less attractive to women as compared with men?

MAY: Well, I think women have a lot of demands that men don't have, like children and, like in my case now, aging parents. So those kinds of demands are not quite as strong for men, and I think there may be something about women's leadership and management styles that maybe doesn't fit quite as well. For instance, the idea of having power has no draw for me at all. I want to have autonomy, I want to be able to do the things I want to do, but I have no interest whatsoever in being able to tell other people what to do. I suppose that, if you like that, and I think a lot of men do, maybe. Maybe they don't. But anyway, that's the stereotype. I mean, in my case, I think that my management style is good, and I think that it comes up with good results. I think we got some very interesting stuff from the project I led, and I think the people that I'm leading now in this informal way through a kind of mentoring are doing very well, so I think my contribution can be very good. But I'm not willing to make the sacrifice to be in one of those formal positions, partly because I think your ability to do those positive things is reduced because you're so busy doing this formalistic political stuff.

INTERVIEWER: Politics is everywhere, though, right?

MAY: It doesn't have to be your whole life. Our DG spends all of his time traveling around from one meeting to another trying to get money. Now, that is not an interesting life to me. I don't want to do that. What I would like to do is talk with people and figure out the best strategy to get to the Millennium Development Goals or whatever you want to go for, but some real substantive purpose. But they have no time for substantive stuff. I just wanted to let you know about the fact that I was not seeking more leadership. I think that has to do with my personal experience within the course, really.

Transformative insights in the WLS course were critical for Asdis and May, albeit in different ways. Asdis received validation and affirmation that the choices she had made prior to the WLS were good ones, this strengthened and bolstered her resolve and strengthened her commitment to context-aligned thinking. May appears not to have explored the implications of the one topic that really hit home for her—the difficulties women had in the WLS attending to both their personal and work lives. She had to see through the successful implementation of the participatory action research project that she was leading before she could allow herself to do this. However, once this project was completed and she began to think about next steps, this issue and particularly the impactful discussions that the WLS alumnae had on managing the demands of work and home, appears to have surfaced and influenced her thinking and decision. In the next section we will discuss what inspired behaviors looked like in the context of Asdis' and May's stories.

Behaviors of Inspired Leadership

The notion of being inspired pertains to a sense of becoming energized, encouraged, galvanized, and excited to do something. Inspiration came from depleted leaders' clarity on what they wanted in the totality of their lives, not just in the domain of work. They wanted to be enlivened by work and at work, and they wanted to feel alert and enlivened in their relationships at home and within themselves. This context-aligned thinking led May and Asdis to seek out opportunities that would engage them in this holistic manner. For Asdis, this meant finding a way to work collaboratively while, for May, using her relational skills was important. For both women, there was the recognition that, how they spent their time at work would impact their personal lives and overall sense of well-being. These were choices motivated by the desire for personal fulfillment. This new outlook demonstrated a fundamental shift towards making decisions on the basis of a holistic consideration for priorities of work and life. This is quite different from the idea of balance which does not entail making choices on the basis of avowed priorities but rather fulfilling external expectations and/or avoiding external recrimination.

Asdis Receiving Recognition

As the reader may recall, prior to the WLS, Asdis had successfully implemented her first project which entailed building a website featuring the various research agendas in her center. While she had specifically disliked the competitive relationship with IT on this project, she had been gratified by the collaborative relationships she had established with the research teams, and she was proud of the resulting product. Later, she had found a way to continue to work in a collaborative mode by learning about the entirely new area of knowledge-sharing and had successfully established a network of contacts as well as developed tools that researchers in her center could use to disseminate their work. This project allowed her to do what she loved—build collaborative relationships resulting in products that met the needs of key constituents in her organization—while avoiding what she disliked—politics and competition. Her work on these two projects earned her the respect and trust of her boss who was increasingly prepared to entrust her with more responsibilities and the opportunity to work in the collaborative mode in which she excelled.

Coincidentally and fortuitously, in the course of working on the knowledge-sharing project, Asdis met and developed a relationship with an internationally recruited consultant. She described this individual as a mentor who greatly encouraged her. This individual mentored Asdis and publicly gave her credit for the success of the knowledge-sharing pilot project. Having an internationally recruited champion was very helpful in changing others' stereotypical perception of her as a national staff with less-specialized skill. The consultant's endorsement and her boss' growing confidence slowly paved a pathway for Asdis to continue to take on more interesting challenges, working in collaborative mode.

An opportunity for continued growth arose when Asdis' boss told her that he had been approached to have his unit lead a knowledge-sharing project for the CGIAR as a whole. This initiative was perfectly suited to Asdis' goals. It presented her with the opportunity to work collaboratively and continue using her skills while also stretching them. Additionally, her boss said that if her center got the project, she would be the person to lead it. However, initially things did not work out as she hoped. The center got the project, but there was a feeling at the higher levels that it should be led by an internationally recruited "expert" rather than by a nationally recruited staff person. Fortunately, at the completion of the first phase of the project, Asdis got her second shot to lead it. This time, her boss stuck up for her, and said, "It's obvious that you will coordinate it. We don't need an international staff. You can do it." She gladly accepted the opportunity.

May's Recall of Transformative Insight

As described in the previous section, when May completed her four-year term as project leader and began looking ahead to what to do next, the latent insights from the WLS became salient. These insights had to do with the difficulties and challenges that women in the WLS had with balancing their roles within the home and at work. May, who had elder parents to care for, reflected on the work-life demands and struggles of the other WLS alumnae. After her four-year term as project leader were completed, she decided that her next career choice would not be shaped by concern for upward mobility but by the goal of achieving autonomy and doing what she valued and what she found fulfilling.

Next she describes her effort mentoring one particularly talented but difficult female scientist.

MAY: I'm not the team leader, but I still have a cadre of junior scientists that I'm sort of mentoring, and there's one that's so difficult. She's so capable, very organized, very proactive, very motivated, but she irritates people. She snaps at them, and it's so disruptive. I'm trying to figure out how to give her that feedback that I'm so terrible at giving, you know. Say, "Listen, you've got to be more patient with people." And I haven't been able to really say it yet the way I want to say it to her. She's very easily offended, and I don't want her to lose her commitment and her enthusiasm for what she's doing, and I still haven't figured out a way to do both of those two things, you know?

INTERVIEWER: Can you explain that more?

MAY: It's a little more tricky in this (Southeast Asian) context because most of the time they're very careful of each others' feelings and talk politely, whereas Americans can have flare-ups and get over it. In (Southeast Asian country) in general, if you have a fight with somebody, that's the end of your relationship. So, that's a problem. It's also a problem in her case because she irritates somebody and then that's the end of their relationship. You know, they're supposed to be on a team together. Now were I in the American context, I could say to her, "I've just been talking with these other people and you've really offended them by doing this particular thing and I really think you need to be careful about that." If I said that to an American, depending on the individual of course, to a lot of them that would be perfectly fine. If I said that to her, she would be very offended.

INTERVIEWER: So, what would she find offensive in that?

MAY: You would not be showing whole-hearted support for her, which is what she would like. I suppose there's more of an expectation of people to be kind to other people. She probably doesn't realize how objectionable she's behaving, and if I say that to her, it would upset her for two reasons. One because I'm not accepting her 100% and two, because she feels that she should be good at treating people carefully, and she's not good at it, so that would make her upset also.

INTERVIEWER: How can you convey your concern in giving feedback in (Southeast Asian country)?

MAY: That's exactly the dilemma I've had. I've been trying to figure out how can I express to her that I care about her and I want her to succeed because she has a lot of potential, but I haven't figured out how to do it.

May's description here demonstrates not only the care with which she approached the task of developing the talented woman, but also how demanding the task is. From her description, May took her time to fully assess the situation and contemplate the options she had. For instance, she considered the expectations of the "problematic" person.

One expectation had to do with the relationship with May, namely that May would need to convey her full support, while also giving negative feedback. May also demonstrated empathy by imagining what this person might feel in response to any negative feedback, especially given the cultural norms of kindness and politeness. She made an astute and very subtle observation that this woman may experience conflict and dissonance because she may actually see herself as kind. May did not want to upset her, not only because this would hurt her feelings, but also because it was more likely to shut her down than make her receptive. May considers the cultural context and the indirect methods used to give negative feedback and determined that this was incongruent with her own style and values. Despite the demanding nature of mentoring the problematic staff, described previously, the biggest difference was that now May was not obliged to do it. She mentored others not because others did not want to deal with difficult people, but out of her own choice and with the desire and ability to provide useful feedback.

Summary

The WLS facilitated a subtle but very powerful shift in depleted leaders' habitual pattern of self-affirming and context-obliged thinking, feeling, and acting. Depleted leaders were effective in that they not only achieved the goals they laid out for themselves but did so by enlisting others' support. In fact, it was their ability to work well with others in the creation and implementation of goals that fostered their effectiveness. However, their stories also suggest that effectiveness is not the only thing we are looking to develop in leaders. In his book, *On Leadership*, Howard Gardner suggested that we also want leaders to develop a moral compass and engage in moral reasoning and action (1990). Beyond this, my analysis of depleted leaders adds to this that we also want leadership to not only be a vehicle of making positive change but also a vehicle for promoting individual well-being and fulfillment. As the stories of depleted leaders showed, although context-obliged thinking motivated them to make valuable contributions to others, it also weighed them down, removed accountability from others, and limited the growth and development of depleted leaders as well as those they sought to serve. As depleted leaders discovered, reacting to others' needs on the basis of obligation alone can become all-consuming and one can lose track of oneself. The WLS gave depleted leaders the opportunity to step back and reflect on this crucial issue. In the case of Asdis, the WLS offered her affirmative feedback that her decision to align her energy expenditure to her priorities—at home and at work—was critical. Although May was not in a position to fully explore the implications of the WLS for her at the time of the course, she was struck by the discussion on women's struggles to address the demands of home and work. These insights were nevertheless powerful and latent, resurfacing once her demanding project came to a successful conclusion. May and Asdis made the transformation to inspired leadership by cultivating and enacting context-aligned thinking. By doing so, they became intentional about the activities into which they would pour their energies. By being intentional, they became inspired—generating energy and enthusiasm—in what they did at work, home, and for themselves.

Notes

1. See Rappaport et al. (2002) for a gendered analysis that shifts the perspective from a rational instrumental preoccupation.
2. See Caproni's (2004) apt critique of the rational instrumental paradigm underlying the work-life balance literature and particularly the prescriptions for how to achieve "balance."
3. See Maslach and Leiter (1997) and Maslach (2015).
4. See Fletcher (1999) for a detailed and insightful gendered analysis of what she calls relational practice.
5. See Wrzesniewski and Dutton (2001) regarding the concept of job crafting, which has to do with the way that individuals use the opportunities and resources available to them to shape their jobs in ways that meet their needs.

References

Caproni, P. J. (2004). Work/life balance: You can't get there from here. *The Journal of Applied Behavioral Science, 40*(2), 208–218.

Debebe, G. (2017). Authentic leadership and talent development: Fulfilling individual potential in sociocultural context. *Advances in Developing Human Resources, 19*(4), 420–438.

Fletcher, J. K. (1999). *Disappearing acts: Gender, power, and relational practice at work*. Boston, MA: MIT Press.

Gardner, H. (1990). *On leadership*. New York, NY: The Free Press.

Luthans, F., Yousseff, C. M., & Avolio, B. J. (2015). *Psychological capital: Developing the human competitive edge*. New York, NY: Oxford University Press.

Maslach, C. (2015). *Burnout: The cost of caring*. Los Altos, CA: Malor Book Publishing.

Maslach, C., & Leiter, M. (1997). *The truth about burnout: How organizations cause personal stress and what to do about it*. New York, NY: John Wiley & Son.

Rappaport, R., Bailyn, L., Fletcher, J. K., & Pruitt, B. H. (2002). *Beyond work-family balance: Advancing gender equity and workplace performance*. San Francisco, CA: Jossey-Bass.

Wrzesniewski, A., & Dutton, J. E. (2001). Crafting a job: Revisioning employees as active crafters of their work. *Academy of Management Review, 26*(2), 179–201.

8 Conclusion

This book has sought to answer three questions related to the impact of the Women's Leadership Series (WLS) of the Consultative Group for International Agricultural Research (CGIAR). These questions are:

- Did the WLS training effect changes in participants' leadership behavior, and if so, what were the nature of these changes?
- Did these changes enable alumnae to exercise leadership more effectively?
- What aspects of the WLS teaching and learning methodology facilitated learning and change, and why were these aspects important?

To answer these questions, I interviewed 24 WLS participants who participated in the week-long training program. The women represented many nationalities, recruitment categories (national, regional, international), disciplines (natural and social sciences), and levels within the organization. Analyzing stories of their leadership experiences prior to the WLS, after the WLS, and their experiences of critical learning during the WLS, I identified four leadership transformations fostered by critical learning in the WLS training. I also argued that these transformations fostered improvements in participants' leadership capacities. My analysis of participants' accounts of their experiences within the WLS also provided insight into how the use of care-practices within the training program fostered psychological safety and facilitated transformational learning. In this final chapter, I summarize these findings and highlight the key contributions of the book.

One contribution of this book is theoretical in nature. In particular, the *dual contingency framework* (Figure 2.1) integrates concepts from several relevant streams of research—leadership effectiveness, transformational learning, habit, and care—to provide an enriched way of thinking about leadership, leadership development, and the learning processes through which leader development occurs. My analysis is particularly sensitive to women's developmental concerns, but there is nothing about the framework that should exclude men. Another contribution of this book is empirical. An aspect of the empirical findings concerning the four transformations of the WLS is incorporated into and *grounds* the dual contingency framework. The contribution of the empirical findings is specifically related to the transformations facilitated by the WLS.

Grounded Dual Contingency Framework

The book has presented a multidisciplinary and multifaceted framework that offers a way of thinking about leadership effectiveness and how people develop as leaders through transformational learning experiences in a classroom setting. This framework was primarily presented in Chapters 1 and 2. Chapter 1 draws on the leadership effectiveness literature to propose a dual contingency framework of leader effectiveness. This framework posits that effective leaders formulate behaviors that account for the dual contingencies of *context* and *authenticity*. Behavior that is inattentive to either of these or relies heavily on consideration of one over the other limits leader effectiveness.

Thus, the dual contingency framework enriches the leadership effectiveness literature by expanding contingency approaches to leader effectiveness. Contingency theories posit that effective leader behaviors are those that are attentive to or appropriate for the demands of context. By incorporating the element of authenticity into this equation of leader effectiveness, the dual contingency model suggests that effective leaders not only seek to understand their environment and the needs and wants of various stakeholders, but they act based on their own priorities as well. These include but are not limited to factors such as values, interests, and aspirations. Thus, effective leadership is a form of *self-expression* in which individuals pursue purposes that are aligned with their sense of self in a way that is appropriate and attentive to external conditions. By doing this, leaders take inspired and energized action and inspire and energize others.

The Differing Paths to Leadership Effectiveness

Chapter 2 further elaborates this framework in two directions. First, it grounds the dual contingency formulation in the analysis derived from the data of the study. Maintaining that effective leaders formulate their leadership behaviors by considering both the demands of the environment and their own inner desires, the interpretive analysis contained in Chapters 4 to 7 has shown that the way that this general idea applies depends on the habitual patterns of thought of the individual involved. The book identified four habitual patterns of thinking, feeling, and acting that limited WLS alumnae leadership efforts prior to the WLS. These patterns produced four types of leadership processes: hidden, inflexible, intuitive, and depleted. For each of these four constraining processes, the

WLS helped alumnae gain awareness of how their leadership challenges stemmed from behaviors based on habitual patterns of thinking and feeling that entailed a problematic attention, or inattention to the demands of either context and/or authenticity. The WLS fostered leadership growth and improved effectiveness by cultivating participant capacity to attend to the dual contingencies in their formulation of leadership behaviors.

Hidden leaders engaged in self-diminishing and context-affirming thinking, a pattern that produced behaviors whose function was to make attributes or characteristics of the self go unnoticed and be easily overlooked. The WLS fostered a transformation to *visible leadership* by effecting a shift towards a new pattern of thought, feeling, and action that I refer to as self-affirming and context-mitigating in which the leader has greater appreciation and trust of previously hidden self-aspects and expresses these more freely.

Inflexible leaders engaged in self-affirming and context-dismissing patterns of thinking and feeling. When met with situations they could not understand, they clung to what they knew, believed, or what had worked for them in the past, dismissing the confusing cues from the environment. The WLS fostered a transformation to *receptive leadership* by effecting a new pattern of thinking that I refer to as self-tempering and context-regarding in which there was relaxation of priors in the face of uncertainty, acknowledgment of the validity of and need to account for both one's own and others' views. This granted receptive leaders the opportunity to learn and more fully account for context.

Except for some areas of chronic difficulty, *intuitive leaders* were generally effective in their leadership efforts. These difficulties arose from intuitive leaders' blind spots or lack of awareness of the principles, assumptions, and ideas upon which they relied to guide their actions. The shift to *deliberate leadership* was characterized by a self-aware and context-discerning thought process in which the capacity to reflect on one's intuitive processes enabled their regulation and the capacity to choose new approaches attuned to the situation and to the self.

For *depleted leaders*, a habitual self-affirming, context-obliged thinking produced behaviors that sapped their energy and enthusiasm. The WLS facilitated a shift to self-affirming and context-aligned thinking that fostered *inspired leadership*, whereby individuals were careful about how they expended their energy, favoring pursuits that allowed them to simultaneously contribute to their organizations and their personal priorities, including their families and themselves.

Creating a Caring Environment for the Transformation of Habitual Patterns

Chapter 2 also enriched the grounded, dual contingency framework by incorporating the notions of *transformational learning* and *care* to explain how the transformation of habitual patterns took place in the WLS. Transformational learning is a process that engages cognition, emotion, and behavior, resulting in insights that are deep and meaningful. Transformative learning produces a paradigm shift that significantly alters how a person perceives, thinks, feels, and behaves. Transformational change in the context of leadership entails a shift in habitual patterns of thinking regarding the dual contingencies of context and authenticity. Although subtle, such shifts can be very significant because, based in schemas, beliefs, and unconscious assumptions, habitual patterns of thinking and feeling frame experiences about the self and context and produce behaviors based on these premises. When habitual patterns are disrupted and schemas modified, sometimes radically, individuals tend to approach a previously problematic situation in an entirely new way.

Transformational learning cannot be planned for or guaranteed. Rather, it is a delicate and subtle process that responds to the willingness of the individual to open up and be vulnerable despite potential risk associated with uncertainty. This occurs when the person feels a sense of psychological safety, that she will not be judged, ridiculed, or punished in any way for the exposure of her true feelings, but rather accepted and gently encouraged to explore her experiences.

We know from the WOT and single-sex education literatures that gender pressure is pervasive and seeps into formal learning contexts, inhibiting psychological safety for women learners. Although mixed-sex environments are particularly problematic for women learners in this regard, single-sex environments can be as well. There is a growing body of research, however, that shows that single-sex settings are promising for women learners if they are designed and delivered in ways that affirm and celebrate women's experiences and values. Affirming environments allow learners to feel relaxed, put down their defenses, and become willing to engage uncertainty.

While the transformational learning literature provides insight into the processes of deep change and highlights the necessity of safety, it does not provide a detailed explanation of the activities that occur to produce this environment. The dual contingency framework therefore incorporates the idea of *care-practice*, a set of activities that are used in facilitating others' growth. The care perspective helped explain the kinds of activities that the WLS participants described and to which they attributed their feeling of safety in the WLS. Chapter 3 described the idea of care and illustrated how it was enacted in the WLS. In particular, the WLS care practices were used to keep the competitive behavioral norms prevalent within the CGIAR centers at bay, and foster an environment in which participants were willing to put down their defenses and allow themselves to be vulnerable. This, in turn, facilitated the expression and exploration of participants' real concerns about their work and life experiences, and this led to greater self-awareness, particularly with regards to the habitual patterns of thinking, feeling, and acting that limited their effectiveness as leaders.

Questions to Consider

The book raises at least three issues that would be fruitful areas of inquiry and further exploration. The first issue is whether the dilemmas and challenges that characterize each of the transformations represent developmental challenges that are part of the leadership journey. The second issue is whether the focus on individual change is enough or whether systemic change is necessary to unleash women's leadership potential. Finally, there is a question of men's leadership development and what relation it might have to that of women.

Dilemmas of the Leadership Journey

Many of us might remember instances when we exhibited the characteristics of all four leadership patterns: hiding, inflexibility, intuitiveness, and depletion. Perhaps this can be explained by the context in which we were attempting to lead. It is also possible that readers identified with some but not all four leadership patterns. And more likely than not, readers may have identified other patterns that have not been captured in this book. This raises the question of whether the pre-WLS leadership stories represent some of the developmental challenges that might be encountered in any leadership development journey. Relatedly, one might wonder whether the transformations represented in the post-WLS patterns of visible, receptive, deliberate, and inspired leadership give some clues about the tasks involved in learning and growing through engaging these developmental challenges.

Assuming for the moment that the four pre-WLS patterns might be challenges commonly encountered in leadership development programs, a question that arises is: What are some of the developmental challenges highlighted in this book? One possibility is to see the four pre-WLS patterns as different ways that people respond to the inherent ambiguity and uncertainty of the environment. Hidden leaders and inflexible leaders displayed two contrasting responses in which, finding the environment overwhelming and threatening, individuals respond by withdrawing from uncertainty and clinging to their comfort zones. Hidden leaders tried to direct attention away from themselves, and they avoided engaging the environment by concealing or cloaking self-aspects they feared might be liabilities. Inflexible leaders did the opposite, clinging to what they knew and what had worked for them in the past and attempting to bend the environment to their will. Neither withdrawal nor control worked, however, and both responses to environmental flux and ambiguity blocked growth, development, and leader effectiveness.

In contrast, intuitive and depleted leaders had more permeable boundaries vis-à-vis their environments. In both cases, the individuals attempted to read their environments and had a sense of clarity and confidence about what they wanted and needed to do, as well as confidence in their capacity to get things done. However, they too encountered difficulties with how they managed the boundaries between themselves and their environment. Intuitive leaders lacked awareness of the prism or lens through which they viewed the environment and therefore did not understand that the difficulties they encountered arose when their preferred way of seeing did not give them an accurate read on their environment. The lens or prism through which they viewed the environment was limited and presented a blind spot in certain circumstances. Depleted leaders, on the other hand, had difficulty filtering out unwelcome needs and demands from the environment. By responding to others' needs out of a sense of obligation, they drained energy from their personal lives and failed to find ways to more selectively participate in their organizations.

The transformations to visible, receptive, deliberate, and inspired leadership give some clues about the developmental tasks in solving each of these problems. It is hoped that the accounts of the WLS alumnae's learning, growth, and transformation can give individuals struggling with similar concerns a way to think about their challenges and their resolution. It is also hoped that these accounts can provide insights to individuals responsible for supporting others' growth.

Change the System or Change the Individual?

The WLS program focused on individual-level change, effecting growth in CGIAR women to enable them to better navigate the many challenges they encountered within their jobs and to better exercise leadership. The G&D program where the WLS is housed had other programs and activities that were specifically focused on organizational change. These have not been the focus of this book, but there was a clear recognition that addressing gender pressures required working on both individual and structural change. The G&D's individual and systemic change efforts were focused on a dual agenda of enabling the organization to tap into the immense leadership potential of women and to give women a sense of effectiveness, satisfaction, and well-being through the exercise of leadership. The WLS participants were aware of the scope of the G&D's activities. While they knew that they had a part to play in bringing about change in their organizations, several mentioned the importance of the on-going organizational change efforts. Thus, the WLS and its impacts are best regarded as just one element of a larger change effort.

How About the Men?

Throughout this book, I have specifically addressed women's leadership development, and this has necessitated investigation of the notion of gender. But it is critical to remember that the notion of gender applies to men as well. In fact, quite a few WLS participants said that, while they benefited greatly from the training, they felt that men also needed a similar learning experience. I interpreted this to mean that WLS alumnae were not recommending that men receive standard leadership training but one centered on giving them the space to engage in transformational learning.

Ironically, this may entail crafting an environment that keeps the unique gender pressures that men experience at bay. The pressures of masculinity can be just as oppressive for men as it is for women, although this is rarely considered. The pressures of masculinity might in fact be particularly pernicious as these are what are expected and rewarded for men. Furthermore, the pressures that men and women face would obviously be different, and this may influence the habitual patterns that men develop.

Despite these differences, it is likely that men too need a safe space crafted by caring practices that free them of the need to comply with hegemonic notions of masculinity and allow them to take off their masks and be vulnerable. This is likely to pose new and interesting challenges but responding to these with care practices would be in order. The questions are what form these care practices might take in light of the emphasis on masculinity in mens' socialization. Nonetheless, care is a universal activity from which men and women have benefited and in which men and women participate. Thus, the problem of creating a safe and caring environment for men raises interesting questions about vulnerability and masculinity and the expansion of men's possibilities.

Final Words

This book was written in a spirit of inquiry into the leadership dilemmas of women. My hope is that the grounded, dual contingency model of women's leadership development will be useful to both leadership researchers and leadership development practitioners. The paths of transformation described in the book are indicative of the struggle women leaders face, and the practices that go into making these transformations possible deserve greater attention. Women are a critical organizational resource and tapping into their leadership potential is a universal challenge. I hope this book contributes to effectively meeting this challenge.

Appendix
Research Methodology

In order to investigate the impact of the WLS on the development of women's leadership in the CGIAR, the goal of this research was to obtain rich descriptive information related to the leadership experiences of participants before the WLS, their experiences during the WLS course itself, and their leadership experiences after the course. Here I provide more detail on the research methodology and the steps taken to assure the trustworthiness of the findings as well as the anonymity of interview participants.

Qualitative Research

Qualitative research is grounded in a set of assumptions and purposes that distinguish it from quantitative research. These include studying individuals in natural settings, discovering the meanings individuals construct to make sense of their experiences, and attending to process and context (Bogdan & Bilken, 2007; Lincoln & Guba, 2005). Unlike quantitative research where research begins with hypotheses and a priori categories, qualitative research begins with questions, and categories are discovered through an iterative process of data collection and analysis (Glaser & Strauss, 1967; Strauss & Corbin, 1996). Consistent with these purposes, I used semi-structured interviews to discover the impact of the WLS training from the perspective of participants. Although external perspectives were not obtained, alumnae perspectives on the impact of the WLS provide insight into the internal changes that are imperceptible to outsiders but form the foundation for noticeable behavior changes. In particular, examining the WLS impact from the perspective of participants provided understanding of and insight into the varieties of habitual patterns of thinking and acting that inhibited their leadership effectiveness prior to the WLS, as well as the ways in which leadership training fostered transformations of earlier patterns of thought and fostered new patterns and behaviors.

All researchers need to establish the trustworthiness of their findings. They must be mindful, however, to use evaluation criteria that are consistent with the paradigmatic assumptions of their research. There are three possible paradigms available in the conduct of qualitative research (Lincoln & Guba, 2005). The first paradigm, post-positivist, represents a modified positivist view in which researchers believe that, while there is an objective reality that is knowable, pure objectivity is impossible. In the second paradigm, interpretivist-constructionist, researchers believe that reality is multiple, co-constructed in the interactions taking place in different contexts and in fluid circumstances. Third, critical-ideological researchers agree with the interpretive view that there are multiple realities, but they attribute this to individuals' differing positions within the social structure. Although qualitative researchers may be primarily guided by one of these paradigms, in practice, the research they undertake may be guided by hybrids of paradigmatic assumptions.

This book is most closely aligned with the interpretive view in that its aim was to understand the impact of the WLS from participants' point of view. Consequently, I sought to create a conversational process in which the interviewee felt engaged and safe enough to describe her experiences and meanings in as much detail as possible. This enabled me to gain an understanding of how and why she saw something as she did. While I am aware that my analysis and interpretation of this information will be shaped by my own frame of reference, I was concerned about "getting it right." However, this did not mean correcting for the interviewee's or my own biases, as is common in quantitative research, but making sure that interviewees agreed that I had captured the details of their story and their intended meanings correctly and that other experts agreed that the description is rich and the interpretation in sync with and contributing to current knowledge in the field. After describing the research setting, interviewees, data collection, and data analysis procedures, this section will conclude with the steps taken to ensure anonymity of interviewees and establish the trustworthiness of the research findings based on the paradigmatic assumptions outlined.

Recruiting Interviewees via Web-Survey and Characteristics of Web-Survey Respondents

The web-survey was administered to alumnae who participated in the WLS between 1995 and 2005. In this time period, approximately 300 women had participated in the WLS courses. Given the global dispersion of WLS alumnae, potential interviewees were identified by means of a web-based survey.

Approximately one quarter of all WLS alumnae, 76 women, responded to the web-survey. Of the 50 who agreed to be interviewed, 24 followed through with signed consent forms and were interviewed. Thus, approximately 8 percent of WLS alumnae were interviewed regarding their leadership experiences prior to and after the WLS, as well as their critical learning moments during the WLS courses. Of the 76 web-survey respondents, 65, or 85.5 percent, were still employed in a CCIAR Center. As for those who agreed to be interviewed; all but one was employed by the CGIAR at the time of the study.

Web-survey respondents were asked to indicate the relevance and impact of the WLS training on their current leadership effectiveness. In terms of relevance, 85.5 percent of respondents indicated that the WLS course was "very relevant" to the leadership issues they encountered in their work, and 14.5 percent felt it was "somewhat relevant." Assessments of course impact among web-survey respondents were more varied than with interviewees, with 56 percent indicating the course had a "very positive" impact, 39.5 percent indicating "somewhat positive" impact, and the remaining 3.9 percent indicating "neither positive nor negative" impact. This breakdown compares to 96 percent of interviewees indicating that the WLS course had a "very positive" impact on their leadership effectiveness. Not surprisingly, interviewees' experience does not reflect all the possible learning experiences of WLS alumnae, but none of the web respondents reported a negative impact of the WLS.

Characteristics of Interviewees

Interviewees represented many nationalities from six regions of the world: East Asia and Pacific (25%), North America (20.8%), Europe and Central Asia (25%), Sub-Saharan Africa (12.5%), South Asia (4.2%), and Latin America and the Caribbean (12.5%). Research centers in the Middle East and North Africa were not represented due to non-response from those regions of the world.

On average, interviewees worked for nine years within their research Centers, with a range from two to 29 years. The interviewees came to their current roles having had a variety of experiences, including working in other CGIAR Centers, war zones, villages, and community organizing. Interviewees' job titles were: program leader/theme leader, scientist/researcher, and manager/administrator. Program and theme leaders have a Ph.D. and a minimum of 20 years' experience, including significant management and leadership experience. Their roles include: developing institutional strategy and policy, identifying and pursuing funding opportunities, preparing and managing large budgets, negotiating on behalf of the center, and participating in major decisions of the management team. Program leaders manage a major scientific unit of the organization, including leading the unit's research and training programs, staffing, fundraising, financial management, and negotiating on behalf of the organization on sensitive and contentious issues. Scientist/researchers are individuals trained in either a physical or social science discipline. Their role is to develop, lead, and carry out science projects as well as initiate and sustain partnerships with the center's partners. At senior levels, scientists are also responsible for negotiating with partners and providing expert scientific leadership on key research themes across the center. Finally, manager/administrators may carry a range of titles including finance manager, personnel officer, and quality manager. Administrators have a university degree or equivalent professional status awarded by a professional institute and at least eight years relevant experience. They perform a wide range of roles including: offering expert advice within their discipline, having a leading role in reviewing, developing, refining, and implementing significant administrative policies and practices and leading and supervising a subset of corporate administrative services (CGIAR internal document).

Data Collection

The author conducted all interviews. A semi-structured interview protocol exploring three broad areas was used. These areas were, participants' pre-WLS leadership experiences, post-WLS leadership experiences, and critical learning within the WLS. The protocol contained a set of questions to start the conversation on topics related to each of these areas. But, as is common in qualitative interviewing, follow-up questions picked up on issues and themes arising in each interview to deeply explore the respondent's point of view. For instance, to start the conversation about pre-WLS experiences, I asked participants to think of one or more problems/issues they were facing in their positions prior to the WLS training. Then I asked them to explain each of the problems/issues one at a time. As they talked about each of these, I followed up with questions about what their goals were in the situation; what they did to achieve their goals; what happened in the course of these efforts; what, if any, obstacles they encountered and how they managed them; what, if any, types of assistance they received; and whether they felt they were successful in achieving their goal and why. As they addressed these initial questions, I followed up with spontaneous questions to gain clarity on topics of interest as well as pursue lines of inquiry the interviewee opened up. I went through a similar set of questions with respect to their post-WLS leadership experiences. I also posed initial questions about the types of learning activities they engaged in during the WLS, the most memorable of these, and what if any learnings they felt they gained. Again I followed up on these questions with more specific ones to get detail on what their most memorable learning experiences were and their reactions to the learning.

One alumnae interview took place in-person and lasted for five and a half hours. The remainder of the interviews were conducted by telephone and lasted between one hour and three and a half hours with an average length of two hours. All interviews were taped and transcribed. In order to maintain the anonymity of information sources: all names used in describing stories are fictitious, names of projects, system-wide initiatives or programs are not identified, centers of alumnae are not named in any of the stories, years in which the participants took the WLS courses are not indicated, some pieces of information from the stories have been altered although the events and meaning of the story has remained unchanged, nationalities are either not included or disguised, position titles have been omitted or changed, and years of employment in a center are not included.

Data collection and in-process analysis were concurrent processes. Although each interview was taped, I also kept notes during the interview to identify issues that needed further development or clarification, as well as to identify emergent issues that needed to be explored. I also developed an interview summary sheet that pertained to key issues from the interview and this was filled out immediately after each interview. Information contained in this document included participants' overall assessment of the usefulness of the WLS, reasons given for their assessment, critical learning during the WLS, and a very brief summary of the leadership stories told by participants. These summaries were continually consulted to write on-going memos and identify themes emerging during the interview process (Emerson et al., 1995). Written after each interview, memos also identified questions that needed to be explored in subsequent interviews (Bogdan & Bilken, 2007; Emerson et al., 1995). No new issues and themes emerged after 17 interviews, but interviews continued through 24 alumnae interviews to ensure data saturation (Bogdan & Bilken, 2007). At this point, data collection came to a close, and a second phase of post-data analysis began.

Analytic Procedures and Analytic Categories

The analytic procedures of grounded theory methodology were used to reduce the data and identify the core themes of the research (Glaser & Strauss, 1967). Grounded theory methodology refers to an approach to developing theoretical ideas from the data. At this point, the goal was to reduce the data and achieve inclusive and local integration (Weiss, 1994). Inclusive integration pertains to the identification of a core or overarching theme that captures all or significant portions of the data corpus (Weiss, 1994). Local integration pertains to the identification of components or sub-themes into which the overarching theme can be categorized (Weiss, 1994).

The collection and analysis of leadership stories was a concurrent process with leadership stories extracted and summarized immediately after each interview. In addition, interviews were compared, emerging themes identified and subsequently, thematic categories were identified and elaborated. As new themes were identified, new theoretical memos were written, and subsequent interviews were compared to emergent themes to determine if there were indeed new categories.

All interviews were transcribed. Analysis refers to the process of working with data, systematically reading through field notes, interview transcripts, archival materials, and the like to group conceptually similar data together (Bogdan & Bilken, 2007). After the data collection process was completed, these interviews were subjected to an intensive and iterative analysis process. In the first cycle of analysis, I read through all the transcripts and memos written during the data collection process a few times (Weiss, 1994; Emerson et al., 1995). I began with a process of open coding and concurrently wrote memos about the emergent codes. Through these activities, I generated the preliminary list of first-order categories. I also continued writing analytic memos until I had three competing, data-driven ideas for a possible second-order thematic category.

The next task was to assess the fit of these first and second-order categories to the emerging ideas about the data. The first idea concerned confidence gained from training, the second was women-only training environment, and the third was leadership transformation. At this point, I assessed the fit of the codes identified during open coding to the three thematic categories, writing short comparative memos in an effort to answer the question of which thematic category best captured the first-order codes. Eventually I dropped the idea of confidence, and determined that the remaining two themes addressed two related but different questions. The theme of leadership transformations addressed the question of the impact of the WLS, while the theme of women-only training addressed the question of how the transformations were cultivated in the training environment.

The process of relating the first-order categories to the leadership transformation theme led me to identify six leadership transformation sub-categories. These sub-categories were used to code the transcripts, and in this process two additional sub-categories were added, resulting in the final eight contrasting leadership transformation pairs. The categories of hidden, inflexible, intuitive, and depleted leadership pertain to pre-WLS leadership stories, while the categories of visible, receptive, deliberate, and inspired leadership pertain to post-WLS leadership stories. The idea of women-only training was revised with further refinement and reconceptualization. I settled on the idea of creating a safe environment for women's transformational learning through gender-sensitive teaching and learning practices. Relating the first-order categories to this theme led me to five caring teaching and learning practices: disruptive physical cues, building an inclusive and accepting environment, caring norms, relaxed learning, and staying in touch.

Next, excerpt files were created for each of the contrasting leadership transformation pairs as well as the themes relating to gender-sensitive teaching and learning practices. Excerpt files are collections of data from many interviews that relate to the idea captured in a category code (Weiss, 1994). Creating excerpt files required grouping stories with the same code labels together. The result of this process was eight excerpt files, one for each leadership type: hidden, visible, inflexible, receptive, attenuated, expanded, discouraged, and inspired. I also created five excerpt files for the caring practices: disruptive physical cues, building an inclusive and accepting environment, caring norms, relaxed learning, and staying in touch. Data in these files were then subjected to line-by-line coding. Here the first-order code labels identified in earlier analysis were used to develop a coding scheme within each file.

In addition to the paired leader types and caring practices, another sub-category of leadership transformation was critical learning. Data in this category pertained to stories of memorable learning moments in the WLS. The data in the excerpt file for the critical learning sub-category were categorized by leader type and subjected to further coding using labels corresponding to the transformational learning process: articulating a leadership dilemma, meaning-making, achieving a transformative insight, and connecting this insight to real-world practice.

My analysis of pre-WLS and post-WLS leadership types showed that critical learning during the WLS contributed to the four leadership transformations. A key question was whether these transformations facilitated improvements in leadership practice. To answer this question, I revisited the leadership effectiveness literature, identifying dimensions of leadership effectiveness: behavior, authenticity, context, and trait. The leadership stories of the WLS contained the first three of these elements. Thus, in my next round of analysis, I coded the pre-WLS and post-WLS leadership stories using labels associated with these theoretical constructs. The context code was applied to segments of text that related to the situational factors an individual felt were important to take into account in the leadership situation and how they thought about these factors. The authenticity code was applied to text in which the individual identified her personal considerations such as values and interests that shaped her preferences in a situation. The behavior code was applied to text where a person describes their actions in light of their thoughts about contextual factors and authenticity considerations. The third order codes in Figure 2.1, pertaining to the thought patterns associated with the four paired leadership transformations, were derived from this analytic process, and help frame the findings in relation to the leadership effectiveness literature. The grounded theory, dual contingency model of women's leadership effectiveness was the result of my data analysis.

A similar theoretically informed process of analysis took place as it related to the category of creating a safe learning environment for women. As I was reading and re-reading the data related to this theme I came across several references to the idea of being cared for. This led me to the care literature where I discovered that the empirical categories of my data fit prior work and conceptualization of care and care-practice. At this point, I reframed the category of "creating safety for women through gender-sensitive teaching and learning practices" to "creating a safe learning environment for women." I then proceeded to frame the five sub-themes related to this idea to the relevant ideas derived from the care literature, by distinguishing between care-giving that involved arrangement of the physical environment for care-giving and providing care in interactions.

Anonymity of Information Sources

Several measures have been taken to maintain the anonymity of information sources. Because of the small number of administrators and instructors among the interviewees, it was not possible to maintain their anonymity. However, after discussing this with them, both administrators and instructors indicated that the lack of anonymity was not problematic. The steps taken to ensure the anonymity of alumnae, and to some extent administrators, are as follows:

- All names used in describing stories are fictitious;
- Names of projects, system-wide initiatives or programs are not identified;
- Centers of alumnae are not named in any of the stories;
- Years in which the participants took the Leadership or Negotiation Course are not indicated;
- Some pieces of information from the stories have been altered although the meaning of the story has not been changed;
- Nationality has not been included in a story along with other identifying facts;
- Position titles have been omitted or changed;
- Years of employment in a center are not included.

Establishing Trustworthiness of the Research

In establishing the validity or trustworthiness of their research, qualitative and quantitative researchers utilize criteria and strategies consistent with their paradigmatic assumptions. Quantitative researchers are additionally concerned with reliability but, because interpretive qualitative researchers do not assume that there is a stable and measurable reality, the notion of reliability, which assumes this, does not play a role in establishing trustworthiness. Post-positivists establish the validity of their research by taking measures to reduce and account for biases that can distort results. In contrast, because interpretivist-constructivists believe that reality is fluid and emergent, shaped by interactions and context, the researcher's task is not to render an objective account of a fixed reality but to understand the meanings created in interactions in particular contexts. To establish trustworthiness, the interpretive researcher seeks to ensure that he or she has interpreted the data correctly from the point of view of respondents.

This paper is primarily based on interpretive assumptions where the goal is discovering the multiplicity of interviewee meanings and perspectives and accurately portraying them. To assess my findings relative to these aims, I draw on Guba's (1981) three criteria for assessing qualitative research: credibility, dependability, and confirmability. Credibility, the most important criterion for assessing a qualitative study, has to do with the truth-value of the findings, determining whether the qualitative study got it right. Establishing credibility implicates not only the final product of the research findings but also the data collection process. The second criterion of dependability requires that the researcher explains variation in findings. Explanations may focus on changes in the interviewee's circumstances, the researcher's deepening understanding, or that findings capture the range (and not just the average) experience. The final criterion, confirmability, refers to the management of researcher and researchers may attempt to manage their subjectivity by means such as semi-structured interviews, expert review, member checks, or reflective journals.

In this study, credibility was sought by activities that occurred during the data collection and writing process. Most of the interviewees indicated that the process of the interview had been thorough and they were satisfied that they had fully "told their stories." Several indicated that the process of telling and reflecting had helped them gain insight into how they had grown as leaders as a consequence of the WLS and how they had built on these learning subsequently. My analysis of findings provides rich descriptions that capture interviewees' points of view, meanings, processes, and the nuances of context. In addition, five individuals from the CGIAR, some of whom were interviewees and other external stakeholders, read the report and performed member checks. Gender experts, also colleagues, provided feedback. Feedback from members and experts contributed to confirmability, as did collecting data by means of semi-structured interview. Detailed description of findings contributed to credibility but also dependability. Finally, dependability was also assured by providing an explanation for the variation of meanings between the interviewees in terms of habitual patterns of thinking, and the variation of meaning within interviewees' stories by change in habitual patterns of thinking.

References

Bogdan, R. C., & Bilken, S. K. (2007). *Qualitative research for education: An introduction to theory and method*. Boston, MA: Pearson Allyn and Bacon.

Emerson, R. M., Fretz, R. I., & Shaw, L. L. (1995). *Writing ethnographic fieldnotes*. Chicago, IL: University of Chicago Press.

Glaser, B. G., & Strauss, A. (1967). *The discovery of grounded theory: Strategies for qualitative research*. Chicago, IL: Aldine.

Guba, E. G. (1981). Criteria for assessing the trustworthiness of naturalistic inquiries. *Educational Communication and Technology, 29*(2), 75–91.

Lincoln, Y. S., & Guba, E. G. (2005). Paradigmatic controversies, contradictions, and emerging confluences. In N. K. Denzin & Y. S. Lincoln (Eds.), *Handbook of qualitative research* (pp. 191–216). Thousand Oaks, CA: Sage Publications.

Strauss, A., & Corbin, J. (1996). *Basics of qualitative research*. Thousand Oaks, CA: Sage Publications.

Weiss, R. S. (1994). *Learning from strangers: The art and method of qualitative interview studies*. New York, NY: The Free Press.

Index

Printed in the United States
by Baker & Taylor Publisher Services